BUCKNILL, John Charles. **The Mad Folk of Shakespeare; Psychological Essays. Burt Franklin, 1969 (orig. pub. 1867). 333p (Research and Source Works/Essays in Literature and Criticism, 33) 71-103835. 12.50. Folcroft, 17.50**

CHOICE   SEPT. '70

Language & Literature

English & American

The essays examine Macbeth, Hamlet, Ophelia, King Lear, Timon of Athens, Constance, Jaques, Malvolio, Christopher Sly, and various characters in *The Comedy of Errors*. Leontes, of *The Winter's Tale*, who would have made one of the best characters to analyze, is unaccountably omitted. Bucknill was a practicing psychologist, editor of a journal of mental science, and co-author of a manual of psychological medicine. He was thoroughly acquainted with Shakespeare. In spite of its age, this book is well worth reading and has not been superseded. The language is simple and clear, completely free from modern critical and professional jargon. The studies are sensible and straightforward, based on evidence drawn from the texts themselves, and reveal Shakespeare's sound and brilliant delineations of various kinds of madness.

THE

MAD FOLK

OF

SHAKESPEARE.

THE

MAD FOLK

OF

SHAKESPEARE.

PSYCHOLOGICAL ESSAYS.

BY

JOHN CHARLES BUCKNILL, M.D., F.R.S.,

FELLOW OF THE ROYAL COLLEGE OF PHYSICIANS.

SECOND EDITION, REVISED.

THE FOLCROFT PRESS, INC.
FOLCROFT, PA.

First Published 1867

Reprinted 1969

THE

MAD FOLK

OF

SHAKESPEARE.

PSYCHOLOGICAL ESSAYS.

BY

JOHN CHARLES BUCKNILL, M.D., F.R.S.,

FELLOW OF THE ROYAL COLLEGE OF PHYSICIANS.

SECOND EDITION, REVISED.

London and Cambridge:

MACMILLAN AND CO.

1867.

PREFACE.

THE shoemaker, who criticised the work of the great painter of antiquity, was listened to with respect, so long as he confined his observations within the limits of his own practical knowledge. If in the following Essays the author has ventured to submit the works of another great master of art to the test of comparison with the special knowledge of a workman, he trusts that his opinions may receive that consideration to which a long and extensive experience of the irregular phenomena of mind may appear fairly to entitle them. As the shoemaker doubtless found it a more easy and agreeable occupation to criticise painted sandals than to make leather ones, so the author of these Essays has found the study of his own science, as it is represented in the works of the immortal dramatist, a delightful recreation from the labours of his practice. If he could by any charm transfer to his readers but a small portion of the pleasure which he has enjoyed

in writing the following pages, he would need to make
no apology for their publication, nor entertain any
fear of their favourable reception.   To have the mind
diverted from the routine of professional work, or of
professional study, is both wholesome and enjoyable,
not for the reason that Lord Bacon gives for physicians
so frequently becoming antiquaries, poets, humourists,
etc., namely, because "they find that mediocrity and
excellence in their own art maketh no difference in
profit or reputation;" but because change in the
habitual subject and mode of thought is a source of
mental recreation and delight.   These pages have,
indeed, been written in the leisure hours of a busy
life; and although the constant care of six hundred
insane persons has afforded ample opportunities of
comparing the delineations of the psychological artist
with the hard realities of existence, it has also denied
that leisure which would have enabled the writer to
have expressed his opinions in a form and manner
more satisfactory to his judgment, and more worthy
of the subject.   Under these circumstances they have
necessarily been written in some haste, and have been
sent to the printer with the ink yet wet: they have
also been written in the country, so that neither their
matter or manner could be submitted to friendly
advice.   The author tenders these explanations in
excuse for imperfections of literary execution, which,

he trusts, may in some measure be atoned for by other qualities in the work, which comes fresh from the field of observation. He claims, indeed, that indulgence which would readily be accorded to a writer whom the active business of life had led into some region of classic interest, and who, taking his ease at his inn, should each evening compare the descriptions of an ancient historian with the scenes he had just beheld during the burden and heat of the day ; the fresh and immediate nature of his knowledge would justify him in assuming a certain kind of authority, without at each step establishing the grounds of his judgment. The author, however, has endeavoured to bear in mind that he was writing, not upon the subject of his own knowledge, but upon that of Shakespeare's ; and although it would have been easy to have supported and illustrated his opinions by the details of observation and the statement of cases, he has abstained from doing so, preferring sometimes to be dogmatic rather than tedious.

Although for many years the dramas of Shakespeare have been familiar to the author, the extent and exactness of the psychological knowledge displayed in them, which a more diligent examination has made known, have surprised and astonished him. He can only account for it on one supposition, namely, that abnormal conditions of mind had at-

tracted Shakespeare's diligent observation, and had
been a favourite study. There is no reason to suppose that when Shakespeare wrote, any other asylum
for the insane existed in this country than the then
poor and small establishment of Bethlem Hospital,
the property of which had been taken from the monks
by Henry the Eighth, and presented to the city of
London for conversion into an asylum, only seventeen
years before the poet's birth. In his time the insane
members of society were not secluded from the world
as they are now. If their symptoms were prominent
and dangerous, they were, indeed, thrust out of sight
very harshly and effectually; but if their liberty was
in any degree tolerable, it was tolerated, and they
were permitted to live in the family circle, or to
wander the country. Thus every one must have been
brought into immediate contact with examples of
every variety of mental derangement; and any one
who sought the knowledge of their peculiarities would
find it at every turn. Opportunities of crude observation would, therefore, be ample; it only required the
alembic of a great mind to convert them into psychological science.

Shakespeare's peculiar capacity for effecting such
conversion would consist in his intimate knowledge
of the normal state of the mental functions in every
variety of character, with which he would be able to

compare and estimate every direction and degree of aberration. His knowledge of the mental physiology of human life would be brought to bear upon all the obscurities and intricacies of its pathology. To this power would be added that indefinable possession of genius, call it spiritual tact or insight, or whatever other term may suggest itself, by which the great lords of mind estimate all phases of mind with little aid from reflected light. The peculiarities of a certain character being observed, the great mind which contains all possibilities within itself, imagines the act of mental transmigration, and combining the knowledge of others with the knowledge of self, every variety of character possible in nature becomes possible in conception and delineation.

That abnormal states of mind were a favourite study of Shakespeare would be evident from the mere number of characters to which he has attributed them, and the extent alone to which he has written on the subject. On no other subject, except love and ambition, the blood and chyle of dramatic poetry, has he written so much. On no other has he written with such mighty power.

Some explanation seems due of the title chosen for this work. Since psychology strictly implies all that relates to the soul or mind of man in contradistinction to his material nature, the character of Othello might have been placed under this title with as much propriety as that of Lear. The derivation and original use of a term, however, not unfrequently differ from its acquired and permanent use, and the term psychology has, of late years, been used to denote all that relates to the department of science which takes cognizance of irregularities and aberrations and diseases of the mind. It serves not to object that the derivation of the word is opposed to such employment, for the same may be said of half the words in the language. Mental pathology would be a far more exact, but also a more cumbrous term ; and no further apology need be made .for the modern use of the shorter term, than that no other suits the purpose to which it is applied with equal convenience. One chooses words, like servants, for their usefulness and not for their pedigree.

The author had intended to append to the following pages a chapter on Shakespeare's knowledge of medicine. When, however, it was partly written, he found that the freedom of expression which the great dramatist had permitted himself on medical subjects was such as would either have prevented the admission and consideration of important passages, or have forbidden the present work to many readers, whom it is hoped may otherwise honour it with a perusal. The inconvenience therefore of a separate publication has been preferred.

It only remains to add that three of the following essays have already appeared in the pages of the " Quarterly Journal of Mental Science," a publication edited by the author.

EXMINSTER,
May 12th, 1859.

CONTENTS.

PSYCHOLOGICAL ESSAYS.

MACBETH.

MACBETH, the most awful creation of the poetic mind, is a study every way worthy of those to whom the storms of passion present the frequent cause of mental disease. The historian studies the temper of the mind in its most ardent heats, that he may gain a clue to the causation of human events ; the statesman, that he may obtain foreknowledge of tendencies to human action ; and the psychologist, for the more beneficent purpose of acquiring that knowledge as the means of alleviating the most terrible of calamities, and of doing that which the terrified physician in this tragedy dared not attempt, of "ministering to the mind diseased." The philosopher studies the laws of storms, that he may teach the mariner to avoid the destructive circle of their influence ; and the physician, whose noble object of study is the human mind, seizes every opportunity of making himself acquainted with the direction and events of its hurricane movements,

B

that he may perchance lead some into a port of safety, or at least that he may assist in refitting the torn and shattered barque. But to stand on one side and calmly contemplate the phenomena of human passion, like the chorus in the old Greek drama, is the lot of few. When the elements of human passion are in fierce strife, there is no near standing-place for the foot of science, like the deck of the great steamer which allowed Scoresby to measure the force and speed of the wild Atlantic wave. The vortex of passion tends to draw in all who float near; and tranquil observation of its turmoil can only be made from a standing-point more or less remote. On all possible occasions, indeed, it behoves the man whose object of study and of care is the human mind, to observe for himself its phenomena, and to test its springs and sources of action ; but it behoves him also to accept the testimony of those who have weathered the storm, and gratefully to appreciate any assistance he may obtain from others who contemplate the same phenomena from different points of view to his own : and there is no one from whom he will derive help of such inestimable value, as from the man whose high faculties enable him to contemplate human nature, as it were, from within. The Poet or maker, the same intrinsically with the Seer or gifted observer, is the best guide and helpmate with whom the psychologist can ally himself. He is like the native of a country to whom mountain and stream

and every living thing are known, acting as instructor
and guide to the naturalist, whose systems and classi-
fications he may hold in slight esteem, but with whom
he has a common love and a more personal knowledge for all their objects. Compared with the assistance which the psychologist derives from the true
poet, that which he obtains from the metaphysician
is as sketchy and indistinct as the theoretical description of a new country might be, given by one who
had never been therein, as the description of Australia
might be, drawn from the parallel of its climate and
latitude with South America or China.

Above all seers with whom a beneficent Providence
has blessed mankind, to delight and instruct them
with that knowledge which is so wondrous that it is
falsely called intuitive, is that heaven-born genius,
who is the pride and glory of this country, the greatest
poet of all ages, and preeminently the most truthful
analyst of human action. Shakespeare not only possesses more psychological insight than all other poets,
but more than all other writers. He has been aptly
called "a nature humanized." He has above all men
the faculty of unravelling the motives of human
action. Compared with his profound knowledge of
the surface and depths of the human soul, the information of other great minds, even of such wondrously
vigorous intelligences as those of Plato and Bacon,
were obscure and fragmentary. Had he not been
a poet, what might he not have been as a philo-

sopher? What essays might he not have written? What Socratic dialogues, sparkling with wit, seething with humour, saturated with truth, might he not have written upon politics and philosophy? An American writer has lately started the idea that Shakespeare's plays were written by Bacon! Verily, were it not for the want of power of imagination and verbal euphony which is displayed in Bacon's Essays, one might rather think that they were some of Shakespeare's own rough memoranda on men and motives, which had strayed from his desk.

Although Macbeth is less pervaded with the idea of mental disease than its great rival tragedies of Hamlet and Lear, and contains fewer scenes in which phases of insanity are actually represented, it is not only replete with passages of deep psychological interest, but in the mental development of the bloody-handed hero and of his terrible mate, it affords a study scarcely less instructive than the wild and passionate madness of Lear, or the metaphysical motive-weighing melancholy of the Prince of Denmark.

It is not within the scope of our intention to comment upon the artistic perfection of this work. This has already been done, and done well, by professed writers of dramatic criticism—by Schlegel especially, and by Hazlitt. The wonderful rapidity of action which obtains in this tragedy, the exquisite adaptation of all its parts to form a perfect and consistent whole, and the inimitable use of violent contrasts which it presents, have been dilated upon by the German with a ripe and critical intelligence—by our countrymen with the eloquence of vehement admiration. Coleridge also has a long essay upon this drama, to which the authority of his name has attached importance. Some of his criticisms, however, appear more subtle than sensible. He discovers that Lady Macbeth's "is the mock fortitude of a mind deluded by ambition. She shames her husband by a superhuman audacity of fancy which she cannot support, but sinks in the season of remorse, and dies in suicidal agony." He discovers that the scene opens "with superstition"; as if Macbeth had dreamt he had seen the Witches. Surely there is a difference between the supernatural and the superstitious! The difference between mere apprehension and sensation, between imagination and apparent existence. The truth of supernatural events may be doubted or denied, but if admitted, to see it as it is, is not superstition. Degrading Lady Macbeth into a fanciful would-be heroine, Coleridge makes her lord a predetermined scoundrel, "rendered temptable (by the Witches) by previous dalliance of the fancy with ambitious thoughts." "His soliloquy shewed the early birth-date of his guilt." According to this view, the temptation of the weird Sisters, and the "concatinating tendency of the imagination," was quite needless. A villain *ab initio*, "who, wishing a temporal end for itself, does in truth will the means," can find no palliation in the direct tempting of supernatural beings, nor in being subject to the masterdom of another human will. Then Macbeth makes the most grievous metaphysical mistakes. Before the deed, "the inward pangs and warnings of conscience are interpreted into prudential reasonings;" and afterwards, he is "ever and ever mistaking the anguish of conscience for fears of selfishness." The idea conveyed is, that conscience is independent of reason; that the inward monitor intuitively decides upon the right and wrong without the aid of the judgment; that the still small voice is an uninstructed sentiment.

We cannot give our adhesion to the theory that Macbeth was originally a treacherous and bad man, prone to deeds of midnight murder. His bold and fierce wife is likely to have known him far better than his metaphysical critic; and she reading his letter, which describes the prophecies of the weird Sisters, says:

> "Glamis thou art, and Cawdor; and shalt be
> What thou art promised: yet do I fear thy nature;
> It is too full o' the milk of human kindness
> To catch the nearest way: thou wouldst be great;
> Art not without ambition, but without
> The illness should attend it: what thou wouldst highly,
> That wouldst thou holily; wouldst not play false,
> And yet wouldst surely win."

Macbeth is introduced as a right brave man. "Valour's minion," he is called by the bleeding captain, and "Bellona's bridegroom" by Rosse. "Oh, valiant cousin! worthy gentleman!" exclaims the King, on hearing the relation of his first victory. Twice in one day he is represented to have saved the kingdom, and the gracious Duncan regrets his inadequate power of reward:

"More is thy due than more than all can pay."

He is "full of the milk of human kindness," but withal so personally brave that his deeds against the Irish gallowglasses and the Norwegians are the theme of general enthusiasm, and win for him "golden opinions from all sorts of people." Evidently he is a man of sanguine nervous temperament, of large capacity and ready susceptibility. The high energy and courage which guides his sword in the battles of his country are qualities of nerve force which future circumstances will direct to good or evil purposes. Circumstances arise soliciting to evil; "supernatural soliciting," the force of which, in these anti-spiritualist days, it requires an almost unattainable flight of imagination to get a glimpse of. It must be remembered that the drama brings Macbeth face to face with the supernatural, with that devil's brood the weird Sisters, so unlike the inhabitants of earth, who, after a prophecy immediately fulfilled, "made themselves air into which they vanished." What would be the effect upon a man of nervous sensibility, of such appearances? Surely most profound. Well

may Hazlitt say, that "he can conceive no common
actor to look like a man who had encountered the
weird Sisters." When they had "melted as breath
into the wind," even the firm tempered and judicious
Banquo exclaims :

> "Were such things here as we do speak about?
> Or have we eaten of the insane root
> That takes the reason prisoner?"

We may disbelieve in any manifestations of the
supernatural; but we cannot but believe that were
their occurrence possible, they would profoundly
affect the mind. Humboldt says, that the effect of
the first earthquake shock is most bewildering, up-
setting one of the strongest articles of material faith,
namely, the fixedness of the earth. Any supernatural appearance must have this effect of shaking
the foundations of the mind in an infinitely greater
degree. Indeed, we so fully feel that any glimpse
into the spirit-world would effect in ourselves a profound mental revulsion, that we readily extend to
Macbeth a more indulgent opinion of his great crimes,
than we should have been able to do had he been led
on to their commission by the temptations of earthly
incident alone.

Macbeth is no villain in-grain, like Richard the
Third or Iago, revelling in the devil's work because
he likes it; but a once noble human nature, struggling but yielding in a net of temptation, whose
meshes are wound around him by the visible hand

of the Spirit of Evil. Slave as he is to that soldier's passion, the love of fame and power, he is not without amiable qualities. He was once loved even by his arch-enemy Macduff, to whom Malcolm says :

> " This tyrant, whose sole name blisters our tongues,
> Was once thought honest; you have loved him well."

And we may even accept the testimony of the Queen of Hell, "the close contriver of all harms," in his favour. She upbraids her foul menials, the Sisters, because they had been serving one who had no pleasure in evil for its own sake, but who had spitefully and wrathfully accepted it only as the means to an end :

> " And, which is worse, all you have done
> Hath been but for a wayward son,
> Spiteful and wrathful; who, as others do,
> Loves for his own ends, not for you."

Let it not be thought that we attempt to palliate the guilt of Macbeth. In a moral point of view this is impossible. If his solicitings to crime are supernatural, combined with fate and metaphysic aid, he is not blinded by them. With conscience fully awake, with eyes open to the foul nature of his double treachery, although resisting, he yields to temptation. He even feels that he is not called upon to act to fulfil the decrees of destiny.

> " If Chance will have me king, why Chance may crown me
> Without my stir."

Had he with more determination resisted the tempt-

ations of the woman, he might have falsified the prophecies of the fiend, put aside from his lips the
poisoned chalice of remorse, maintained from rancours
the vessel of his peace, and rescued the eternal jewel
of his soul.

Though here and elsewhere Shakespeare has admitted the doctrine of destiny, no one more pitilessly
tore, aside this veil from the features for wickedness.
Edgar, in Lear, says : " This is the excellent foppery
of the world ! That when we are sick in fortune [often
the surfeit of our own behaviour] we make guilty of
our disasters, the sun, the moon, and the stars : as if
we were villains on necessity ; fools by heavenly com-
pulsion ; knaves, thieves, and treachers by spherical
predominance ; drunkards, liars, and adulterers, by
a forced obedience of planetary influence ; and all
that we are evil in by a divine thrusting on : an
admirable evasion———"

To the Christian moralist, Macbeth's guilt is so
dark that its degree cannot be estimated, as there
are no shades in black. But to the mental physi-
ologist, to whom nerve rather than conscience, the
function of the brain rather than the power of the
will, is an object of study, it is impossible to omit
from calculation the influences of the supernatural
event, which is not only the starting-point of the
action, but the remote cause of the mental phenomena.

The professed moralist is slow to accept the teaching of the drama ; but where shall we find a more impressive lesson of the manner in which the infraction of the moral law works out its own punishment, than in the delineation of the agonizing soul torture of Macbeth ? In this, as in all other instances, the true psychological is not opposed to the true moral doctrine of human life. In the attempt to trace conduct to its earliest source or motive, and to deduce the laws of emotional progression, the psychological, or to use the stricter and better term, the physiological moralist teaches the importance of establishing an early habit of emotional action, which may tend to virtuous conduct, and form a prepared defence against temptation. By shewing how invariably in the moral world evil leads on to evil, he teaches in the best manner the wisdom of opposing the beginnings of evil, and he developes the ethical principle laid down by our Great Teacher, that an evil emotion is in the heart the living representative of the bad action.

The great interest of this drama is most skilfully made to depend upon the conflicting emotions of sympathy with a man struggling under fearful temptation, horror excited by treachery and foul murder, awful amazement at the visible grasp of the Spirit of Evil upon the human soul, and of satisfied justice at the hell of remorse into which he is plunged. In this respect there is an obvious parallelism between Macbeth and Faust ; since in both the hero-criminal of the piece is not responsible as a free agent, so far as he is but the mortal instrument of the fiend in deeds of evil. The conduct of Faust, however, is not comparable to that of the fierce and bloody Scotch tyrant, and he is saved from our utter disgust and hatred by the more immediate intervention of the fiend in the execution of the murders, both of Margaret's mother and her brother. Had the action not been thus arranged, had Faust himself poisoned the mother and slain the brother, all sympathy with him as a human soul in the hands of fate would have been destroyed by the irrepressible feelings which attach to a base and dastardly criminal.

In Macbeth the fiercer temptation, fanned not only by the evil solicitings of the devil, but by the agency of his dark and terrible human tempter and colleague, renders it possible to commit the perpetration of crimes to his own hand, without destroying those traces of sympathy, without which any deep interest in his fate could not have been invoked.

The temptation of the weird Sisters has an immediate effect on Macbeth. In the presence of others, he soliloquises, and calls upon himself the remark from Banquo:

"Look how our partner's wrapt."

The immediate fulfilment of two parts of the prophecy come as "happy prologues to the swelling act," while murder is thought of as an "horrible imagining," and an indication that the supernatural soliciting was evil in its nature.

> " This supernatural soliciting
> Cannot be ill, cannot be good : if ill,
> Why hath it given me earnest of success,
> Commencing in a truth? I am thane of Cawdor :
> If good, why do I yield to that suggestion
> Whose horrid image doth unfix my hair
> And make my seated heart knock at my ribs,
> Against the use of nature? Present fears
> Are less than horrible imaginings :
> My thought, whose murder yet is but fantastical,
> Shakes so my single state of man, that function
> Is smother'd in surmise, and nothing is
> But what is not."

Let not this early and important testimony be over-
looked, which Macbeth gives to the extreme excitability of his imagination. The supernatural soliciting
of the weird Sisters suggests to him an *image*, not
a thought merely, but an image so horrible that its
contemplation

> " doth unfix my hair
> And make my seated heart knock at my ribs,
> Against the use of nature."

This passage was scarcely intended to describe an
actual hallucination, but rather that excessive predominance of the imaginative faculty which enables
some men to call at will before the mind's eye the
very appearance of the object of thought; that faculty
which enabled a great painter to place at will in the
empty chair of his studio the mental delineation of
any person who had given him one sitting. It is a
faculty bordering on a morbid state, and apt to pass
the limit, when judgment swallowed in surmise yields

her function, and the imaginary becomes as real to the mind as the true, "and nothing is but what is not." This early indication of Macbeth's tendency to hallucination is most important in the psychological development of his character.

We are not to understand that Macbeth had entertained any idea of his great crime, before the suggestion of it arising from the devil's interview on Forres heath. That he yields to it is only too evident from the passage beginning "Stars hide your fires." That his wife should form the same guilty purpose, upon the mere recital in his letter of the supernatural information he had obtained of that which was in the "coming on of time," proves not that he had suggested it to her, but that she was prone to entertain it on slighter grounds, and that there was between them that unity of thought and desire which is common between man and wife who are much wrapt in each other.

The struggle of Macbeth before he yields to the suggestion is so fierce that horror and pain are forthwith stamped upon his features. His wife exclaims, when he meets her :

> "Your face, my thane, is like a book, where men
> May read strange matters."

For herself, she hath no faltering ; she hath no need of supernatural appearances to "prick the sides of her intent." Ambition and the desire "of sovereign sway and masterdom" are to her undaunted metal the all-sufficient motives of the terrible deed which she plotted and instigated, and would have perpetrated, had not a touch of filial piety withheld her hand. Strange inconsistency of humanity which leaves not the darkest moments of the lost soul without stray gleams of light.

> " Had he not resembled
> My father as he slept, I had done 't."

This is one of the " compunctious visitings of nature," against which she invokes the murdering ministers whose sightless substances wait on nature's mischief, in that expression of sublimated wickedness in which she welcomes the fatal entrance of Duncan under her battlements.

The wavering of Macbeth, expressed in his first soliloquy, appears to us very different from the " prudential reasonings," which, according to Coleridge, he mistakes for conscience. Surely it indicates a sensitive appreciation of right motive, and the fear of punishment in the life to come ; the acknowledgment also that crime, even in this world, receives its due reward from the operation of even-handed justice ; the acknowledgment of the foul nature of treachery to a kinsman and disloyalty to a king. Moreover, that expression of sincere pity for the gracious Duncan, whose meek and holy character is depicted in so fine a contrast to his own fierce and wayward passions, is a sentiment far removed from "prudential reasonings." Thus he convinces himself against the deed, and concludes :

> "I have no spur
> To prick the sides of my intent, but only
> Vaulting ambition, which o'erleaps its'sell,
> And falls on the other."

When Lady Macbeth joins him, he expresses his virtuous resolve, and for the first time adds "prudential reasonings" :

> "We will proceed no further in this business :
> He hath honour'd me of late ; and I have bought
> Golden opinions from all sorts of people,
> Which would be worn now in their newest gloss,
> Not cast aside so soon."

Then mark the temptation to which the terrible woman subjects him ; the taunts of cowardice and weakness ; taunts to which a soldier gifted with sensitive personal bravery would be keenly alive, especially coming from the lips of a beautiful woman whom he loved :

> "Was the hope drunk
> Wherein you dress'd yourself ? hath it slept since ?
> And wakes it now, to look so green and pale
> At what it did so freely ? From this time
> Such I account thy love. Art thou afeard
> To be the same in thine own act and valour
> As thou art in desire ?"

Further she urges the temptation by comparing his vacillating desire with her own fell purpose, in that terrible passage :

> "I have given suck, and know
> How tender 'tis to love the babe that milks me :

> I would, while it was smiling in my face,
> Have pluck'd the nipple from his boneless gums,
> And dash'd the brains out, had I so sworn as you
> Have done to this."

Fearing that his better nature would relent, she had sworn him to the treacherous and bloody deed. She concludes by shewing clearly the opportunity. She will ply the two chamberlains with wine and wassail, until

> " Memory, the warder of the brain,
> Shall be a fume, and the receipt of reason
> A limbeck only : when in swinish sleep
> Their drenched natures lie as in a death——."

Well may Macbeth exclaim in astonishment :

> " Bring forth men-children only ;
> For thy undaunted mettle should compose
> Nothing but males."

He reels under the fierce battery of temptation, and when she has thus poured her spirits into his ear, and chastised his compunctions with the valour of her tongue, he falls, without time for further thought, rushing into the commission of his first great crime.

> " I am settled, and bend up
> Each corporal agent to this terrible feat.
> Away, and mock the time with fairest show :
> False face must hide what the false heart doth know."

As in earliest time, the temptation was urged by the woman. Woman, infinitely the most virtuous, distances her partner when she has once entered the career of crime.

> " Denn, geht es zu des Bösen Haus,
> Das Weib hat tausend Schritt voraus."

C

The dagger scene is an illustration of Shakespeare's finest psychological insight. An hallucination of sight resulting from the high-wrought nervous tension of the regicide, and "the present horror of the time," and typifying in form the dread purpose of his mind is impressed upon his senses, but rejected by his judgment is recognised as a morbid product of mental excitement, and finally its existence altogether repudiated, and the bloody business of the mind made answerable for the foolery of the senses.

> "Is this a dagger which I see before me,
> The handle toward my hand? Come, let me clutch
> thee.
> I have thee not, and yet I see thee still.
> Art thou not, fatal vision, sensible
> To feeling as to sight? or art thou but
> A dagger of the mind, a false creation,
> Proceeding from the heat-oppressed brain?
> I see thee yet, in form as palpable
> As this which now I draw.
> Thou marshall'st me the way that I was going;
> And such an instrument I was to use.
> Mine eyes are made the fools o' the other senses,
> Or else worth all the rest; I see thee still,
> And on thy blade and dudgeon gouts of blood,
> Which was not so before. There's no such thing:
> It is the bloody business which informs
> Thus to mine eyes."

The deed is done! and the terrible punishment of guilt commences from the very moment. Remorse dogs the murderer's heels even from the chamber of death.

> "*Macb.* One cried *God bless us!* and *Amen* the other;

As they had seen me with these hangman's hands.
Listening their fear, I could not say 'Amen,'
When they did say 'God bless us !'
    Lady M.   Consider it not so deeply.
    Macb. But wherefore could not I pronounce 'Amen'?
I had most need of blessing, and 'Amen'
Stuck in my throat.
    Lady M.   These deeds must not be thought
After these ways ; so, *it will make us mad.*"

Guilt hath instantly changed the brave man into a coward.

> " I am afraid to think what I have done ;
>   Look on't again I dare not."
> " How is't with me, when every noise appals me ?"

The sting of remorse extorts from him the direct expression of regret :

> " To know my deed, 'twere best not know myself."
> " Wake Duncan with thy knocking ! *Would thou could'st !*"

Compare this with the woman's firmer nerve, rebuking him :

> " You do unbend your noble strength, to think
>   *So brainsickly of things.*"

>   " Infirm of purpose !
> Give me the daggers : the sleeping and the dead
> Are but as pictures : 'tis the eye of childhood
> That fears a painted devil."

She enters the murder chamber, to do that which her mate dare not do, and shewing her hands, gilded like the faces of the grooms with Duncan's blood, says :

> " My hands are of your colour ; but I shame
> To wear a heart so white."

And this is the lady whom Mr. Coleridge describes as courageous in fancy only!

The passage, "Methought I heard a voice," &c., is scarcely to be accepted as another instance of hallucination, an hallucination of hearing parallel to that of sight in the appearance of the dagger. It is rather an instance of merely excited imagination without sensual representation, like the "suggestion whose horrid image" is spoken of on Forres heath. The word "*methought*" is sufficient to distinguish this voice of the fancy from an hallucination of sense. The lengthened reasoning of the fancied speech is also unlike an hallucination of hearing; real hallucinations of hearing being almost always restricted to two or three words, or at furthest, to brief sentences. How exquisite is this description of sleep! How correct, psychologically, is the threat that remorse will murder sleep! How true the prediction to the course of the drama, in which we find that hereafter the murderer did "lack the season of all natures, sleep!"

> " *Macb.* Methought I heard a voice cry, *Sleep no more!*
> *Macbeth doth murder sleep, the innocent sleep,*
> *Sleep that knits up the ravell'd sleave of care,*
> *The death of each day's life, sore labour's bath,*
> *Balm of hurt minds, great nature's second course,*
> *Chief nourisher in life's feast,—*
>   *Lady M.*   What do you mean?
>   *Macb.* Still it cried *Sleep no more!* to all the house:
> *Glamis hath murder'd sleep, and therefore Cawdor*
> *Shall sleep no more; Macbeth shall sleep no more.*"

When the first agony of remorseful excitement has

passed, its more settled phase is expressed in the life-weary, Hamlet-like melancholy of the passage :

> "Had I but died an hour before this chance,
> I had lived a blessed time ; for, from this instant,
> There's nothing serious in mortality :
> All is but toys : renown and grace is dead ;
> The wine of life is drawn, and the mere lees
> Is left this vault to brag of."

The description of the night of murder is conceived to add to the supernatural. By lamentings in the air, earthquake, eclipse, prodigies in animal life, things "unnatural, even like the deed that's done," the mental effect of awe is skilfully produced, and the feeling of Macbeth's balance between fate and free-will is maintained just at that point which enables us both to sympathize and condemn.

Macbeth at last hath obtained the "All hail hereafter ;" but the furies of conscience rack his soul with cowardly and anxious thoughts. He is cowed by the presence of a brave and honest man, his old friend and colleague, whose royalty of nature, dauntless temper, and the prudence with which he acts, make him an object of fear, and his presence a rebuke. Jealousy, moreover, of the greatness which the weird Sisters had promised to the issue of Banquo, rankles in his mind, now debased by guilt and the fertile seed-ground of all evil passion.

> "For Banquo's issue have I filed my mind ;
> For them the gracious Duncan have I murder'd ;
> Put rancours in the vessel of my peace

Only for them ; and mine eternal jewel
Given to the common enemy of man,
To make them kings, the seed of Banquo kings !
Rather than so, come fate into the list,
And champion me to the utterance !"

Strange inconsistency ! He yields to Fate when its
decrees jump with his own desires ; but when the
tide turns he resolves to breast its irresistible wave.
One is inclined, however, to the belief, that the first
reason assigned for Banquo's death was the most
potent, that "there is none but he whose being I do
fear." Macbeth had no children, and the descent of
the crown could not touch his feelings or interests.
When he learns that Fleance has escaped, he feels
"bound in to saucy doubts and fears ;" but, on the
whole, he treats the escape as a light matter, and as
the cause of future danger to himself, rather than
of anxiety respecting the succession.

How awful is the retribution which the Nemesis
of conscience works upon the guilty pair ; and that
before they have cause to dread any earthly retribution. Duncan's sons are fugitives in foreign lands.
The peers gather freely round the court of the new
king. Suspicions have indeed arisen in the mind of
Banquo, but he breathes them only to himself, and
commends his indissoluble duties to the king. All
without seems fair ; but within ? Listen to the deep
sound of melancholy surging from the heart of the
imperious woman :

"Nought's had, all's spent,

> Where our desire is got without content :
> 'Tis safer to be that which we destroy
> Than by destruction dwell in doubtful joy."

From these sad lonely thoughts she rouses herself to chide her lord for permitting similar thoughts to be expressed legibly on his more sensitive organization.

> "*Lady M.* How now, my lord ! why do you keep alone,
> Of sorriest fancies your companions making,
> Using those thoughts which should indeed have died
> With them they think on ?   Things without all remedy
> Should be without regard : what's done is done.
>   *Macbeth.* We have scotch'd the snake, not kill'd it :
> She'll close and be herself, whilst our poor malice
> Remains in danger of her former tooth.
> But let the frame of things disjoint, both the worlds suffer,
> Ere we will eat our meal in fear and sleep
> In the affliction of these terrible dreams
> That shake us nightly : better be with the dead,
> Whom we, to gain our peace, have sent to peace,
> Than on the torture of the mind to lie
> In restless ecstasy."

Well might she feel it needful to urge upon him the policy of sleeking o'er his rugged looks, and of being bright and jovial among his guests ; but how deep the agony of the reply :

> " O, full of scorpions is my mind, dear wife !"

The banquet scene following the murder of Banquo is unrivalled in dramatic force and psychological truth.   The kingly host hath put on a a forced cheerfulness.   He will play the humble host, and sit in the midst.   He commands his guests to be large in mirth. He has something like a grim jest for the murderer

who appears at the side door, to whom he makes the
only play on words in the tragedy, the porter's
ribaldry excepted.

"*Macbeth.* There's blood upon thy face.
Murderer. 'Tis Banquo's then.
Macb. 'Tis better thee *without* than he *within.*"
"Thou art the best o' the cut-throats: yet he's good
That did the like for Fleance: if thou didst it,
Thou art the *nonpareil.*"

The short-lived effort to be gay subsides into the
usual abstracted mood, and Lady Macbeth needs to
chide him: "You do not give the cheer," &c. He
makes an effort, giving that physiological grace before meat:

"Now good digestion wait on appetite,
And health on both!"

He playfully challenges the absence of Banquo as an
act of unkindness, thus by a voluntary mental act
calling before his mind's eye the image of the murdered man. When invited to sit, "The table's full."
He says—"Here's a place reserved, sir."—"Where?
which of you have done this?" None see the shadowy
form except Macbeth himself, and his first impression
is that it is a sorry jest; but how quickly does he
believe in the supernatural nature of his visitor:
"Thou canst not say I did it; never shake thy gory
locks at me." He looks "on that which might appal
the devil," but which no eyes but his own can see.
Although "quite unmann'd in folly," fear turns to
daring, and he threatens the ghost:

"Prithee, see there! behold! look! lo! how say you?
Why, what care I? If thou canst nod, speak too.
If charnel-houses and our graves must send ·
Those that we bury back, our monuments
Shall be the maws of kites."

The hallucination fades, and his natural high courage allows him on the moment to philosophize upon the appearance:

"Blood hath been shed ere now, i' the olden time,
Ere human statute purged the gentle weal;
Ay, and since too, murders have been perform'd
Too terrible for the ear: the times have been,
That, when the brains were out, the man would die,
And there an end; but now they rise again,
With twenty mortal murders on their crowns,
And push us from our stools: this is more strange
Than such a murder is."

Again roused from reverie by his wife, he excuses his behaviour by the same reference to a customary infirmity, which is twice alluded to for the same purpose by his wife:

"I do forget.
Do not muse at me, my most worthy friends;
I have a strange infirmity, which is nothing
To those that know me."

He proposes a bumper health to the general joy of the whole table, and to that in particular of "our dear friend Banquo," this second reference shewing how his mind is fascinated with the idea of the dead man, and having the immediate effect of re-establishing the hallucination. Then comes that burst of despairing defiance, when the extremity of fear changes to audacity:

> "Avaunt! and quit my sight! let the earth hide thee!
> Thy bones are marrowless, thy blood is cold;
> Thou hast no speculation in those eyes
> Which thou dost glare with!"
> "What man dare, I dare:
> Approach thou like the rugged Russian bear,
> The arm'd rhinoceros, or the Hyrcan tiger;
> Take any shape but that, and my firm nerves
> Shall never tremble: or be alive again,
> And dare me to the desert with thy sword;
> If trembling I exhibit then, protest me
> The baby of a girl. Hence, horrible shadow!
> Unreal mockery, hence!—Why, so: being gone,
> I am a man again. Pray you, sit still."

He is astonished that the others present are not moved by the object of his dread. Unlike the air-drawn dagger, which he recognised as an hallucination, he believes this appearance to have been most real. He does this notwithstanding his wife's assurance that—

> "This is the very painting of your fear:
> This is the air-drawn dagger which, you said,
> Led you to Duncan."

She gives no credence to matters which

> "Would well become
> A woman's story at a winter's fire,
> Authorized by her grandam."

She taunts him, and assures him:

> "Why do you make such faces? When all's done,
> You look but on a stool."

It is markworthy that the ghost of Banquo is seen to no one but Macbeth, differing in this respect from that of Hamlet's father. Moreover, Banquo's ghost is silent : Hamlet's ghost is a conversational being, subject to disappearance at cock-crow and other ghost laws ; points indicating the poet's intention to represent the ghost of Banquo as an hallucination, not as an apparition, a creation of the heat-oppressed brain, not a shadowy messenger from spirit-land. It is the pathological Nemesis of guilt, not a spiritual existence returned to the confines of the day actively to assist in the discovery of guilt. The progress of the morbid action is depicted with exquisite skill. First, there is the horrible picture of the imagination not transferred to the sense, then there is the sensual hallucination whose reality is questioned and rejected, and now there is the sensual hallucination whose reality is fully accepted.

Are we to accept the repeated assurance, both from Macbeth and from his wife, that he is subject to sudden fits of mental bereavement ? or was it a ready lie, coined on the spur of the moment, as an excuse for his strange behaviour ?

> " Sit, worthy friends : my lord is often thus,
> And hath been from his youth : pray you, keep seat ;
> The fit is momentary ; upon a thought
> He will again be well : if much you note him,
> You shall offend him, and extend his passion."

And again :

> " Think of this, good peers,

> But as a thing of custom : 'tis no other ;
> Only it spoils the pleasure of the time."

Macbeth is at this juncture in a state of mind closely bordering upon disease, if he have not actually passed the limit. He is hallucinated, and, in respect to the appearance of Banquo, he believes in the hallucination, and refers it to the supernatural agencies which discover the "secret'st man of blood." The reality of the air-drawn dagger he did not believe in, but referred its phenomena to their proper source, with as much truth, though not with as much phlegm, as Nicolai or any other sane subject of hallucination could have done. Unlike the hallucinations of Nicolai and Ben Jonson, it caused terror although its unreality was fully recognised, because it suited with "the horror of the time" of which it was a reflex. But between this time and the appearance of Banquo, the stability of Macbeth's reason had undergone a fearful ordeal. He lacked "the season of all natures —sleep ;" or, when he did sleep, it was

> " In the affliction of those terrible dreams
> That shake us nightly."

Waking, he made his companions of the "sorriest fancies ;" and, "on the torture of the mind," he lay "in restless ecstacy." Truly, the caution given by his wife was likely to become a prophecy :

> "These deeds must not be thought on
> After these ways ; so, it will make us mad."

In the point of view of psychological criticism, this

fear appears on the eve of being fulfilled by the man, when to sleepless nights and days of brooding melancholy are added that undeniable indication of insanity, a credited hallucination. It was in reality fulfilled in the instance of the woman, although, at the point we have reached, when she with clear intellect and well-balanced powers is supporting her horror-struck and hallucinated husband, she offers a character little likely, on her next appearance, to be the subject of profound and fatal insanity. The man, on the other hand, appears to be almost within the limits of mental disease. Macbeth, however, saved himself from actual insanity by rushing from the maddening horrors of meditation into a course of decisive resolute action. From henceforth he gave himself no time to reflect ; he made the firstlings of his heart the firstlings of his hand ; he became a fearful tyrant to his country ; but he escaped madness. This change in him, however, effected a change in his relation to his wife, which in her had the opposite result. Up to this time her action had been that of sustaining him ; but when he waded forward in a sea of blood, without desire of the tedious return, when his thoughts were acted ere they were scanned, then his queen found her occupation gone. Her attention, heretofore directed to her husband and to outward occurrences, was forced inwards upon that wreck of all-content which her meditation supplied. The sanitary mental influence of action is thus impressively shewn. Even the stings of conscience, if not blunted, can for a time be averted, by that busy march of affairs, which attracts all the attention outwardly, and throws the faculty of reflection into disuse.

The rapid deterioration of Macbeth's moral nature deserves notice. The murder of the king, to which he had the greatest temptation, was effected in the midst of a storm of conscientious rebuke. The murder of Banquo was attended with no expression of remorse, although it highly stimulated the imagination; for this also he had temptation. But shortly afterwards we find him committing a wholesale and motiveless deed of blood, in the assassination of the kindred of Macduff—far more atrocious and horrible, if there can be degrees in the guilt of such deeds, than all he has done before. At first we find him "infirm of purpose" in guilt. Referring either to his want of sleep or to his hallucination, he says:

> "My strange and self-abuse
> Is the initiate fear, that wants hard use :—
> We are yet but young in deeds."

Afterwards he becomes indeed "bloody, bold, and resolute;" and he orders the massacre of Macduff's kindred without hesitation or compunction.

> "From this moment
> The very firstlings of my heart shall be
> The firstlings of my hand. And even now,
> To crown my thoughts with acts, be it thought and done :
> The castle of Macduff I will surprise ;

> Seize upon Fife; give to the edge o' the sword
> His wife, his babes, and all unfortunate souls
> That trace him in his line.   No boasting like a fool;
> This deed I'll do before this purpose cool."

Subsequently to this foul deed, the tyrant supported his power with many acts of sudden and bloody violence : for, notwithstanding the great rapidity of action in the drama, an interval in reality of some years must be supposed between the first and last acts, during which time

> " Each new morn,
> New widows howl; new orphans cry; new sorrows
> Strike heaven on the face."

See also the fine description of the country under the tyrant's sway given by Rosse :

> " The dead man's knell
> Is there scarce ask'd for who; and good men's lives
> Expire before the flowers in their caps,
> Dying or ere they sicken."

The change in Macbeth's nervous system, from its early sensibility, when he was young in deeds of guilt, to the obtuseness brought on by hard use, is later in the piece described by himself :

> " *Seyton.* It is the cry of women, my good lord.
> *Macbeth.* I have almost forgot the taste of fears :
> The time has been, my senses would have quail'd
> To hear a night-shriek; and my fell of hair
> Would at a dismal treatise rouse and stir
> As life were in 't : I have supp'd full with horrors;
> Direness, familiar to my slaughterous thoughts,
> Cannot once start me.—Wherefore was that cry?
> *Sey.* The queen, my lord, is dead."

To the last, the shadow of madness is most skilfully
indicated as hovering around Maebeth, without the
reality actually falling upon him.   When finally
brought to bay in his stronghold, the opinion of his
madness is positively expressed :

> "Great Dunsinane he strongly fortifies :
> Some say he's mad ; others that lesser hate him
> Do call it valiant fury : but, for certain,
> 'He cannot buckle his distemper'd cause
> Within the belt of rule."

The cause of his reputed madness is conscience.

> "Who then shall blame
> His pester'd senses to recoil and start,
> When all that is within him does condemn
> Itself for being there ?"

The defiant fierceness of his resistance is not within
the belt of rule.   He'll fight till from his bones the
flesh is hacked ; put on his armour before 'tis needed ;

> "Send out more horses ; skirr the country round ;
> Hang those that talk of fear."

But with all this valiant fury, he is sick at heart,
oppressed with profound weariness of life : "I 'gin to
be a-weary of the sun."   What exquisite pathos in
the melancholy passages :

> "My way of life
> Is fall'n into the sear, the yellow leaf ;
> And that which should accompany old age,
> As honour, love, obedience, troops of friends,
> I must not look to have ; but, in their stead,
> Curses, not loud but deep, mouth-honour, breath,
> Which the poor heart would fain deny, and dare not."

And in this, so Hamlet like :

> " She should have died hereafter ;
> There would have been a time for such a word.
> To-morrow, and to-morrow, and to-morrow,
> Creeps in this petty pace from day to day,
> To the last syllable of recorded time,
> And all our yesterdays have lighted fools
> The way to dusty death.   Out, out, brief candle !
> Life's but a walking shadow, a poor player
> That struts and frets his hour upon the stage
> And then is heard no more : it is a tale
> Told by an idiot, full of sound and fury,
> Signifying nothing."

When all hope has fled, his superabundant activity rejects the very idea of self-destruction. He will not play the Roman fool, and die on his own sword. Gashes look best on others. In the last scene, in which the lying juggle of the fiend is unmasked, and he falls by the sword of Macduff, some remaining touches of conscience and of nature are shewn. At first he refuses to fight :

> " My soul is too much charged
> With blood of thine already."

When even fate deserts him, and his better part of man is cowed, he fights bravely to the last, and falls in a manner which the poet takes care to mark, in the scene which immediately follows, as the honourable end of a soldier's life. He descends from the light a fearful example of a noble mind, depraved by yielding to the tempter ; a terrible evidence of the fires of hell lighted in the breast of a living man by his own act.

D

The character of Lady Macbeth is less interesting
to the psychological student than that of her husband.
It is far less complex; drawn with a classic simplicity
of outline, it presents us with none of those balancing
and contending emotions which make the character
of Macbeth so wide and varied a field of study. It
does not come within the scope of this criticism to
enquire at length into the relative degree of wickedness and depravity exhibited by the two great crimi-
nals. Much ingenious speculation has been expended
on this subject, one upon which writers are never
likely entirely to agree so long as different people
have antipathies and preferences for different forms
of character. The first idea of the crime undoubtedly
comes into the mind of Macbeth before he sees his
wife; the suggestion of it fills his mind immediately
after his interview with the weird Sisters, and he
indicates the strong hold which the horrible imagination takes on him.

> "Stars, hide your fires;
> Let not light see my black and deep desires:
> The eye wink at the hand; yet let that be,
> Which the eye fears, when it is done, to see."

But in Macbeth's letter to his wife there is not
a word by which the enterprise can be said to be
broken to her, and she expresses her own fell purpose
before their meeting. At the first moment of their
meeting she replies to his assertion, that Duncan
goes hence to-morrow:

"O, never
Shall sun that morrow see !"

The idea of the crime arises in the minds of both
man and wife, without suggestion from either to the
other ; though in Macbeth the idea is a "horrible
imagining," while in Lady Macbeth it is a "fell
purpose."

Lady Macbeth's subsequent taunt,—

"What beast was't, then,
That made you break this enterprise to me ?"

"Nor time nor place did then cohere,
And yet you would make both,"—

appears to us, though we dare hardly say it, a flaw
in the plot. It is certainly inconsistent with Lady
Macbeth's language at her first meeting with her lord.
The truthfulness of these expressions can only be
saved by supposing them to have referred to con-
fidences between husband and wife on Duncan's
murder, before Macbeth went to the wars ; a supposition inconsistent with the development of the
wicked thought as it is pourtrayed after the meeting
with the weird Sisters.

The terrible remorseless impersonation of passionate ambition delineated in the character of Lady
Macbeth is not gradually developed, but is placed
at once in all its fierce power before us in that awful
invocation to the spirits of evil :

"Come, you spirits
That tend on mortal thoughts, unsex me here,
And fill me from the crown to the toe top-full

Of direst cruelty ! make thick my blood ;
Stop up the access and passage to remorse,
That no compunctious visitings of nature
Shake my fell purpose, nor keep peace between
The effect and it ! Come to my woman's breasts,
And take my milk for gall, you murdering ministers,
Wherever in your sightless substances
You wait on nature's mischief ! Come, thick night,
And pall thee in the dunnest smoke of hell,
That my keen knife see not the wound it makes,
· Nor heaven peep through the blanket of the dark,
To cry *Hold, Hold !*"

With what vehemence and unchanging resolution
does she carry out this fell purpose ; how she domi-
nates the spirit of her vacillating husband ; with what
inflexible and pitiless determination she pursues that
one great crime which gives her sovereign sway and
masterdom ! It is, however, to be remarked, that she
is not exhibited as participating in her husband's
crimes after the murder of Duncan. Having seized
upon " the golden round," her high moral courage and
self-contained nature save her from those eternal suspicions and that restlessness of imagination which
lead her husband onward from crime to crime. Her
want of imagination, her very want of sympathy,
would save her from that perversion of sympathy,
which in her husband resulted in useless deeds of
blood. There are some characters capable of committing one great crime, and of resting upon it ; there
are others in whom the first crime is certainly and
necessarily followed by a series of crimes. A bad,
cold, selfish, and unfeeling heart may preserve a

person from that fever of wickedness which a more sympathising nature is prone to run into when the sympathies are perverted, and the mobile organization lends itself to effect their destructive suggestions. We have above indicated the turning point of Lady Macbeth's madness to have been the state of inactivity into which she fell when her husband broke away from her support into that bloody, bold, and resolute career which followed the murder of Banquo. We can only speculate upon her course of conduct from this time. She probably in some manner gave her countenance to her husband's career, or she would scarcely have been called his "fiend-like queen"; for it must be remembered, that, although the reader is well aware of her guilt, no suspicion of her participation in Duncan's murder has been excited in the other personages of the drama. We may suppose, then, that without active participation in that career of tyranny which desolated Scotland, she looked on with frigid and cruel indifference, while her imagination having no power to throw itself outwardly, it became the prey of one engrossing emotion, that of remorse. Giving no outward expression of it in word or deed, she verified the saying of Malcolm—

> " The grief that does not speak,
> Whispers the o'erfraught heart, and bids it break."

Cold, stedfast, and self-contained, she could no more escape from the gnawing tooth of remorse, than Prometheus, chained upon his rock, could escape from

the vulture-talons for ever tearing his vitals. In
Macbeth's more demonstrative and flexible nature
passion was explosive; in her it was consuming. In
him the inward fires found a volcanic vent; in her
their pent-up force shook in earthquake the deep
foundations of the soul.

Lady Macbeth's end is psychologically even more
instructive than that of her husband. The manner
in which even-handed justice deals with her, "his
fiend-like wife," is an exquisite masterpiece of dramatic skill. The undaunted metal which would have
compelled her to resist to the last, if brought face to
face with any resistible adversaries, gradually gives
way to the feeling of remorse and deep melancholy
when left to feed upon itself. The moral object of
the drama required that the fierce gnawing of remorse
at the heart of the lady should be made manifest;
and, as her firm self-contained nature imposes upon
her a reticence in her waking moments in strong
contrast to the soliloquising loquacity of her demonstrative husband, the great dramatist has skilfully
availed himself of the sleep-talking state in which
she uncovers the corroding ulcers of her conscience.
Whether the deep melancholy of remorse often tends
to exhibit itself in somnambulism, is a fact which may
on scientific grounds be doubted. Shakespeare makes
the Doctor himself express the doubt: "This disease
is beyond my practice; yet I have known those which
have walked in their sleep, who have died holily in

their beds." The phenomena of sleep-walking are painted with great truthfulness. In this slumbrous agitation "the benefit of sleep" cannot be received, as the Doctor thinks. It neither exerts its soothing effects on the mind, nor is it "chief nourisher in life's feast" to the body.—Light must be left by her continually. Was this to avert the presence of those "sightless substances" once so impiously invoked?— She "seems washing her hands," and "continues in this a quarter of an hour." What a comment on her former boast, "A little water clears us of this deed." —The panorama of her crime passes before her, searing the eye-balls of the fancy; a fancy usually so cold and impassive, but now in agonising erethism. A wise and virtuous man can "thank God for his happy dreams," in which "the slumber of the body seems to be but the waking of the soul"; dreams of which he says "it is the ligation of sense, but the liberty of reason, and our waking conceptions do not match the fancies of our sleep." "There is surely a nearer apprehension of anything that delights us in our dreams than in our waked senses." "Were my memory as faithful as my reason is then fruitful, I would never study but in my dreams; and this time also would I chuse for my devotions." *(Religio Medici.)* But the converse? Who can tell the torture of bad dreams! Surely, 'tis better in the mind to lie in restless ecstacy, than thus to have the naked fancy stretched upon the rack; all its defences gone, all

power of voluntary attention and abstraction, all
guidance of the thoughts, all judgment abrogated.
What more lurid picture of hell can be formed than
that it is one long bad dream!

"*Gentlewoman.* Since his majesty went into the field, I
have seen her rise from the bed, throw her night-gown upon
her, unlock her closet, take forth paper, fold it, write upon't,
read it, afterwards seal it, and again return to bed; yet all
this while in a most fast sleep.

Doctor. A great perturbation in nature, to receive at once
the benefit of sleep, and do the effects of watching! In
this slumbery agitation, besides her walking and other actual
performances, what, at any time, have you heard her say?"

    *   *   *   *   *   *

"*Gent.* Lo you, here she comes! This is her very
guise; and, upon my life, fast asleep. Observe her; stand
close.

Doct. How came she by that light?

Gent. Why, it stood by her: she has light by her continually; 'tis her command.

Doct. You see, her eyes are open.

Gent. Ay, but their sense is shut.

Doct. What is it she does now? Look, how she rubs
her hands.

Gent. It is an accustomed action with her, to seem thus
washing her hands: I have known her continue in this
a quarter of an hour.

Lady Macbeth. Yet here's a spot.

Doct. Hark! she speaks: I will set down what comes
from her, to satisfy my remembrance the more strongly.

Lady M. Out, damned spot! out, I say!—One: two:
why, then 'tis time to do't.—Hell is murky!—Fie, my
lord, fie! a soldier, and afeard? What need we fear who
knows it, when none can call our power to account?—Yet
who would have thought the old man to have had so much
blood in him.

Doct. Do you mark that?

Lady M. The thane of Fife had a wife: where is she

now?—What, will these hands ne'er be clean?—No more
o' that, my lord, no more o' that: you mar all with this
starting.

Doct. Go to, go to; you have known what you should
not.

Gent. She has spoke what she should not, I am sure of
that: heaven knows what she has known.

Lady M. Here's the smell of the blood still: all the
perfumes of Arabia will not sweeten this little hand. Oh,
oh, oh!

Doct. What a sigh is there! The heart is sorely charged.

Gent. I would not have such a heart in my bosom for
the dignity of the whole body."

The diagnosis arrived at by the judicious and
politic Doctor appears to have been, that she was
scarcely insane, but so sorely troubled in conscience
as to be prone to quit the anguish of this life by
means of suicide.

> " Unnatural deeds
> Do breed unnatural troubles : infected minds
> To their deaf pillows will discharge their secrets :
> More needs she the divine than the physician.
> God, God forgive us all ! Look after her ;
> Remove from her the means of all annoyance,
> And still keep eyes upon her."

A passage at the very end of the drama indicates,
though it does not assert, that the fear of the Doctor
was realized—

> " his fiend-like queen,
> Who, as 'tis thought, by self and violent hands
> Took off her life."

This diagnosis of the Doctor, that actual disease was
not present, is again expressed in his interview with
Macbeth :

Macb. How does your patient, doctor?
Doct. Not so sick, my lord,
As she is troubled with thick-coming fancies,
That keep her from her rest.
Macb. Cure her of that.
Canst thou not minister to a mind diseased,
Pluck from the memory a rooted sorrow,
Raze out the written troubles of the brain,
And with some sweet oblivious antidote
Cleanse the stuff'd bosom of that perilous stuff
. Which weighs upon the heart?
Doct. Therein the patient
Must minister to himself.
Macb. Throw physic to the dogs; I'll none of it."

This contempt of physic was not ill-founded upon the want of reliance which the Doctor expressed on the resources of his art. In those early times the leech and the mediciner had not learnt to combine the moral influences which are the natural means of ministering to a mind diseased after the manner of Lady Macbeth's, with those sleep-producing oblivious antidotes which at present form the remedies of melancholia. Such a patient would not now be given over, either to the divine, or to the unresisted ravages of conscience. What indeed could the divine effect without the aid of the physician? or, rather, until the physician had done his work? In such a state of nervous system as that of this wretched lady, no judicious divine would attempt to excite religious emotion; indeed, all thoughts of the world to come would act as fuel to the fire of a conscience so remorseful. The treatment of such a case as that of

Lady Macbeth would be, to remove her from all scenes suggesting unhappy thoughts, to attract her attention to new objects of interest, and to find, if possible, some stimulus to healthy emotion. If she had been thrown from her high estate, and compelled to labour for her daily bread, the tangible evils of such a condition would have been, most likely, to have rooted out those of the imagination and of memory. The judicious physician, moreover, would not in such a case have neglected the medicinal remedies at his command, especially those which Macbeth himself seems to indicate, under the title of some sweet oblivious antidote. He would have given the juice of poppy, or some "drowsy syrup," to prevent thick-coming fancies depriving her of rest. He would thus have replaced the unrefreshing, nay, exhausting sleep of somnambulism, for that condition so beautifully described, earlier in the play, as that which

> " knits up the ravell'd sleave of care,
> The death of each day's life, sore labour's bath,
> Balm of hurt minds, great nature's second course,
> Chief nourisher in life's feast."

When these remedies had produced their effect, and the patient's remorse was no longer of that " brain-sickly" kind accompanying disorders of the organization, then, and only then, might the divine step in with those consolations of religious faith which assure us that "though your sins be as scarlet, they shall be as white as snow; though they be red like crimson, they shall be as wool."

What was Lady Macbeth's form and temperament? In Maclise's great painting of the banquet scene, she is represented as a woman of large and coarse development; a Scandinavian amazon, the muscles of whose brawny arms could only have been developed to their great size by hard and frequent use; a woman of whose fists her husband might well be afraid; but scarcely one who would present that Satanic spiritualization of character which we find in this awful impersonation of dauntless and ruthless ambition; an instrument, in fact, to do coarse things coarsely; a butcher's cleaver perhaps, but by no means the keen scimitar whose rapid blow destroys ere it is seen. We do not so figure Lady Macbeth to the mind's eye—no, not even as the large and majestic figure of Siddons, whose impersonation of the character so moved our fathers. Shakespeare was not in the habit of delineating big and brawny women. There is a certain femininity in his female characters, which is distinguishable even in those whom he has filled with the coarser passions. But that Lady Macbeth, whose soul is absorbed and whose devilish deeds are instigated by ambition, the highest of all earthly passions, "the last infirmity of noble minds," which, like Aaron's rod, consumes and destroys the meaner desires,—that this woman should have had the physical conformation of a cook, is a monstrous

libel upon the sex. Regan and Goneril, whom we
not only hate, but who excite disgust in our minds,
might have been such women, coarse and low natures
as they were; and indeed they are represented as
using their fists with a freedom proving the reliance
they placed in the efficiency of that safety-valve to
passion; and Lear threatens the wolfish visage of
one with the nails of the other. But was Lady Macbeth such a being? Did the fierce fire of her soul
animate the epicene bulk of a virago? Never! Lady
Macbeth was a lady beautiful and delicate, whose one
vivid passion proves that her organization was instinct
with nerve-force, unoppressed by weight of flesh.
Probably she was small; for it is the smaller sort
of women whose emotional fire is the most fierce, and
she herself bears unconscious testimony to the fact
that her hand was little. The drama contains many
indications that to outward appearance she was
gentle and feminine. Duncan greets her by the
name of "most kind hostess"; and, after the murder,
Macduff says:

> "Gentle lady,
> 'Tis not for you to hear what I can speak:
> The repetition in a woman's ear
> Would murder as it fell."

Although she manifests no feeling towards Macbeth
beyond the regard which ambition makes her yield, it
is clear that he entertains for her the personal love
which a beautiful woman would excite. Returning

from the wars, he greets her with "Dearest love!" "Dearest partner of my greatness!" Afterwards he lavishes upon her the terms of endearment, "Love!" "Dear wife!" "Dearest chuck!" "Sweet remembrancer!" Above all, she makes use of his love to taunt him with his change of purpose, when it looked green and pale at the contemplated murder of Duncan. "From this time," she says, "such I account thy love." She relies upon this threat of disbelief in his love as a goad to urge him to his first great crime; and she applies this motive with the confident assurance that the love was there to give it force. Moreover, the effect of remorse upon her own health proves the preponderance of nerve in her organization. Could the Lady Macbeth of Mr. Maclise, and of others who have painted this lady, have been capable of the fire and force of her character in the commission of her crimes, the remembrance of them would scarcely have disturbed the quiet of her after years. We figure Lady Macbeth to have been a tawny or brown blonde Rachel, with more beauty, with grey and cruel eyes, but with the same slight dry configuration and constitution, instinct with determined nerve-power.*

The scene with the Doctor at the English court

---

* Since the above was written, we have been informed that Mrs. Siddons herself entertained an opinion of Lady Macbeth's physique similar to our own; and that in Mrs. Jameson's critique on this character, which we have not had the opportunity of consulting, the same opinion is expressed.

has several points of interest, besides that of antiquarian medicine. It fixes the date of Macbeth's
history as that of Edward the Confessor's time. It
was doubtless introduced as a compliment to James
the First, who assumed the power of curing scrofula,
the king's evil, by means of the king's touch. Another
passage indicates that it was written in this reign, and
thus that it was one of the later productions of the
poet. James was descended from Banquo, and in the
last Witch scene Macbeth thus refers to the lineage of
his rival :

> "And some I see
> That two-fold balls and treble sceptres carry."

HAMLET.

ALL critical study of Hamlet must be psychological;
and as there are few subjects which have been more
closely studied, and more copiously written upon, than
this magnificent drama, criticism upon it might seem
to be exhausted. But human nature itself is still
more trite; yet, study it profoundly as we can,
criticise and speculate upon it as we may, much will
ever be left outside the largest grasp of those minds
who undertake to elucidate so much of it as they can
comprehend. Hamlet is human nature, or at least
a wide range of it, and no amount of criticism can
exhaust the wealth of this magnificent storehouse.
It invites and evades criticism. Its mysterious pro-
fundity fascinates the attention; its infinite variety
and its hidden meanings deny exhaustive analysis.
Some leavings of treasure will always be discoverable
to those who seek for it in an earnest and reverent
spirit. Probably no two minds can ever contemplate
Hamlet from exactly the same point of view, as no
two men can ever regard human life under exactly
the same aspect. Hence truthful criticism of this
great drama is not only various as mind itself, but is
apt to become reflective of the critic. The strong

sense of Johnson, the subtle insight of Coleridge, the fervid eloquence of Hazlitt, the discriminating tact of Schlegel, are nowhere more evident than in their treatment of this mighty monument of human intellect. Every man who has learned to think, and has dared to question the inward monitor, has seen some part of the character of Hamlet reflected in his own bosom.

It will form no part of the subject of this essay to criticise the dramatic construction of Hamlet. We may, however, confess ourselves to be among those who cannot see in its construction that perfect art which has been so abundantly shewn by Shakespeare in many other pieces. Of the petty anachronisms which sent Hamlet to school in Wittenberg, which allow Ophelia to call for a coach, and the King's palace to resound with salvos of artillery, we make small account; like spots on the sun's surface, they only impress themselves upon those who look upon the great work through some medium capable of obscuring its glories. The great length appears by no means an imperfection of this drama as a composition, whatever it may be as an acting play. The analysis of the motives of human action, which is the great object of this work, could not have been effected if the action had been rapid. Rapidity of action is inconsistent with philosophic self-analysing motives and modes of thought; while the slow and halting progress of the action in this drama not only affords to

E

the character space and verge enough to unfold the inmost peculiarities of thought and feeling, but develops in the mind of the reader a state of receptivity scarcely less essential to its full appreciation.

Once for all, let us say, in pointing out what appear to us difficulties to a logical apprehension of this piece from that point of view which contemplates the development of character and the laws of mind, we do not urge these difficulties as objections to this great drama, which we love and prize more than any other human piece of composition. We venture to find no fault with Hamlet; we revere even its irregularities, as we prefer the various beauties of forest landscape to the straight walks and trim parterres of a well-kept garden. There are more irregularities and unexpected turns of action in Hamlet than in any other of Shakespeare's plays. Our belief is, that the poet became charmed with the creature of his own imagination as it developed itself from his fertile brain ; and that as he gave loose reign to poetic fancy and philosophic reverie, he more than ever spurned the narrow limits of dramatic art. The works of Shakespeare's imagination, contrasted with those of the Greek dramatists, have been said to resemble a vast cathedral, combining in one beautiful structure various forms of architecture, various towers and pinnacles,—the whole irregular, vast, and beautiful. The drama of the Greeks, on the other hand, has been said to resemble their temples, finished in one style, perfect and regular. The *simile* is true and instructive, and in no case more so than in its application to Hamlet. If in our admiration of its whole effect,—if in our reverent examination of its parts, its pinnacles of beauty, its shrines of passion, its gorgeous oriels of many-coloured thought,—we venture to express the difficulties we experience in understanding how one part grew out of another, and the many parts grew to form the wondrous whole, let our criticism be accepted as that of one who examines only to learn and to enjoy.

It is known that Shakespeare devoted more time to this than to any other of his works, and that in its construction he altered and re-altered much. The work bears evident traces of this elaboration, both in its lengthy and slow action, in its great diversity of incident and character, and in the perfection of its parts contrasted with some loss of uniformity as a whole. Some of his plays (as the Merry Wives of Windsor) Shakespeare is said to have thrown off with incredible rapidity and facility ; but this certainly is not one in which he "warbled his native wood-notes wild." It was the laboured and elaborate result of years of toil, of metaphysical introspection and observation. It was the darling child of its great author, and ran some risk of being a little spoiled. A singular trace of this remodeling, which the commentators appear to have overlooked, is left in the different ages which are assigned to Hamlet in the earlier part and

at the end of the drama. The Prince is introduced
as a mere youth, whose intent,

"In going back to school in Wittenburg,"

the King opposes. His love is described as

"A violet in the youth of primy nature;"

and he is so "young" that he may walk with a large
tether in such matters. He has not even attained his
full stature, for

"Nature, crescent, does not grow alone
In thews and bulk; but, as this temple waxes,
The inward service of the mind and soul
Grows wide withal."

To his mistress he appears in the "unmatched form
and feature of *blown youth.*" In fact, he is a young
gentleman of eighteen or thereabouts. The inconsistency of attributing such profound powers of reflection, and such a blasé state of emotion, to a youth
who could scarcely have had beard enough to be
plucked, appears so forcibly to have struck Shakespeare, that he condescends to that which with him
is a matter of the rarest occurrence, an explanation
or contradiction of the error. With curious care he
makes the Sexton lay down the age of the Prince
at thirty years. He came to his office "the very day
that young Hamlet was born;" and he had been
"sexton here, man and boy, thirty years." As if this
were not enough, he confirms it with the history of
Yorick's skull, which "has been in the earth three

and twenty years ;" Yorick, whose qualities were well remembered by Hamlet, "a fellow of infinite jest, of most excellent fancy ; he hath borne me on his back a thousand times ;" a kind of memory not likely to have stamped itself before the age of seven ; and thus we have Hamlet presented to us not as an unformed youth, but a man of age competent to his power of thought, and of the age most liable to his state of feeling.

The first scene, where the Ghost appears to the sentinels on watch, is constructed with exquisite dramatic verisimilitude, and is admirably adapted to prepare the mind for that contest between the materialism of sensation and that idealism of passion, that doubting effort to discriminate between the things which are and the things which seem, which is the mark thread in the philosophy of the piece.

The Ghost appears at cold and silent midnight. "'Tis bitter cold, and I am sick at heart." "Not a mouse stirring," says Francisco. On this Coleridge remarks, that "in all the best attested stories of ghosts and visions, the ghost-seers were in a state of cold or chilling damp from without, and of anxiety inwardly." As far as visions are concerned, this observation might have psychological importance, as tending to indicate the conditions of the nervous system favourable to the production of hallucination; but with regard to ghosts seen by many persons at the same time, if such things have been, it could only indicate that, escaped for

a while from "sulphurous and tormenting flames,"
these airy existences preferred to walk on cold nights.

We cannot consent to reduce the Ghost of Hamlet
to physiological laws.

> "We do it wrong, being so majestical,
>   To offer it the shew of" *science.*

The Ghost in Hamlet can in no wise be included
within the category of illusions or hallucinations; it
is anti-physiological, and must be simply accepted as
a dramatic circumstance calculated to produce a
certain state of mind in the hero of the piece.
Hazlitt well says, that actors playing Macbeth have
always appeared to him to have seen the weird sisters
on the stage only. He never had seen a stage
Macbeth look and act as if he had been face to face
with the supernatural. We have experienced the same
feeling in seeing the most approved representations
of Hamlet; and doubtless Goëthe had felt the same,
since in the representation of Hamlet in Wilhelm
Meister he produces upon the stage that which the
tyro player takes for a real ghost. No person to act
the part had been provided, and something marvellous had been mysteriously promised; but he had
forgotten it, probably intending to dispense with the
appearance. When it came, "the noble figure, the
low inaudible breath, the light movements in heavy
armour, made such an impression on him that he
stood as if transformed to stone, and could only utter
in a half-voice, 'Angels and ministers of grace defend

us.' He glared at the form, drew a deep breathing once or twice, and pronounced his address to the Ghost in a manner so confused, so broken, so constrained, that the highest art could not have hit the mark so well." Besides the part it takes in the development of the plot, the *rôle* of the Ghost is to account for, if not to produce, a high-wrought state of nerve in the hero: and in the acting play to produce the same effect in lesser degree on the audience. Fielding has described this, when Tom Jones takes Partridge to see Garrick in the character of Hamlet. The life-like acting of the English Roscius, combined with the superstition of the schoolmaster, produces so thorough a conviction of the actual presence of the Ghost, that the result is one of the drollest scenes ever painted by that inimitable romancist.

Hamlet is from the first moment represented in that mood of melancholy which vents itself in bitter sarcasm: "A little more than kin, and less than kind." He is "too much i' the sun." Sorry quips truly, but yet good enough for the hypocritical King, who wishes to rejoice and to lament at the same moment:

> "With an auspicious and a dropping eye,
> With mirth in funeral and with dirge in marriage,
> In equal scale weighing delight and dole."

To the King's unfeeling arguments that the son ought not to grieve for the death of his father, because it is a common theme and an unavailing woe, Hamlet vouchsafes no reply. But to his mother's rebuke, that the common grief "seems" particular to him, he answers with a vehemence which shews that the clouds which hang on him are surcharged with electric fire :

> "Seems, madam ! nay, it is ; I know not 'seems'.
> 'Tis not alone my inky cloak," &c.

He has that within which passes show ; and, when left alone, he tells us what it is in that outburst of grief :

> "O, that this too too solid flesh would melt,
>   Thaw and resolve itself into a dew !
>   Or that the Everlasting had not fix'd
>   His canon 'gainst self-slaughter !   O God ! O God !
>   How weary, stale, flat, and unprofitable,
>   Seem to me all the uses of this world !
>   Fie on't ! ah fie ! 'tis an unweeded garden,
>   That grows to seed ; things rank and gross in nature
>   Possess it merely.   That it should come to this !
>   But two months dead !" &c.

It is the conflict of religious belief with suicidal desire. In his pure and sensitive mind the conduct of his mother has produced shame and keen distress. His generalising tendency leads him to extend his mother's failings to her whole sex—"Frailty, thy name is woman ;" and from thence the sense of disgust shrouds as with foul mist the beauty of the world, and all its uses seem "weary, stale, flat, and unprofitable." To general dissatisfaction with men and the world succeeds the longing desire to quit the scene of shame and woe. In the subsequent arguments which the Prince holds with himself on suicide, he acknowledges the constraining power to be the fear of future punishment : but in this passage the higher motive of religious obedience without fear is acknowledged ; a higher and a holier motive for the duty of bearing the evils which God permits, and refusing to break His law to escape from them, whatever their pressure may be. A bold man may "jump the life to come" in the very spirit of courage ; but a true servant and soldier of God will feel that there is unfaithfulness and cowardice in throwing off by voluntary death whatever burden of sorrows may freight the frail vessel of his life.

The concluding line equally marks profound sorrow, and the position of dependence and constraint in which Hamlet feels himself :

"But break, my heart, for I must hold my tongue."

And yet what rapid recovery to the quick-witted complaisance of social intercourse, when his friends break in upon these gloomy thoughts ; and, again, mark the natural contiguity, in a mind equally sensitive and melancholic, of bantering sarcasm and profound emotion :

"Thrift, thrift, Horatio ! the funeral baked-meats
Did coldly furnish forth the marriage tables.
Would I had met my dearest foe in heaven
Or ever I had seen that day !"

This early passage seems to give the key-note of Hamlet's temper, namely, soul-crushing grief in close alliance with an ironical, often a broad humour, which

can mock at despair.   Profound life-weariness and
suicidal desire indicate that from the first his emotions
were morbid, and that the accusation of the King that
he had

> "A heart unfortified, a mind impatient,
>   An understanding simple and unschooled,"

was as true of the heart as it was false of the intellect.
Yet his rapid recovery from brooding thoughts, and
his entire self-possession when circumstances call
upon him for action trivial or important, prove that
his mind was not permanently off its poise.   Profoundly reflective, capable of calling up thoughts and
ideas of sense at will, of seeing his father "in his
mind's eye," he is equally capable of dismissing them
and throwing himself into the present.   How thoroughly self-possessed is he in his interview with his
friend and fellow-student and the soldiers, and the
reception he gives to their account of the apparition,
by which they were "distilled almost to jelly by the
act of fear;" how unhesitating his decision to see and
speak to it, "though hell itself should gape!" and in
the seventh scene, when actually waiting for the
Ghost, what cool reflection in his comments on the
wassail of the country.   Yet he heard not the clock
strike midnight, which the less pre-occupied sense of
Marcellus had caught.   His address to the Ghost,

> "Angels and ministers of grace defend us!
>   Be thou a spirit of health or goblin damned?" &c.

is marked by a bold and cool reason, at a time when
the awful evidences of the future make

> "us fools of nature
> So horridly to shake our disposition
> With thoughts beyond the reaches of our souls."

The courage of the Prince is of the noblest temper,
and is made the more obvious from its contrast with
the dread of his companions, who suggest that *it*, the
neutral *thing*, as it has before been called, may tempt
him to the summit of the cliff,

> "And there assume some other horrible form,
> Which might deprive your sovereignty of reason
> And draw you into madness.   Think of it :
> The very place puts toys of desperation,
> Without more motive, into every brain
> That looks so many fathoms to the sea
> And hears it roar beneath."

But Hamlet is beyond all touch of fear.

> "My fate cries out,
> And makes each petty artery in this body
> As hardy as the Nemean lion's nerve."

Horatio says, "He waxes desperate with imagination;"
but his state really appears to be that of high-wrought
yet reasonable courage.   After following the Ghost
to some distance he'll "go no further"; but if this is
said with any touch of fear it soon becomes pity :
"Alas, poor Ghost!"   And this, again, changes to
revengeful resolution.   He demands quickly to know
the author of his father's murder, that he

> "May sweep to his revenge."

But when the Ghost has told his terrible tale, and has disappeared, with the solemn farewell, "Adieu, adieu, adieu! remember me," the reaction comes. Then it is that Hamlet feels his sinews fail their function, and invokes them to bear him stiffly up ; then he recognises a feeling of distraction in the globe of his brain ; then he vows forgetfulness of all things but the motive of revenge. He becomes wild at the thoughts of the "smiling damned villain" who had wrought all this woe ; and then, passing from the terrible to the trivial, he sets down in his tables a moral platitude :

> "My tables ! meet it is, I set it down,
> That one may smile, and smile, and be a villain ;
> At least I am sure it may be so in Denmark."

We regard this climax of the terrible in the trivial, this transition of mighty emotion into lowliness of action, as one of the finest psychological touches any-where to be found in the poet. There is something like it in Tennyson's noble poem, Maud. When the hero has shot the brother of his mistress in a duel, he passes from intense passion to trivial observation :

> "Strange that the mind, when fraught
> With a passion so intense,
> One would think that it well
> Might drown all life in the eye,—
> That it should, by being so overwrought,
> Suddenly strike on a sharper sense
> For a shell, or a flower, little things
> Which else would have been past by !
> And now I remember, I,

> When he lay dying there,
> I noticed one of his many rings,
> (For he had many, poor worm,) and thought,
> It is his mother's hair."

When the mind is wrought to an excessive pitch of emotion, the instinct of self-preservation indicates some lower mode of mental activity as the one thing needful. When Lear's passions are wrought to the utmost, he says, "I'll *do!* I'll *do!* I'll *do!*" But he does nothing. Had he been able, like Hamlet, to have taken out his note-book, it would have been good for his mental health. Mark the effect of the restraint which Hamlet is thus able to put upon the tornado of his emotion. When the friends rejoin him, he is self-possessed enough swiftly to turn their curiosity aside. Horatio, indeed, remarks on his manner of doing so, and on his expression of the intention, for his own poor part, to go pray:

> "These are but wild and whirling words, my lord."

Doubtless the excitement of manner would make them appear to be more deserving of this comment than they do in reading. Yet Hamlet knows thoroughly well what he is about, and proceeds to swear his friends to secrecy on his sword. The flippant comments on the awful underground voice of the Ghost "the fellow in the cellarage," "old mole," "truepenny," are another meeting point of the sublime and the ridiculous, or rather a voluntary refuge in the trivial from the awful presence of the terrible. They

are thoroughly true to the laws of our mental being.
How often have men gone out of life upon the scaffold
with a jest upon their lips.   Even the just and cool-
tempered Horatio, who takes fortune's buffets and
rewards with equal thanks, is astounded and terrified
at that underground voice which provokes but mocking retorts from the Prince.   Horatio exclaims :

"O, day and night, but this is wondrous strange !"

That Hamlet's mockery was the unreal opposite to
his true feeling, like the hysteric laughter of acute
grief, is evident from his last earnest adjuration :

"Rest, rest, perturbed spirit !"

How it is that the resolution of Hamlet to put on the
guise of madness follows so quick upon the appearance
of the Ghost to him, (indeed, while the spirit is yet
present, though unseen, for the resolution is expressed
before the final unearthly adjuration to swear,) we
are unable to explain.   His resolutions are not usually
taken with such quick speed ; and indeed the wings
of his meditation, which he refers to as swift, commonly beat the air with long and slow strokes, the
very reverse of Macbeth's vehement action, framed
upon the principle "that the flighty purpose never
is o'ertook, except the act goes with it."   It may,
however, be said that the word *"perchance"* shews
that Hamlet has not yet decided to act the madman
when he swears his friends to secrecy.

> "Never, so help you mercy !
> How strange or odd soe'er I bear myself,
> As I *perchance* hereafter shall think meet
> To put an antic disposition on."

And yet the intention must have resolve in it, even at this time, or he would not swear his friends in so solemn a manner to maintain inviolate the secret of his craft. The purport of Hamlet's feigned madness is not very obvious. It does not appear to have been needful to protect him, like that of the elder Brutus. It may be that under this disguise he hopes better to obtain proof of his uncle's guilt, and to conceal his real state of suspicion and vengeful gloom. Still more probable is it that Shakespeare adopted the feigned madness as an essential part of the old story on which the drama is founded.

The old history of Hamlet relates how he counterfeited the madman to escape the tyranny of his uncle Fengon, whose expedients resemble those in the drama which were resorted to by the King to ascertain whether his madness were counterfeited or not. The feigned madness, therefore, of the Prince was so leading a feature in the original history, that Shakespeare could by no means have omitted it, even if by doing so he would not have deprived himself of a magnificent canvass on which to display his psychological knowledge. As it stands however in the drama, the counterfeit madness would seem to bring Hamlet into more danger than security. What if the King had accepted his madness from the first, and shut him up, as he might have justified himself in doing, in some strong castle. After the death of Polonius, the King says:

> " His liberty is full of threats to all;
> To you yourself, to us, to every one.
> Alas! how shall this bloody deed be answer'd?
> It will be laid to us, whose providence
> Should have kept short, restrain'd, and out of haunt,
> This mad young man."

And again—

> " How dangerous is it that this man goes loose."

He puts not the strong law upon him indeed, as he says, because " he's loved of the distracted multitude," and because " the Queen lives but in his eyes." These motives may explain the King's conduct, but they do not shew that, in assuming the guise of madness, Hamlet was not incurring the risk of the limitation of his own freedom.

The first demonstration of the antic disposition he actually does put on, is made before his mistress, the fair Ophelia.

> "*Polonius.*   How now, Ophelia! what's the matter?
> *Ophelia.* O, my lord, my lord, I have been so affrighted!
> *Pol.* With what, i' the name of God?
> *Oph.* My lord, as I was sewing in my closet,
> Lord Hamlet, with his doublet all unbraced;
> No hat upon his head; his stockings foul'd,
> Ungarter'd, and down-gyved to his ancle;
> Pale as his shirt; his knees knocking each other;
> And with a look so piteous in purport
> As if he had been loosed out of hell
> To speak of horrors,—he comes before me.
> *Pol.* Mad for thy love?

Oph. My lord, I do not know;
But truly, I do fear it.
 Pol. What said he?
 Oph. He took me by the wrist and held me hard;
Then goes he to the length of all his arm;
And, with his other hand thus o'er his brow,
He falls to such perusal of my face
As he would draw it. Long stay'd he so;
At last, a little shaking of mine arm
And thrice his head thus waving up and down,
He raised a sigh so piteous and profound
That it did seem to shatter all his bulk
And end his being: that done, he lets me go:
And, with his head over his shoulder turn'd,
He seem'd to find his way without his eyes;
For out o' doors he went without their help,
And, to the last, bended their light on me.
 Pol. Come, go with me: I will go seek the king.
This is the very ecstasy of love,
Whose violent property fordoes itself
And leads the will to desperate undertakings
As oft as any passion under heaven
That does afflict our natures. I am sorry.
What, have you given him any hard words of late?
 Oph. No, my good lord, but, as you did command,
I did repel his letters and denied
His access to me."

We are at a loss to explain this part of Hamlet's
conduct towards his sweet mistress, unless it be accepted as the sad pantomime of separation, love's
mute farewell. That his noble and sensitive mind
entertained a sincere love to the beautiful and virtuous
girl, there can be no doubt. Surely it must have
been this love which he thus refers to in that paroxysm
of feeling at the close of the Ghost scene:

  " Yea, from the table of my memory
  I'll wipe away all trivial fond records."   F

Indeed, love is an autocratic passion not disposed
to share the throne of the soul with other emotions
of an absorbing nature. Hamlet, however, might feel
his resolution, to wipe from his memory the trivial
fond records of his love, strengthened into action by
the conduct of Ophelia herself, who repelled his letters
and denied his access, thus taking upon herself the
pain and responsibility of breaking off the relationship
in which she had stood to him, and in which with so
keen a zest of pleasure she had sucked in the honey-
music of his vows, and the reaction from which cost
her so dear. In his interview with Ophelia, arranged
by Polonius and the King, he speaks to her of his
love as a thing of the past. That that love was
ardent and sincere we learn from his passionate grief
at the grave of his dead mistress, a grief which, on
his own acknowledgment to his friend, we know to
have been no acting, but the demonstration of which
was due to the fact that he had forgot himself in the
presence of Laertes, the bravery of whose grief had
put him "into a towering passion." It is at this time,
when he had forgot himself, that he exclaims with
passionate vehemence,

> " I loved Ophelia ; forty thousand brothers
> Could not, with all their quantity of love,
> Make up my sum."

That Hamlet's conduct to Ophelia was unfeeling, in
thus forcing upon her the painful evidence of the
insanity he had assumed, can scarcely be denied.

Hamlet, however, was no perfect character, and in the matter of his love there is no doubt he partook of the selfishness which is the common attribute of the passion wherever its glow is the warmest. His love was not of that delicate sentimental kind which would above all things fear to disturb the beatitude of its object, and feel its highest pleasure in acts of self-denial. It was rather of that kind which women best appreciate—an ardent passion, not a sentimental devotion; and hence its tinge of selfishness. Yet, having put on his antic disposition with the trappings and suits of madness, he might feel that the kindest act he could perform towards Ophelia would be to concur with her in breaking off their courtship. He might, indeed, have allowed others to tell her that he had gone mad, and have saved her a great fright and agitation of mind; but, under the circumstances, it cannot be considered unnatural that he should selfishly enough have rushed into her presence to take leave of her in the mad pantomime which she describes. His conduct to Ophelia is a mixture of feigned madness, of the selfishness of passion blasted by the cursed blight of fate, of harshness which he assumes to protect himself from an affection which he feels hostile to the present purpose of his life, and of that degree of real unsoundness, his unfeigned "weakness and melancholy," which is the subsoil of his mind.

In the following scene the King explains to Rosen-

crantz and Guildenstern the condition of the Prince
in a manner which implies that at that time he entertained no doubt of the reality of his madness :

> "Something have you heard
> Of Hamlet's transformation ; so I call it,
> Since not the exterior nor the inward man
> Resembles that it was.   What it should be,
> More than his father's death, that thus hath put him
> So much from the understanding of himself,
> I cannot dream of."

The King's anxiety to ascertain "if aught to us unknown afflicts him thus," indicates the unrest of his
conscience, and the fear that some knowledge of his
own great crime may lie at the bottom of his nephew's
inward and outward transformation.   The same fearful anxiety shews itself immediately afterwards, when
on the vain half-doting Polonius at the same time
asserting that the Ambassadors from Norway are
joyfully returned, and that he has found "the very
cause of Hamlet's lunacy," the King exclaims, "Oh!
speak of that, that I do long to hear ;" thus bringing
upon himself the retort courteous of the old man,
that the news respecting Hamlet should be kept to
follow the pressing business of the moment, as dessert
fruit follows a feast.

From Polonius's exposition of Hamlet's madness,
which, in a manner so contrary to his own axiom
"that brevity is the soul of wit," he dilates upon with
such tediousness and empty flourishes of speech as to
draw upon himself the rebuke of the Queen, "more

matter with less art," one would almost think that
Shakespeare might have heard some lawyer, full of
his quiddets and cases, endeavouring by the sophistry
of abstract definitions to damage the evidence of
some medical man to whose experience the actual
concrete facts of insanity were matters of familiar
observation, but whose verbal expression had more
of pedantry than power:

> "I will be brief: your noble son is mad:
> Mad call I it; for, to define true madness,
> What is't but to be nothing else but mad?"

In the following lines, the old man recognises madness
to be a phenomenon, for which, like every other phenomenon, some cause or other must exist; and, moreover, that madness is not in itself a distinct entity,
something apart from the mind, but a *defect* in the
mind.

> "Mad let us grant him then: and now remains
> That we find out the cause of this effect,
> Or rather say, the cause of this defect,
> For this effect defective comes by cause."

Hamlet's letter to Ophelia is a silly-enough rhap-
sody; of which, indeed, the writer appears conscious.
It reads like an old letter antecedent to the events of
the drama. The spirit it breathes is scarcely consistent with the intense life-weariness under which its
author is first introduced to notice. The signature,
however, is odd. "Thine evermore, most dear lady,
whilst this *machine* is to him," and agrees with the

spirit of Hamlet's materialist philosophy, which is so strongly expressed in various parts of the play, and which forms so strange a contrast with the revelations from the spirit-world, of which he is made the recipient. The description which Polonius gives of the course of Hamlet's madness, after his daughter had locked herself from his resort and refused his messages and tokens, is vain and pedantic in its expression, but pregnant in meaning :

> " And he, repulsed—a short tale to make—
> Fell into a sadness, then into a fast,
> Thence to a watch, thence into a weakness,
> Thence to a lightness, and, by this declension,
> Into the madness wherein now he raves."

Translated into the dulness of medical prose, the psychological opinion of the old courtier may be thus expressed. Disappointed and rejected in his ardent addresses to Ophelia, Hamlet became melancholy and neglected to take food ; the result of fasting was the loss of sleep ; loss of sleep and loss of food were followed by general weakness ; this produced a lightness or instability of the mental functions, which passed into insanity. The suggestion made by Polonius to test the soundness of his view, that the Prince loved his daughter and had fallen from his reason thereon, was plain and practical, namely, to arrange and to watch in ambuscade interviews between him and the persons most likely to excite his emotion. Moreover, Shakespeare was in some sort bound to introduce these interviews, inasmuch as they formed an important part of the old history.

The Queen did not partake of the King's anxiety to ascertain the cause of her son's madness. When he tells her that Polonius

> "Hath found
> The head and source of all your son's distemper,"

she replies—

> "I doubt it is no other but the main;
> His father's death, and our o'erhasty marriage."

Hamlet now for the first time appears in his feigned character. The feint is so close to nature, and there is underlying it withal so undeniable a substratum of morbid feeling, that in spite of ourselves, in opposition to our full knowledge that in his antic disposition Hamlet is putting on a part, we cannot from the first dispossess ourselves of the idea, that a mind fallen, if not from the sovereignty of reason, at least from the balance of its faculties, is presented to us. So much is undirection of mind blended with pregnant sense and apprehension, both however perverted from the obvious line of sane thought; so much is the universal and caustic irony tinged with melancholic self-depreciation, and that longing for death which in itself alone constitutes a form of mental disease. In the various forms of partial insanity, it is a question of intricate science to distinguish between the portions of a man's conduct which result from the sound operations of mind, and those which result from disease.

Hamlet's own assertion, "I am but mad north-north-
west : when the wind is southerly I know a hawk from
a hand-saw," is pregnant with a psychological truth
which has often engaged the most skilful and laborious
investigation both of medical men and of lawyers.
It has often been a question of life or death, of wealth
or poverty, whether a criminal act was done, or a civil
one performed, by a half-madman, when the mental
wind was in the north-west of disease, or blowing
from the sanatory south.

That in his actual unfeigned mental condition
Hamlet is far from being in a healthy state of mind,
he is himself keenly conscious, and acknowledges it
to himself in his soliloquy upon the players :

> "The spirit that I have seen
> May be a devil : and the devil hath power
> To assume a pleasing shape ; yea, and perhaps
> *Out of my weakness and my melancholy,*
> As he is very potent with such spirits,
> Abuses me to damn me."

Upon this actual weakness of mind and suicidal
melancholy, combined with native humour and the
biting irony into which his view of the world has
sharpened it, is added the feigned form of insanity,
the antic disposition wilfully put on, the dishevelled
habiliments of person and wild converse. The characteristics of this feigned form are those of mania,
not indeed violent, acute, and demonstrative, but
mischievous, reckless, and wayward, and so mingled
with flashes of native wit, and disguised by the

ground colour of real melancholy, shewing through
the transparency of the feigned state, that Hamlet's
character becomes one of the most interesting and
complicated subjects of psychological study anywhere
to be met with.

He is first introduced to us in his feigning condition with a fine touch to excite pity :

" *Queen.* But, look, where sadly the poor wretch comes
reading.
Polonius. Do you know me, my lord ?
Hamlet. Excellent well ; you are a fishmonger."

Coleridge and others remark upon this, that Hamlet's
meaning is, You are sent to fish out this secret. But
we are not aware that fishmongers are in the habit
of catching their fish. May it not rather be that
a fishmonger was referred to as a dealer in perishable
goods, and notoriously dishonest ; and thus to give
point to the rejoinder—

" Then I would you were so honest a man."

The writers who insist upon a profound meaning, even
in Hamlet's most hurling words, have been mightily
puzzled with the lines :

" For if the sun breed maggots in a dead dog, being
a god kissing carrion," &c.

Coleridge refers to "some thought in Hamlet's
mind, contrasting Ophelia with the tedious old fool
her father." Is it not rather a wild taunt upon the
old man's jealous suspicion of his daughter, as if he
had said, since the sun causes conception in such

vile bodies, "let not your precious daughter walk in the sun."

Perhaps he only intended to convey to Polonius, by a contemptuous simile, the intimation that he cared not for the daughter, and thus to throw him off the scent of his quest. The intention to offend the tedious old fool, and thus to disembarrass himself of his presence, becomes still more obvious in the description of old age which immediately follows, "Slanders, sir," &c.

The point of the satire, and the absence of un-reason, strikes Polonius.

"*Polonius.* Though this be madness, yet there is method in't. Will you walk out of the air, my lord?
Hamlet. Into my grave.
Pol. Indeed, that is out o' the air. How pregnant sometimes his replies are! a happiness that often madness hits on, which reason and sanity could not so prosperously be delivered of."

In this, again, the old man shews that though his wits may be somewhat superannuated, yet, either from reading or observation, he has no slight knowledge of mental disease.

What depth of melancholy and life-weariness is there not apparent in the conclusion of the interview.

"*Pol.* I will most humbly take my leave of you.
Ham. You cannot, sir, take from me anything that I will more willingly part withal: except my life, except my life, except my life!"

But when his old schoolfellows arrive, how frank

and hearty his greeting ; how entirely is all disguise
for the moment thrown aside ! The noble and generous native nature is nowhere made more manifest than
in his reception of these friends of his youth, men to
whom he once adhered, neighbours to his youth and
humour. Until his keen eye discovers that they have
been "sent for," and are mean instruments, if not spies,
in the hands of the king, he throws off all dissimula-
tion with them, greeting them with right hearty and
cheerful welcome. Yet how soon his melancholy
peers through the real but transient cheerfulness.
The world is a prison, "in which there are many
confines, wards, and dungeons ; Denmark being one
of the worst." If it is not so to his friend, yet is it
so to him from thinking it so, for "there is nothing
either good or bad, but thinking makes it so : to him
it is a prison." The real prison, then, is his own
mind, as, in the contrary mental state, a prison is no
prison, for

> "Stone walls do not a prison make,
> Nor iron bars a cage."

Hamlet feels that he could possess perfect independ-
ence of circumstance if the mind were free.

"*Rosencrantz.* Why then, your ambition makes it one ;
'tis too narrow for your mind.
Hamlet. O God, I could be bounded in a nutshell and
count myself a king of infinite space, were it not that I have
bad dreams."

The spies sound him further on the subject of
ambition, thinking that disappointment at losing the

succession to the crown may be the true cause of his morbid state. In this intention they decry ambition: "it is but a shadow's shadow." Hamlet replies logically enough, that if ambition is but a shadow, something beyond ambition must be the substance from which it is thrown. If ambition represented by a King is a shadow, the antitype of ambition represented by a beggar must be the opposite of the shadow, that is, the substance. "Then are our beggars, bodies; and our monarchs, and outstretch'd heroes, the beggars' shadows." He reduces the sophistry of his false friends to an absurdity, and closes the argument by declining to carry it further: "By my fay, I cannot reason." But Mr. Coleridge declares the passage to be unintelligible, and perhaps this interpretation of it may be too simple.

So far from being able to examine and recover the wind of Hamlet, his old schoolfellows are put by him to a course of questioning as to the motives of their presence, as to whether it is a free visitation of their own inclining, or whether they have been "sent for". Their want of skill in dissemblance and their weaker natures submit to him the secret that they had been "sent for," and the old "rights of fellowship," "the obligations of ever-preserved love," are immediately clouded by distrust: "Nay, then, I'll have an eye of you," he says. Yet notwithstanding he freely discloses to them the morbid state of his mind; and, be it remarked, that in this exquisite picture of life-weariness, in which no image could be altered, no word omitted or changed, without obvious damage to its grand effect, he does not describe the maniacal state, the semblance of which he has put on before Ophelia and Polonius, but that morbid state of weakness and melancholy which he really suffers, of which he is thoroughly self-conscious, and which he avows in his first speech, before he has seen the Ghost:

"I have of late—but wherefore I know not—lost all my mirth, foregone all custom of exercise; and indeed it goes so heavily with my disposition that this goodly frame, the earth, seems to me a sterile promontory, this most excellent canopy, the air, look you, this brave o'erhanging firmament, this majestical roof fretted with golden fire, why, it appears no other thing to me than a foul and pestilent congregation of vapours. What a piece of work is a man! how noble in reason! how infinite in faculty! in form and moving how express and admirable! in action how like an angel! in apprehension how like a god! the beauty of the world! the paragon of animals! And yet, to me, what is this quintessence of dust? man delights not me: no, nor woman neither, though by your smiling you seem to say so."

How exquisitely is here portrayed the state of the reasoning melancholiac, (melancholia without delusion,) who sees all things as they are, but feels them as they are not. All cheerfulness fled, all motive for action lost, he becomes listless and inert. He still recognises the beauty of the earth and the magnificence of the heavens, but the one is a tomb, and the other a funereal pall. His reason still shews him the place of man, a little lower than the angels, but the sources of sentiment are dried up, and, although no man-hater, he no longer derives pleasure from kindly affections. The waters of emotion are stagnant ; the pleasant places of the soul are sterile and desert.

Hamlet is not slow to confess his melancholy, and indeed it is the peculiarity of this mental state, that those suffering from it seldom or never attempt to conceal it. A man will conceal his delusions, will deny and veil the excitement of mania, but the melancholiac is almost always readily confidential on the subject of his feelings. In this he resembles the hypochondriac, though not perhaps from exactly the same motive. The hypochondriac seeks for sympathy and pity ; the melancholiac frequently admits others to the sight of his mental wretchedness from mere despair of relief and contempt of pity.

Although Hamlet is ready to shew to his friends the mirror of his mind, he jealously hides the cause of its distortion. "But wherefore I know not" is scarcely consistent with the truth. In his first soliloquy, which we take to be the key-note of his real mental state, he clearly enough indicates the source of his wretchedness, which the Queen also, with a mother's insight, has not been slow to perceive:

"His father's death, and our o'erhasty marriage."

He is jealous that his friends should not refer his melancholy to love-sickness. The opinion propounded by Polonius, that he was mad for love, could not have escaped him ; a theory, of his malady, which would be likely to wound his pride severely. Polonius had already made, in his presence, sundry aside observations on this point; and the significant smile of Rosencrantz at his observation, "Man delights not me," would be likely to stimulate the sleeping suspicion that he was set down as a brain-sick, rejected lover; and some annoyance at an attempt to explain his madness as the result of his rejection by Ophelia, may combine with the suspicion that he is watched to explain his harshness towards her in his subsequent interview with her.

How are we to understand his confession to the men he already distrusts, that in the appearance of his madness the King and Queen are deceived, except by his contempt for their discrimination, and his dislike to wear his antic disposition before all company?

When Polonius returns, he immediately puts on the full disguise, playing upon the old man's infirmities with the ironical nonsense about Jephtha, king of Israel, who had a daughter, etc., and skilfully leading Polonius by the nose on the scent of his own theory, "Still on my daughter."

When the players enter, however, he thoroughly throws off not only the antic counterfeit, but the melancholy reality of his disposition: he shakes his faculties together, and becomes perfectly master of himself in courtesy, scholarship, and solid sense. His retort to Polonius, who objects to the speech of the player as too long, seems a valuable hint of Shakes-

peare's own opinion respecting the bad necessity
he felt to introduce ribald scenes into his plays : " It
shall to the barber's, with your beard.   Prithee, say
on : he's for a jig or a tale of bawdry, or he sleeps."
A noble sentiment in homely phrase is that in which
he marks the right motive of behaviour towards in-
feriors, and indeed towards all men.   To Polonius's
assurance that he will use the players according to
their desert, the princely reply is—

> "God's bodykins, man, much better : use every man
> after his desert, and who should 'scape whipping ? Use them
> after your own honour and dignity : the less they deserve,
> the more merit is in your bounty."

Although he freely mocks the old lord chamberlain himself, he will not permit others to do so.   His
injunction to the player, " Follow that lord, and look
you mock him not," not only indicates that the absurdities of Polonius are glaring, but that there is less
real malice in Hamlet's heart towards the old man
than he assumes the appearance of.

Hamlet decides upon the use he will make of the
players with a promptitude that shews that his resolve,
"sicklied o'er with the pale cast of thought," is but
the inactivity of an over-reflective melancholic mind,
and that there is energy enough in him to seize some
forms of opportunity.

Hamlet's soliloquy, " O, what a rogue and peasant
slave am I !" resembles, with a difference, the one
following his interview with the Captain : " How all

occasions do inform against me." The latter one, after he has obtained satisfactory proof of his uncle's guilt, is by far the least passionate and vehement, justifying in some degree the remark of Schlegel, that "in the last scenes the main action either stands still or appears to retrograde." There is, however, an important distinction between these two soliloquies. The passionate outburst of the first has been stimulated by emotional imitation. The feigned passion of the player has touched the most sensitive chord of feeling, and given occasion to the vehemence of his angry self-rebuke. The account of the soldier's temper, "greatly to find quarrel in a straw when honour's at the stake," sets him calmly to reflect and philosophize upon the motives of action. In these two soliloquies we have to some extent Shakespeare's own exposition of Hamlet's natural character, and the motives of his conduct.

"The whole," says Schlegel, "was intended to shew that a consideration which would exhaust all the relations and possible consequences of a deed to the very limits of human foresight, cripples the power of acting." In this tragedy of thought we have delineated a highly sensitive, reflecting, self-introspective mind, weak and melancholic, sorrow-stricken and life-weary. In a manner so awful that it might shake the soundest mind, this man is called upon to take away the life of a king and a relative for a crime of which there exists no actual proof.

G

Surely Hamlet is justified in pausing to weigh his motives and his evidence, in concluding not to act upon the sole dictation of a shadowy appearance, who may be the devil tempting his "weakness and his melancholy;" of resolving to "have grounds more relative than this," before he deliberately commits himself to an act of revenge which, even had the proof of his uncle's crime been conclusive and irre-fragable, would have been repulsive to his inmost nature. Hamlet's indecision to act, and his over-readiness to reflect, are placed beyond the reach of critical discovery by his own analytical motive-hunt-ing, so eloquently expressed in the abstruse reasoning in which he indulges. Anger and hatred against his uncle, self-contempt for his own irresolution, incon-sistent as he feels it with the courage of which he is conscious; disgust at his own angry excitement, and doubts of the testimony upon which he is yet dis-satisfied that he has not acted, present a state of intellectual and emotional conflict perfectly consistent with the character and the circumstances. If Hamlet had had as much faith in the Ghost as Macbeth had in the Weird Sisters, he would have struck without needing further evidence. If he had been a man of action, whose firstlings of the heart are those of the hand, he would have struck in the earliest heat of his revenge. He feels while he questions, that it is not true that he is "pigeon-liver'd, and lacks gall to make oppression bitter;" but he does lack that resolution which "makes mouths at the invisible event;" he does make "I would, wait upon, I will:" he does hesitate and procrastinate, and examine his motives, and make sure to his own mind of his justification, and allow us to see the painful labour of a noble and sensitive being struggling to gain an unquestionable conviction of the right thing to do, in circumstances most awry and difficult; he does feel balancing motives, and painfully hear the ring of the yes and no in his head.

"Che sì, e nò nel capo mi tenzona."

Shall we think the less nobly of him because his hand is not ready to shed kindred blood; because, gifted with God-like discourse of reason, he does look before and after; because he does not take the law in his own hands upon his oppressor until he has obtained conclusive evidence of his guilt; that he seeks to make sure he is the natural justiciar of his murdered father, and not an assassin instigated by hatred and selfish revenge?

The report given to the King and Queen by the young courtiers is conceived to hide their failure in the mission of inquiry. The Prince, they say, "does confess he feels himself distracted," while he refuses to yield to them the cause:

"But, with a crafty madness, keeps aloof,
When we would bring him on to some confession
Of his true state."

He behaves

"Most like a gentleman ;"
"But with much forcing of his disposition,"

and he is falsely stated to have been "niggard of
question," but "most free in his reply."

They must, however, have been surprised to hear
the condition in which they found their friend described by the King, as "turbulent and dangerous
lunacy," since, up to this time, this is an untrue
description of Hamlet's state, whatever cause the
King may subsequently have to apply it, when the
death of Polonius makes him feel that Hamlet's
"liberty is full of threats to all." The expression
used by the King, that Hamlet "puts on this confusion," would seem to point to a suspicion, even at
this early time, that his madness is but counterfeit.
The Queen, however, appears to accept its reality,
and, notwithstanding all the arguments of Polonius,
she adheres to her first opinion of its cause. She
doth *wish*, indeed, that Ophelia's "good beauties be
the happy cause of Hamlet's wildness ;" since, if so,
she entertains the hope that her virtues may bring
the remedy. It seems here implied that the King
and Queen have been made aware of Ophelia's love
for Hamlet ; and both in this speech of the Queen,
and in the one she makes over Ophelia's grave,

"I hoped thou shouldst have been my Hamlet's wife,"

it appears that the remedy by which the Queen at

this time hopes to attain his recovery to "his wonted way again," is by his marriage. This understanding, however, or arrangement, is nowhere expressed ; and indeed, although the Queen may desire to think with Polonius respecting the cause and nature of her son's malady, her mother's knowledge and woman's tact lead her conviction nearer to the truth, when she avows the real cause to be "his father's death, and our o'erhasty marriage."

The soliloquy which follows, "To be, or not to be," is one of the most exquisite pieces of poetic self-communing ever conceived. Imbued with a profoundly melancholy view of human life, which is relieved by no gleam of cheerfulness, illumined by no ray of hope, the mind of the unhappy Prince dwells with longing desire, not on a future and happier state of existence, but on annihilation. He wishes to end the troubles of life in a sleep without a dream, and is restrained alone from seeking it by the apprehension of

> " What dreams may come
> When we have shuffled off this mortal coil ;"

by the fear, in fact, of a future state, in which the calamities of this life may be exchanged for others more enduring, in the undiscovered country of the future. This "dread of something after death" scarcely deserves the name of conscience which he applies to it. The fear of punishment is the lowest motive for virtuous action, and is far removed in its nature from the inward principle of doing right for its own sake.

The word, however, does not seem to be here applied
in its higher sense, as the arbiter of right, but rather
in that of reflective meditation. It is this that makes
"cowards of us all." It is this that prevents Hamlet
seeking his own rest in the annihilation he longs for.
It is by this also that his hand is withheld from the
act of wild justice and revenge upon which his mind
sits on brood. It is thus that he accurately describes
the *timbre* of his own mind, so active to think, so
inert to act, so keen to appreciate the evils of life, so
averse to take any active part against them :

> "Thus conscience does make cowards of us all ;
> And thus the native hue of resolution
> Is sicklied o'er with the pale cast of thought,
> And enterprises of great pith and moment
> With this regard their currents turn awry,
> And lose the name of action."

The motive against suicide here adduced is undoubtedly a mean and fallacious one. It is mean,
because it is cowardly ; the coward want of patience
manfully to endure the evils of this mortal life being
kept in check by the coward fear of future punishment. It is fallacious, because it balances the evils
of this life against the apprehended ones of the future ;
therefore when, in the judgment of the sorely afflicted,
the weight of present evils more than counterpoises
those which their amount of religious faith may point
to in the threatening future, the argument here advanced would justify suicide. There is nothing in
which men differ more than in the various degrees

with which they are endowed with the courage of
fortitude and the courage of enterprise; and it is
certain that of two men equally groaning and sweat-
ing under a weary life, and oppressed by the same
weight of calamity, if solely actuated by the reasoning here employed by Hamlet in the contemplation
of suicide, one would have the courage to endure the
present, and the other would have the courage to face
the perils of the future. Courage has been described
as the power to select the least of two evils; the evil
of pain and death, for instance, rather than that of
shame. If this be so, it must yet be admitted that
either one of two given evils may be the greatest to
different men; and courage may urge one man to fight
and another to flee, either in the vulgar wars of Kings
and Kaisars, or in the more earnest trials of the battle
of life. The converse of the proposition must also be
true, and cowardice may either make us stand by
our arms or basely desert. The terrible question of
suicide, therefore, is not to be thus solved; indeed the
only motive against suicide which will stand the test
is that which Hamlet in his first speech indicates,
namely, obedience to the law of God; that obedience
which, in the heaviest calamities, enables the Christian
to "be patient and endure"; that obedience which, in
the most frantic desire to put off this mortal coil, can
withhold the hand by this one consideration, that

"The Eternal hath set His canon 'gainst self-slaughter."

The motives made use of by Hamlet in his earlier

and later contemplation of suicide, indicate his religious and his philosophic phase of character. Faith
in the existence of a God, and of a future state of
existence, is so ingrained in his mind that it powerfully influences his conduct, and constantly turns up
to invalidate, if not to refute, that sceptical philosophy
with which he is indoctrinated, and which leads him
so constantly to trace the changes of matter, as in

> "Imperious Cæsar, dead and turn'd to clay,
>   Might stop a hole to keep the wind away."

This, perhaps, was the philosophy which Horatio and
he had learned at Wittenburg, the fallacy of which
the Ghost had seemed at first to prove. Yet it is
strange how entirely Hamlet appears at times to have
forgotten the Ghost and its revelations. The soliloquy "To be, or not to be" is that of a man to whom
any future state of existence is a matter of sincere
doubt. He reasons as one of those who would not
be persuaded "though one rose from the dead."

After the soul-harrowing recital made to him by
the perturbed spirit of his father, in which the secrets
of the purgatorial prison-house are not indeed unfolded, but in which they are so broadly indicated
that no man who had seen so much of the "eternal
blazon" of the spirit-world could find a corner in his
soul for the concealment of a sceptical doubt, after
this, the soliloquy "To be, or not to be" presumes
either an entire forgetfulness of the awful revelation
which had been made to him, or the existence of a

state of mind so overwhelmed with suicidal melancholy as to be incapable of estimating testimony. Now it is well enough known that the most complete sensorial and intellectual proofs go for nothing when opposed to the stubborn strength of a morbid emotion; and when Hamlet reasons thus upon the future life, and hunts matter through its transmigrations with sceptical intent, it must be accepted as the result of the perverted instinct of self-preservation, which made him desire nothing so much as simple unconditional annihilation.

In his interview with the much-enduring Ophelia which follows the soliloquy, Hamlet has been accused of unworthy harshness. Two considerations will tend to modify, though not altogether to remove, this judgment. The reader is aware that Ophelia entertains the fondest love towards Hamlet; but he, ignorant of this, only knows that, after accepting the tender of his affections, she has repulsed him with every appearance of heartless cruelty. He feels her to be the cause of his "pangs of despised love;" yet he at first addresses her in a manner indicating his own faithfulness and fond appreciation of all her goodness and virtue, as if he could best approach Heaven through her gracious intercession :

> "The fair Ophelia ! Nymph, in thy orisons
> Be all my sins remember'd."

What follows is so opposed to the tenderness of this

greeting, that we are compelled to assume that he sees through the snare set for him ; and that in avoiding it he works himself into one of those ebullitions of temper to which he is prone. He sees that Ophelia is under the constraint of other presence, as what keen-sighted lover would not immediately distinguish whether his mistress, in whatever mood she may be, feels herself alone with him, or under the observation of others ? He has before shewn his repugnance to the idea that he is love-sick mad. He knows that Polonius thus explains his conduct ; and his harshness to Ophelia is addressed to Polonius, and to any others who may be in hiding, more than to Ophelia herself. Yet the harshest words, and those most unfit to be used to any woman, are the true reflex of the morbid side of his mind, which passion and suspicion have cast into the bitterest forms of expression. The true melancholy and the counterfeit madness are strangely commingled in this scene. The latter is shewn by disjointed exclamations and half-reasonings. " Ha, ha ! are you honest ?" " Are you fair ?" " I did love you once." " I loved you not" etc., and by the wild form in which the melancholy is here cast. " Get thee to a nunnery : why wouldst thou be a breeder of sinners ?" " What should such fellows as I do crawling between earth and heaven !" " Where's your father ?" Ophelia tells a white lie. " At home, my lord." Hamlet knows better, and sends a random shaft into his ambuscade. " Let the doors be shut upon him, that he may play the fool nowhere but in his own house."

"*Hamlet.* Get thee to a nunnery : why wouldst thou be a breeder of sinners? I am myself indifferent honest; but yet I could accuse me of such things that it were better my mother had not borne me : I am very proud, revengeful, ambitious, with more offences at my beck than I have thoughts to put them in, imagination to give them shape, or time to act them in. What should such fellows as I do crawling between earth and heaven? We are arrant knaves, all; believe none of us. Go thy ways to a nunnery. Where's your father?"

"*Ham.* If thou dost marry, I'll give thee this plague for thy dowry : be thou as chaste as ice, as pure as snow, thou shalt not escape calumny. Get thee to a nunnery, go : farewell. Or, if thou wilt needs marry, marry a fool; for wise men know well enough what monsters you make of them. To a nunnery, go, and quickly too. Farewell.

Ophelia. O heavenly powers, restore him!

Ham. I have heard of your paintings too, well enough; God has given you one face, and you make yourselves another : you jig, you amble, and you lisp, and nick-name God's creatures, and make your wantonness your ignorance. Go to, I'll no more on't; it hath made me mad. I say, we will have no more marriages : those that are married already, all but one, shall live; the rest shall keep as they are. To a nunnery, go."

Partly dictated by jealous fear that Ophelia may solace her pain with some other lover, it is yet an attempt to wean from himself any fondness which may remain. The burden is, Grieve not for me, but do not marry another. The latter part of the speech is directed to the Queen in ambush.

What exquisite pathos! what wail of despairing love in Ophelia's lament over the ruin of her lover's mind! What fine discrimination of the excellencies marred! What forgetfulness of self in the grief she feels for him! Not for her own loss, but for his fall, is she "of ladies most deject and wretched," although it is the dying swan-song of her own sanity.

> "O, what a noble mind is here o'erthrown!
> The courtier's, soldier's, scholar's, eye, tongue, sword;
> The expectancy and rose of the fair state,
> The glass of fashion and the mould of form,
> The observed of all observers, quite, quite down!
> And I, of ladies most deject and wretched,
> That suck'd the honey of his music vows,
> Now see that noble and most sovereign reason,
> Like sweet bells jangled, out of tune and harsh;
> That unmatch'd form and feature of blown youth
> Blasted with ecstasy: O, woe is me,
> To have seen what I have seen, see what I see!"

The King, in the meanwhile, whose keenness of vision has not been dimmed by the mists of affection, like that of Ophelia, nor by self-conceit, like that of Polonius, has detected the prevalence of melancholy and sorrow in the assumed wildness of the Prince:

> "Love! his affections do not that way tend;
> Nor what he spake, though it lack'd form a little,
> Was not like madness. There's something in his soul,
> O'er which his melancholy sits on brood;
> And I do doubt the hatch and the disclose
> Will be some danger."

Polonius thinks well of the King's scheme to get Hamlet out of the way by pretext of benefiting his health by change of scene, though with senile obstinacy he still holds to his opinion that the com-

mencement of his grief sprung from neglected love. To
test this further he proposes the interview with the
Queen, who is to be round with her son, and whose
conference Polonius will hear. If this scheme fails,
let him be sent to England without delay, or be put
into confinement.

In his speech to the players, Hamlet's attention,
abstracted for a moment from the view of his sorrows,
leaves his mind free from the clouds of melancholy,
and permits him to display his powerful and sarcastic
intelligence without let or hindrance. His innate
nobleness of mind is not less clearly pourtrayed in
the conversation with Horatio which immediately
follows. The character of this judicious and faithful
follower, as it is manifested throughout the piece, and
especially as it is here pourtrayed by Hamlet himself,
forms a pleasing contrast to that of his princely friend.
The one passionate in emotion, inert in action ; the
other cool in temper, prompt in conduct. The maxim
noscitur a sociis may be narrowed to the closer and
truer one, "Shew me your friend, and I'll tell your
mind ;" and in a true and deep friendship there will
always be found much uniformity of sentiment, though
it may be, and indeed often is, combined with great
diversity of temperament. Deep friendship rarely
exists between persons whose emotional tendencies
closely resemble. A true friend is generally chosen
in some contrast of disposition, as if the basis of this
rare and noble affection were the longing to remedy

the imperfections of one's nature by complementing ourselves with those good qualities of another in which we are deficient.

Before this time Hamlet has confided to his friend the terrible secret of the Ghost's message, the truth of which he proposes to test by the scheme of the play, and thus to sting the conscience and unkennel the occult guilt of his uncle.

When the court enter, Hamlet puts on his antics in his ironical half-reasonings with the King and Polonius, and his banter with Ophelia. The manners and playhouse licence of the time explain the broad indelicacy of the latter; but that he so publicly indulged it may be accepted as proof of his desire to mark his indifference to the woman who had, as he thought, heartlessly jilted him, and whose love he had reason to think had been "as brief as the posy of a ring."

As the play within the play draws to its climax, Hamlet becomes so excited and reckless that it is a wonder he does not spoil his scheme by exposing it to the King, who, on the point of taking the alarm, exclaims, "Have you heard the argument? Is there no offence in't?" He is little likely to be reassured by Hamlet's disclaimer, "They poison in jest; no offence i' the world."

When the crisis has come, and the King's guilt has been unkenneled, and Hamlet is again left alone with Horatio, before whom he would not feign, his

real excitement borders so closely upon the wildest
antics of the madness he has put on in craft, that
there is little left to distinguish between the two.
He quotes senseless doggerel, will join "a fellowship
in a cry of players," will "take the Ghost's word for
a thousand pound," and is altogether in that state of
flippant merriment which men sometimes assume to
defend themselves from deep emotion ; as they sometimes jest in the face of physical horrors or mental
woe. It is like the hysterical laughter of intense
emotion, though not quite. It is partly that levity
of mind which succeeds intense strain of thought and
feeling, as naturally as it is to yawn and stretch after
one long-continued wearisome position. This mood
of unfeigned flippancy continues after the re-entrance
of his treacherous school friends, well expressing its
tone in the doggerel,

> "For if the king like not the comedy,
> Why then, belike,—he likes it not, perdy."

To the courtier's request, that he will put his "discourse into some frame," he rejoins, "I am tame, sir :
pronounce." He affects a display of politeness, but
the "courtesy is not of the right breed." To the entreaty to give "a wholesome answer" to the Queen's
message, he affords an indication that some at least
of his wildness is also not of the right breed, since he
appeals to it as a reality. "Make you a wholesome
answer ; my wit's diseased." Of a disease, however,
which leaves the wit too quick for their play. He

sees through them thoroughly. To the silly-enough inquiry of Rosencrantz, "Good my lord, what is your cause of distemper? you do surely but bar the door of your own liberty, if you deny your griefs to your friend;" he gives answer, laying bare the selfish motives of the questioner, "Sir, I lack advancement." Suppressing irony, he becomes for a moment serious with them: "Why do you go about to recover the wind of me, as if you would drive me into a toil?" And then that lesson of sarcastic earnestness, to prove that he knew the breed of their friendship and so-licitude for him:

"Why, look you now, how unworthy a thing you make of me! You would play upon me; you would seem to know my stops; you would pluck out the heart of my mystery; you would sound me from my lowest note to the top of my compass: and there is much music, excellent voice, in this little organ; yet cannot you make it speak. S'blood, do you think I am easier to be played on than a pipe? Call me what instrument you will, though you can fret me, yet you cannot play upon me."

The veil which he deigns to put on before these mean and treacherous ephemera of the court is of the thinnest counterfeit; but with Polonius the mental antics are more pronounced, for with him he rejoices in spiteful mischief, as when the tiresome old man "fools him to the top of his bent." "Do you see yonder cloud?" etc. The soliloquy immediately fol-lowing fully proves how thoroughly on the surface all this flippancy is. The dread purpose is gathering to action, and the mind was never more sad than all this while, under the mask of intellectual buffoonery, for 'tis even now he

> " could drink hot blood,
> And do such bitter business as the day
> Would quake to look on."

At this juncture the King re-appears, with his mind thoroughly made up on the point that Hamlet has in him something dangerous, if his doubts are not also solved on the point of his madness. The play which has discovered the King to Hamlet, must also have discovered his knowledge of the murder to the King. Before this time Claudius thinks his nephew's madness must be watched, and although he fears that the hatch and disclose of his melancholy will be some danger, it does not appear that he yet proposes to send him to England with purpose against his life. After the play, and before the death of Polonius, the King's apprehension is excited :

> " I like him not, nor stands it safe with us
> To let his madness range."
> " The terms of our estate may not endure
> Hazard so dangerous as doth hourly grow
> Out of his lunacies."
> " We will fetters put upon this fear,
> Which now goes too free-footed."

Although the King speaks to the courtiers of dispatching their commission to England forthwith, and desires them to arm to this speedy voyage, it can scarcely be that at this time he is guilty of that

H

treacherous design on Hamlet's life which he unfolds
after the death of Polonius. The agony of repentance
for his past crime, so vehemently expressed in the
soliloquy, "O, my offence is rank," etc., appears
scarcely consistent with the project of a new murder
on his mind. The King has no inconsiderable mental
endowments and moral courage, though personally he
is a coward and a sottish debauchee. But, notwithstanding this personal cowardice, we must accept
Hamlet's abuse of him, in contrast to the manly
perfection of his father, as applying rather to his
appearance, and to his deficiency in those soldier-like
qualities which would command respect in a nation
of warriors, than to his intellect. Although the King
holds fencing, that quality of Laertes which hath
plucked envy from Hamlet, "as of the unworthiest
siege ;" although a plotter, "a cut-purse of the empire
and the rule," and, according to the description of his
son-in-law, altogether a contemptible person, intel-
lectually he is by no means despicable. Yet that
burst of eloquent remorse seems too instinct with the
longing for real repentance to have been uttered by
this cowardly fratricide, who even in the act of prayer
is juggling with heaven itself. We feel no pity for
the scheming hypocrite, in spite of the anguish which
wrings from him the cry :

> "O wretched state ! O bosom, black as death !
> O limed soul, that, struggling to be free,
> Art more engaged !"

If in that fine appreciation of mercy and of Heaven's justice in which

> " There is no shuffling, there the action lies
> In his true nature ; and we ourselves compell'd,
> Even to the teeth and forehead of our faults,
> To give in evidence,"

if these thoughts appear too just to be expressed by so foul a mouth, even as the polished wisdom of the precepts given to Laertes appears inconsistent with the senile incapacity of Polonius, we must somewhat attribute it to that lavish wealth of power and beauty which we find only in Shakespeare, who sometimes in wanton extravagance sets pearls in pinchbeck, and strews diamonds on the sanded floor, who pours nectar into the wooden cup, and feeds us with ambrosia when we should have been satisfied with bread.

It will scarcely be denied by those who have escaped that blindness of bigotry, which the intense admiration Shakespeare naturally excites in those who study him closely accounts for and excuses, that he sometimes gives to one of his personages an important speech, somewhat out of harmony with the general delineation of the character ; his characters being in other parts so thoroughly natural and consistent, that he is able to do this without injury to the general effect. But when he does so, what breadth of wisdom and beauty of morality does not the discursive caprice afford !

The soliloquy of the King, a homily in thirty lines, on the mercy and justice of God, and the utter folly of hypocrisy in prayer, is followed by the speech of Hamlet, "Now might I do it pat," etc., containing sentiments which Johnson designates as atrocious.

We are inclined to think that in writing both this speech and the King's soliloquy, Shakespeare had in mind the intention of conveying instruction on the nature and office of prayer, rather than that of developing his plot. From the King's speech we learn that the mercy of the sweet Heavens is absolutely unlimited, that the force of prayer is two-fold to bring aid and pardon, that the condition of forgiveness is a true repentance which does not shame justice by retaining the offence, and the worthlessness of word prayers. We know that the prayers of the King are hollow and unavailing, but so does not Hamlet, who is made to bear testimony to the all-sufficient efficacy of prayer, since it can save so damnable a villain as his uncle. His father had been

> "Cut off even in the blossom of his sin,
> Unhousel'd, disappointed, unanel'd."
> "He took my father grossly, full of bread ;
> With all his crimes broad blown, as flush as May ;"

so that his audit with Heaven was likely to stand heavy with him. Villain as his uncle was,

> "Bloody bawdy villain !
> Remorseless, treacherous, lecherous, kindless villain !"

still there was that in prayer which would fit and

season him for his passage to the future life, and, if
taken "in the purging of his soul," why, "so he goes
to Heaven."

Both of these speeches seem to have been written
to impress most forcibly the efficacy of sincere and
prayerful repentance. It was to the religious sentiment that the revival of play-acting was due; but
when Shakespeare wrote, it had already ceased to
be a common subject of theatrical representation, and
(*Measure for Measure* perhaps excepted) in no other
of his dramas has it been very prominently brought
forward. The motive for delay assigned in this
speech was certainly neither Christian nor merciful.
Yet the act itself was merciful, and the more horrid
bent with which Hamlet excused his inaction was
but speculative. A conscience yet unsatisfied that
his purposed deed was a just and righteous one,
rather than a cruel thirst for the full measure of
revenge, appears to have been Hamlet's real motive
for delay at this period. His opportunities for assas-
sinating the King, had he so desired, were certainly
not limited to this moment, yet he forbore to use
them, until his uncle's murderous treachery towards
himself at length resolved him to quit accounts with
his own arm. Moreover, it is the Romanist theology
which is represented in this play, and its doctrines
must be taken into consideration in judging of the
excuse which Hamlet makes for delaying to kill the
King, until "about some act what has no relish of

salvation in't."   The future state of punishment is
represented as a terminable purgatory; Hamlet's
father is doomed "for a certain time" to fast in fires
until his crimes are burnt and purged away.   Hamlet
swears by the rood, and he lays the stress of a catholic
upon the incest of the Queen in becoming her husband's brother's wife.   At the funeral of Ophelia it
is the catholic ritual which is in abeyance.   Great
command has overswayed *the order* of priory or
abbey, where the funeral is taking place.   The priest
says "her death was doubtful;" and,

> "We should profane the service of the dead
>   To sing a *requiem* and such rest to her
>   As to peace-parted souls."

In this passage the Romanist idea is for the third
time produced, that the soul's future depends upon
the mode of leaving this life, rather than upon the
manner in which this life has been spent.

   In the interview with his mother, the idea of
Hamlet's profound affection for her has been most
skilfully conveyed in the painful effort with which he
endeavours to make her conscious of her position, to
set before her a glass where she may see her inmost
part, to speak daggers to her, to be cruel, but not
unnatural.   From the speech,

> "A bloody deed! almost as bad, good mother,
>   As kill a king, and marry with his brother,"

it would appear that he entertained some suspicions

of his mother's complicity in the murder of his father,
and that these words were tentative to ascertain
whether her conscience was sore on that side. From
what follows we must suppose this suspicion allayed.
The readiness with which Hamlet seizes the opportunity to strike the blow which kills Polonius,
under the belief that he strikes the King, is of a piece
with a character too meditative to frame and follow
a course of action, yet sometimes sudden and rash
in action when the opportunity presents itself. The
rapid action with which he utilizes the players, with
which he circumvents his treacherous schoolfellows,
with which he at last kills the King, resembles the
quick blow which sends to his account "the wretched,
rash, intruding fool," whom he mistakes for his betters.
So long as resolution can be "sicklied o'er with the
pale cast of thought," so long as time is allowed for
any scruple to be listened to, he thinks too precisely
on the event, and lives to say the thing's to do. But
let the opportunity of action present itself, and he is
quick to seize it, as he would have been dilatory in
seeking it. It is the meditative, inactive man, who
often seizes opportunities for action, or what he takes
for such, with the greatest eagerness. Unable to form
and follow a deliberate course of action, he is too
ready to lend his hand to circumstances, as they arise
without his intervention. Sometimes he fails miser-
ably, as in the death of Polonius ; sometimes he succeeds, as when he finds occasion to praise that rash-

ness, which too often stands him in the place of steady purpose.

> " Rashly,
> And praised be rashness for it, let us know,
> Our indiscretion sometimes serves us well,
> When our deep plots do pall : and that should teach us
> There's a divinity that shapes our ends,
> Rough-hew them how we will."

The comments of Hamlet upon the death of Polonius, if they had been calmly spoken by a man holding the even tenor of his way through life, would have deserved the moralist's reprobation quite as much as his speech over the praying King. To us they tell of that groundwork of unsound emotion upon which the almost superhuman intellectual activity of the character is founded. In Hamlet's life-weary, melancholy state, with his attention fixed elsewhere, such an event as the death of Polonius would have a very different effect to that which it would have had upon so sensitive and noble a mind, if its condition were healthy. His attention at the time is concentrated upon one train of ideas, his feelings are preoccupied, his sympathies somewhat indurated to the sufferings of others, and his comments upon them are likely, therefore, to appear unfeeling.

The Queen indeed, with affectionate invention, represents to the King the very opposite view. She says "he weeps for what he's done;" his natural grief shewing itself pure in his very madness, like a precious ore in a base mineral. It is, however, not thus that

Hamlet is represented "to draw toward an end" with the father of his mistress, and to deposit "the carrion."

The ideas which almost exclude from Hamlet's thoughts the wrong he has done Polonius now become expressed with a vehemence inconsistent with sound mind. The manner in which he dallies with the idea of his mother's incest, using images of the grossest kind—the blighting comparison of that mildewed ear, his uncle, with his warrior father—the vehement de-nunciation of his uncle—"a murderer and a villain, a slave," "a vice of kings, a cutpurse of the empire and the rule," "a king of shreds and patches," "a toad," "a bat, a gib,"—all this verifies his own sneer on himself, that while he cannot act he can curse "like a very drab." Although he succeeds in his purpose of turning the Queen's eyes into her very soul, and shewing black and grained spots there, it must be admitted that this excessive vehemence is not merely so much out of the belt of rule as might be justified by the circumstances, but that it indicates a morbid state of emotion; and never does Hamlet appear less sane than when he is declaring

> "That I essentially am not in madness,
> But mad in craft."

Hamlet's behaviour in the second Ghost scene is more excited and terrified than in the former one. The apparition comes upon him when in a less firm and prepared mood. The first interview is expected, and

each petty artery is knit to hardihood. The second
is wholly unexpected, and comes upon him at a time
when his mind is wrought to passionate excitement;
and it is far easier for the mind to pass from one
state of emotional excitement to the opposite, than
from a state of self-possessed tranquillity to one of
excitement. It is thus with Hamlet's rapid transition
from the passionate vehemence, with which he is
describing his uncle's crimes and qualities, to the
ecstasy of fear, which seizes him when his father's
shade once more stands before him. The sting of
conscience also adds force to the emotion of awe.
He has neglected the dread command, the sacred
behest, of the buried majesty of Denmark. With
unworthy doubts and laggard procrastination, his
purpose has become almost blunted. His doubts,
however, have now vanished; he no longer entertains
the thought that "the spirit he has seen may be the
devil;" he no longer questions whether it is "a spirit
of health, or goblin damned;" but accepts the appearance implicitly as the gracious figure of his father.
Since the first appearance of the unearthly visitant
he has caught the conscience of the fratricide King,
and unkenneled the dark secret of his guilt; therefore
it is that at this second visitation the feeling of awe
is unmixed with doubt and that touch of defiance
which is so perceptible on the former one. Since
then, moreover, his nerves have been rudely shaken;
he has lived in the torture of extreme anxiety and

profound grief, and the same cause naturally produces upon him a greater effect. Even while he is
vehemently railing at the criminal whom he had been
called upon to punish, the Ghost appears.

> "*Hamlet.*   How is it with you, lady?
> *Queen.* Alas, how is't with you,
> That you do bend your eye on vacancy
> And with the incorporal air do hold discourse?
> Forth at your eyes your spirits wildly peep;
> And, as the sleeping soldiers in the alarm,
> Your bedded hair, like life in excrements,
> Starts up, and stands an end.   O gentle son,
> Upon the heat and flame of thy distemper
> Sprinkle cool patience."

> "*Queen.* This is the very coinage of your brain:
> This bodiless creation ecstasy
> Is very cunning in.
> *Ham.* Ecstasy!
> My pulse, as yours, doth temperately keep time,
> And makes as healthful music: it is not madness
> That I have utter'd: bring me to the test,
> And I the matter will re-word; which madness
> Would gambol from.   Mother, for love of grace,
> Lay not that flattering unction to your soul,
> That not your trespass, but my madness speaks:
> It will but skin and film the ulcerous place,
> Whilst rank corruption, mining all within,
> Infects unseen."

It is in this agony of awe that he calls upon the
heavenly guards to save and protect him, that his
eyes wildly indicate alarm, that his bedded hairs
stand on end, that the heat and flame of his distemper
appear to lack all patience. It is in this agony of
awe that he feels himself so unnerved, that he entreats his father not to look upon him, lest he should

be thus rendered incapable of all action, and only live
to weep. During the brief space of the Ghost's second
appearance, Hamlet's extremity of fear can scarcely
be overrated. Still it is the sentiment of awe, not
of that horror which petrifies Macbeth in the banquet
scene. Moreover, in Hamlet the reaction tends to
tears, in Macbeth it is to rage.

There is something exquisitely touching in the
regard which the poor Ghost shews towards the frail
partner of his earthly state. The former injunction

> "Taint not thy mind, nor let thy soul contrive
> Against thy mother aught"

had scarcely been obeyed ; and now the entreaty

> "O, step between her and her fighting soul"

is a fine touch of the warrior's heart, whose rough and
simple silhouette is thrown upon the page in those
two lines of unsurpassable descriptive terseness,

> "So frowned he once, when in an angry parle
> He smote the sleded Polack on the ice."

The Ghost, indeed, is a character as never ghost
was before. So far from being a neutral *it*, a *thing*,
the buried majesty of Denmark is now highly personal
in his simple Sclavonic majesty. Though he in-
stigates revenge in the old viking, rather than in the
Christian spirit, though he protests against the luxury
and damned incest which defiles his royal bed, yet
is he nobly pitiful to the wretched woman through
whose frailty the transgression arises ; and it is worthy

of remark that after the intercession of the Ghost,
Hamlet's manner to his mother entirely changes. In
his former reference to the incest he makes her a full
partner of the crime. In his subsequent one he represents the King as the tempter, and supposes her
future conduct as that of "a queen fair, sober, wise ;"
and to the end he gives her his affection and confidence.

That the apparition is not an hallucination, as the
Queen thought, a bodiless creation caused by the
diseased brain, is known to Hamlet and the reader
of the play by its previous appearance, and by its
reference to the disclosure then made. Its use of
speech distinguishes it from the silent ghost of
Banquo. It seems an error to put the Ghost on the
stage clad in armour on this second occasion.

" My father, in his *habit* as he lived !"

indicates that this time the design of the poet was
to represent the dead king in the weeds of peace.
The quarto edition, indeed, gives as a stage direction,
" Enter the Ghost, in his night-gown." The appearance in this form would be suited to the place, even
as the *cap-à-pie* armament to the place of warlike
guard. Unlike the appearance on the battery, which
is seen by all who were present, on this occasion it is
only visible to Hamlet, and invisible to his mother.
Ghosts were supposed to have the power to make
themselves visible and invisible to whom they chose ;

and the dramatic effect of the Queen's surprise at Hamlet's behaviour was well worth the poetic exercise of this privilege. The Queen, indeed, must have been thoroughly convinced of her son's madness, in despite of his own disclaimer, and of the remorseless energy with which he wrings her own remorseful heart. Her exclamation, "Alas, he's mad !" is thoroughly sincere ; and though her assurance that she has "no life to breathe" the secret that he is "but mad in craft" seems to imply her assent to the fact, Hamlet's language and demeanour are certainly not such as are calculated to convince her of the truth of this avowal. She is therefore likely to have spoken not falsely, but according to her convictions, when she immediately afterwards says that her son is

> "Mad as the sea and wind, when both contend
>   Which is the mightier."

The Queen in this ghost scene, and Lady Macbeth in the banquet scene, are placed in very similar circumstances. They both refer the appearances, by which the son of the one and the husband of the other are so terribly moved, to a morbid state of the brain ; they both, but in very different degrees, are endeavouring to conceal remorse. But the Danish Queen is affrighted at the behaviour of her son ; the Scottish Queen, incapable of fear, is mainly anxious about the effect which her husband's conduct will have upon the bystanders. The one gives free expression to her alarm,—she allows amazement to sit visible in her expression and attitude; the other, firm and self-possessed, is the ruling spirit of the hour. The one is a middle-aged voluptuary who, incestuously married to a drunkard of degraded appearance, has feelings so little refined that, until her son holds up the mirror to her soul, she is barely sensible of her own shameless position; the other, a great criminal, is as self-conscious as she is outwardly confident. The one is animated with the spirit of Belial, the other with that of Satan.

Hamlet finds that his assumed madness, which he puts on and off rather capriciously, is likely to become an impediment to a right understanding with his mother. He sees her ready to deny the reality of her own trespass, because it is mirrored to her with the demeanour and, in some sort, with the words of ecstasy. He therefore offers as tests of his sanity, that his pulse is temperate, that his attention is under command, and his memory faithful; tests which we are bound to pronounce about as fallacious as could well be offered, and which could only apply to febrile delirium and mania. The pulse in mania averages about fifteen beats above that of health; that of the insane generally, including maniacs, only averages nine beats above the healthy standard: the pulse of melancholia and monomania is not above the average. That a maniac would gambol from reproducing in the same words any statement he had made, is true enough in the acute forms of the disease; but it is not so in numberless instances of chronic mania, nor in melancholia or partial insanity. The dramatic representations which are in vogue in some asylums prove the power of attention and memory preserved by many patients; indeed, the possessor of the most brilliant memory we ever met with was a violent and mischievous maniac. He would quote page after page from the Greek, Latin, and French classics. The Iliad, and the best plays of Molière in particular, he seemed to have at his fingers' ends. In raving madness, however, the two symptoms referred to by Hamlet are as a rule present. The pulse is accelerated, and the attention is so distracted by thick-flowing fancies, that an account can scarcely be given of the same matter in the same words. It is, therefore, to this form alone that the test of verbal memory applies.

The death of "the unseen good old man" Polonius, which Hamlet in his "lawless fit" and "brainish apprehension" had effected, adds to the alarm of the King, already excited by the "pranks too broad to bear with" of the play. The courtiers and the Queen do not seem to have inquired how it was that the King was so marvellously distempered with choler, wherefore he became so much offended with the catastrophe of the play. Like good courtiers, they accept his humour unquestioning. Now, however, the King has a good presentable excuse for alarm.

> "O heavy deed!
> It had been so with us, had we been there:

His liberty is full of threats to all;
To you yourself, to us, to every one.
Alas, how shall this bloody deed be answer'd?
It will be laid to us, whose providence
Should have kept short, restrain'd and out of haunt,
This mad young man : but so much was our love,
We would not understand what was most fit;
But, like the owner of a foul disease,
To keep it from divulging, let it feed
Even on the pith of life."

From which it appears that the all-observing eye of the poet had noted the custom of the world to conceal the occurrence of insanity within the family circle, a custom which still prevails, and from which much evil is wrought. To keep secret the existence of this dreaded malady, the relatives of an insane person oftentimes postpone all effectual treatment until the time of its usefulness is past; and they forego measures of security until some terrible calamity results. Accepting the ignorant and wicked opinion that disease of the brain is disgraceful, they give grounds to others for holding this opinion, by the sacrifices they are willing to make that the existence of insanity in the family may be concealed. They not only sacrifice to this the safety of the public, but that of the patient himself, with his present comfort and the probable means of restoration. From motives variously compounded of selfishness and ignorance, they ignore the two great principles in the successful treatment of insanity, that it must be early, and that it must be conducted in

I

scenes remote from those influences in which it has its origin. Under a real or assumed regard for the feelings of the unhappy patients, they retain them at homes which may once have been happy, but which now have become places of moral torture, where every look inflicts a wound, every word probes a sore. When the patient is removed to fresh scenes, and to that skilfully arranged repose of the excited mental functions, which is provided for in a judicious system of treatment, the misery inflicted by the disease abates, even as the anguish of a broken limb is allayed by simple rest and well-arranged position.

In the following scene with Rosencrantz, Guilden-stern, and the King, Hamlet is again in his most antic disposition of mind. His sarcastic irony to his two old schoolfellows, whom he now trusts as he would adders fanged, is more directly insulting than before. They are sponges that soak up the King's countenance, the ape's first morsel, first mouthed, last swallowed. Still he throws a thicker cloak of counter-feit unreason over his sarcasm than he has done be-fore. His replies,

> " The body is with the king, but the king is not with the body. The king is a thing—"
> " — of nothing : bring me to him. Hide fox, and all after ;"

his answers to the King, " Farewell, dear mother," " My mother : Father and mother is man and wife ; man and wife is one flesh ; and so, my mother"—are

fairly on a par in unreasoning suggestiveness with his
reply to Polonius, "For if the sun breed maggots,"
etc. These mad absurdities are never altogether
meaningless, and never altogether foreign to the
natural train of his own thoughts. The description
of Polonius at supper, "not where he eats, but where
he is eaten," is the foreshadowing idea of the serious
and earnest meditations on the mutability of matter
in which he afterwards indulges over the churchyard
skulls. "A man may fish with a worm that hath
eat of a king; and eat of the fish that hath fed of
that worm." And thus, "A king may go a progress,"
etc. 'Tis the very same speculation as that so
seriously expressed to his friend:

"To what base uses we may return, Horatio! Why may
not imagination trace the noble dust of Alexander, till he
find it stopping a bung-hole?"

This is the philosophy he had learnt at Wittenburg,
and which he toyed with to the last. He had learned,
indeed, its inadequacy to explain all things by im-
material evidence, sights which make

"us fools of nature,
So horribly to shake our disposition
With thoughts beyond the reaches of our souls."

He had been compelled to acknowledge that there
"are more things in heaven and earth than are dreamt
of" in this philosophy. Still this form of speculation
was the habit of the mind, and whether in antic
disposition of madness, or in earnest converse with

his friend, it is found his frequent topic. Might not this habit of dwelling upon the material laws to which our flesh is subject, have been resorted to as a kind of antidote to those "thoughts beyond the reaches of the soul" to which his father's apparition had given rise,—his father, whose "bones had burst their cerements," whose sepulchre had oped its ponderous jaws to cast him up again. Was not this materialist speculation a struggle against these thoughts, and akin to the unconscious protest against the Ghost, that beyond the grave is

> "The undiscover'd country, from whose bourn
> No traveller returns."

Alas for Hamlet! What with his material philosophy and his spiritual experiences, there was contention enough in that region of the intellect which abuts upon veneration, to unhinge the soundest judgment; let alone the grief, and shame, and just anger, of which his uncle's crimes and his mother's frailty were the more than sufficient cause in so sensitive a mind.

In the following scene with the captain of the army of Fortinbras, we have a comment upon the folly of useless war, and an occasion for another fine motive-weighing soliloquy; like the prayer scene, useless indeed to the progress of the piece, but exquisite in itself. Never does Shakespeare seem to have found a character so suited to give noble utterance to his own most profound meditations as in

Hamlet.   It is on this account that we unconsciously
personify Shakespeare in this character, as we personify Byron in Childe Harold, or Sterne in Yorick,
and, may we not add, Goëthe in Faust.

The soliloquy "How all things do inform against
me" marks a state of inclination to act, in advance
of that manifested in the soliloquy beginning "Oh,
what a rogue and peasant slave am I !" but still not
screwed up to the point of resolve.   The gross example of soldiers, who "for a fantasy and trick of
fame" are so lavish of life and limb, places before
Hamlet in the strongest light his own craven scruples,
and, as he chooses to say, his apprehension of results.
But on this point he does not do himself justice.   His
personal courage is of the most undaunted temper.
In his first interview with the Ghost he does not set
his "life at a pin's fee"; and the independent evidence
of Fortinbras testifies to his high promise as a soldier.
It is not the lack of courage, but the inability to carry
the excitements of his reason and his blood into an
act so repugnant to his nature as the assassination of
his uncle, that yet withholds his hand ; and although
he concludes,

> " O, from this time forth
> My thoughts be bloody, or be nothing worth !"

he leaves his purpose unfulfilled, and allows himself
to be sent out of the country—a proceeding likely
to postpone his revenge indefinitely, or to defeat it
altogether ; and it is not until he discovers the King's

villainous plot against his own life, that he determines
to "quit him with this arm."

The colloquy with the grave-digger and Horatio
in the churchyard affords abundant proof that the
biting satire and quaintness of thought, which have
been accepted as the antic garb of Hamlet's mind,
are quite natural to him when he is playing no part.
The opening observation on the influence of custom
is a favourite theme with him.   When he wishes to
wring his mother's heart, he is apprehensive whether

> " damned custom have not brass'd it so
> That it is proof and bulwark against sense."

And when he dissuades her from her incestuous intercourse, he says :

> " That monster, custom, who all sense doth eat,
> Of habits devil, is angel yet in this,
> That to the use of actions fair and good
> He likewise gives a frock or livery,
> That aptly is put on."
> " For use almost can change the stamp of nature,
> And either curb the devil, or throw him out
> With wondrous potency."

Custom, therefore, brazes the heart in vice ; custom
fortifies the body in habits of virtue ; it also blunts
the sensibilities of the mind ; so that grave-making
becomes "a property of easiness."

> " 'Tis even so : the hand of little employment hath the
> daintier sense."

This, however, is but half truth.   The "hand of little
employment" hath not always "the daintier sense" in

use. Does custom blunt the fingers of a watchmaker, the eyes of a printer, or the auditory nerve of a musician? Did the grave-digger do his own sombre work with less skill because he had been accustomed to it for thirty years? Custom blunts our sensations to those impressions which we do not attend to, and sharpens them to those which we do. Custom in Hamlet himself had sharpened the speculative faculties which he exercised, while it had dulled the active powers which depend upon that resolution which he did not practise.

Hamlet's comments upon the skulls,—upon the politicians, who could circumvent God,—on the courtiers, who praised my lord Such-a-one's horse when he meant to beg it,—on the lawyers, whose fine of fines is to have his fine pate full of fine dirt, and whose vouchers vouch him for no more of his purchases than the length and breadth of a pair of indentures,—are the quaint prosaic expression of his melancholy, his gloomy view of the nothingness of life, combined with his peculiar speculations upon death as the mere corruption of the body. He revolts at the idea of this ignoble life, as he thinks it, ending in annihilation, and he equally recoils at the idea that it may end in bad dreams. He thinks that if death is an eternal sleep, such an end of the ills of life is a consummation devoutly to be wished, but the fear that it is an eternal dream is unendurable. His fancy is too active to permit him to rush into an eternity of unknown consciousness. Like Prince Henry, in the *Spanish Student,* he feels,

> " Rest ! rest ! O give me rest and peace !
> The thought of life that ne'er shall cease
> Has something in it like despair,
> A weight I am too weak to bear."

To return to his mother earth an unconscious clod seems his most earnest hope; yet when the offensive *débris* of mortality meets his eyes, such an ignoble termination of mental activity revolts both his sensibility and his reason. " Here's a fine revolution, if one had the trick to see't" His bones ache to think on't. When he sees the skull of his old friend the jester, from whose companionship he may have derived much of his own skill in word-fence and poignancy of wit, his imagination is absolutely disgusted.

> "Alas, poor Yorick ! I knew him, Horatio : a fellow of infinite jest, of most excellent fancy : he hath borne me on his back a thousand times ; and now, how abhorred in my imagination it is ! my gorge rises at it. Here hung those lips that I have kissed I know not how oft. Where be your gibes now ? your gambols ? your songs ? your flashes of merriment, that were wont to set the table on a roar ? Not one now, to mock your own grinning ? quite chap-fallen ? Now get you to my lady's chamber, and tell her, let her paint an inch thick, to this favour she must come ; make her laugh at that."

The grave-digger's jest that Hamlet's madness will not matter in England, since " 'twill not be seen in him : there the men are as mad as he," is legitimate enough in the mouth of a foreigner, since for ages have the continentals jested upon the mad English, who hang themselves by scores every day, and who, in November especially, immolate themselves in hecatombs to the dun goddess of spleen. By this time the jest has somewhat lost its point. At least, it may be said that if the English furnish as many madmen as their neighbours, they are somewhat better acquainted with the means of ameliorating their sad condition. Madness, however, and suicide are now known to be as prevalent in the great neighbour nation, whose writers jest upon the universal diffusion of the curse.

All men are mad, writes Boileau, the grand distinction among them being the amount of skill employed in concealing the crack : and if statistics prove anything with regard to suicides, it is that our once volatile neighbours have an unhappy advantage over us in that respect, both in numbers and variety. If it was ever a habit with us, it has now become a fashion with them.

The funeral of Ophelia, and the bravery of her brother's grief, are the occasion of conduct in Hamlet which cannot be considered either that of a reasonable man or of a counterfeit madman. He acknowledges to his friend that he forgot himself, and that he was in a towering passion. The more probable explanation is, that the shock of Ophelia's death, made known to him so suddenly, strangely, and painfully, gave rise to an outburst of passionate excitement referrible to the latent unsoundness of his mind, and that the Queen's explanation of his conduct is the true one :

> "This is mere madness :
> And thus awhile the fit will work on him ;
> Anon, as patient as the female dove,
> When that her golden couplets are disclosed,
> His silence will sit drooping."

It indeed looks like madness ; for why should a brother's phrase of sorrow over the grave of a sister, however exaggerated its expression, excite a sane lover to such rage,—the rage of passion, not of grief. A sane man would have been struck dumb by overwhelming grief, if he had thus accidentally met at the verge of the tomb the body of a mistress whom he devotedly loved, and whose stinted ritual betokened that with desperate hand she had foredone her own life. In Hamlet's state of mind the occurrence gives birth to rash conduct and vehement passion ; passion, be it remarked, not caused by the struggle in the grave, but by the bravery of the brother's grief.

Although after this scene Hamlet converses with thorough calmness with his self-possessed friend, there are passages which strongly indicate the morbid state of his mind. Speaking of his condition on shipboard, he says :

> "Sir, in my heart there was a kind of fighting,
> That would not let me sleep : methought I lay
> Worse than the mutines in the bilboes."

And again, referring to his present feelings, he says : "Thou wouldst not think how ill all's here about my heart; but it's no matter." "It is but foolery; but it is such a kind of gain-giving as would, perhaps, trouble a woman."

Above all, if his conduct in the churchyard is not the result of morbidly violent emotion, uncontrolled by reason, what can we say of his own explanation:

> "Give me your pardon, sir: I've done you wrong;
> But pardon 't, as you are a gentleman.
> This presence knows, and you must needs have heard,
> How I am punish'd with a sore distraction.
> What I have done,
> That might your nature, honour and exception
> Roughly awake, I here proclaim was madness.
> Was't Hamlet wrong'd Laertes? Never Hamlet:
> If Hamlet from himself be ta'en away,
> And when he's not himself does wrong Laertes,
> Then Hamlet does it not, Hamlet denies it.
> Who does it, then? His madness: if 't be so,
> Hamlet is of the faction that is wrong'd;
> His madness is poor Hamlet's enemy.
> Sir, in this audience,
> Let my disclaiming from a purposed evil
> Free me so far in your most generous thoughts,
> That I have shot mine arrow o'er the house,
> And hurt my brother."

Except the above brief reference to the inner wretchedness, which Horatio takes for an evil augury, Hamlet shews no disposition to melancholy after the rough incidents of his sea voyage. The practice of the King upon his life appears to have fixed his resolve: He'll wait till no further evil is hatched. He that hath

> "Thrown out his angle for my proper life,
> And with such cozenage; is't not perfect conscience

> To quit him with this arm? and is't not to be damn'd
> To let this canker of our nature come
> In further evil?"

Moreover, what there is to do he'll do quickly. The issue of the business in England, with Rosencrantz and Guildenstern, will quickly be known, but

> "the interim is mine;
> And a man's life's no more than to say, one."

In this temper it would have been frivolous in him to have accepted the challenge of Laertes, were it not that he saw in it an opportunity to right himself with his old friend, by the image of whose cause he read the portraiture of his own. It is after a seeming reconciliation thus obtained, that he determines to accept "this brother's wager." Might not also the challenge be accepted as likely to offer a good opportunity to meet the King, and "quit him with this arm," an opportunity which he now resolves to seize whenever it offers? The sentiment of coming evil lends probability to the thought.

> "Not a whit, we defy augury: there's a special providence in the fall of a sparrow. If it be now, 'tis not to come; if it be not to come, it will be now: if it be not now, yet it will come: the readiness is all: since no man has aught of what he leaves, what is't to leave betimes?"

The final scene of indiscriminate slaughter, which, as Fortinbras says, would more become a battle-field than a palace, points the moral so obvious throughout the piece, that the end of action is not within the hands of the human agents. The blow which finally

quits the King was fully deserved for his last act.
His end has an accidental suddenness about it, which
disappoints the expectation of judicial revenge. Like
Laertes, he is a woodcock caught in his own springe.
Retribution is left to the terrible future, whose mys-
teries have been partially unveiled; and the mind,
prepared by the revelations of the Ghost, accepts the
death of the King but as the beginning of his quittance.

The death of Hamlet has been objected to as cruel
and needless; but would it not rather have been cruel
to have left him alive in this harsh world, drawing his
breath in pain? Heart-broken, and in that half-mad
state which is vastly more painful than developed insanity, what could he do here, after the one act for
which he was bound to live had been accomplished.
Had he survived he must have sank into inert
motiveless melancholy, or have struggled on in the
still more painful state of contention between conscience and suicidal desire. To prevent a wounded
name being left behind him, he can command his
friend to "absent him from felicity awhile"; but for
himself the best is the dark mantle of oblivion, the
rest with hope which his friend so gracefully expresses:

"Now cracks a noble heart. Good night, sweet prince;
 And flights of angels sing thee to thy rest!"

There is no attempted poetical justice in this
bloody finale to the drama. The way of the world
rather is followed in the indiscriminate mischief. Sweet
Ophelia and noble Hamlet meet the same fate which

attends the incestuous Queen, the villanous King, the
passionate Laertes, and the well-meaning Polonius.
The vortex of crime draws down the innocent and
the guilty, the balance of desert being left for adjust-
ment in the dark future.   The intricacy of the action
and the unexpected nature of the events are copied
from life as closely as that marvellous delineation of
motive and feeling which brings Hamlet so intimately
home to the consciousness of reflective men.   Those
dramas in which we accurately foresee the event in
the first act are as little like the reality of human life
as a geometric problem is like a landscape.   Granted
that there is nothing like accident in human affairs,
that if a special providence in the fall of a sparrow
may be doubted, the subjection of the most trivial
circumstances to general laws is beyond question ;
still, in human affairs the multiplicity and mutual
interference of these laws are such, that it is utterly
beyond human foresight to trace forward the thread
of events with any certainty.   In Hamlet this uncertainty is peculiarly manifested.   Everything is
traceable to causes, which operate, however, in a
manner which the most astute forecaster of events
could never have anticipated ; though, after their
occurrence, it is easy enough to trace and name them,
as Horatio promised to do.

> "So shall you hear
> Of carnal, bloody, and unnatural acts,
> Of accidental judgments, casual slaughters,
> Of deaths put on by cunning and forced cause,

> And, in this upshot, purposes mistook
> Fall'n on the inventors' heads : all this can I
> Truly deliver."

Although we arrive at the conviction that Hamlet is morbidly melancholic, and that the degree to which he puts on a part is not very great; that, by eliminating a few hurling words, and the description which Ophelia gives of the state of his stockings, there is little either in his speech or conduct which is truly feigned ; let us guard ourselves from conveying the erroneous impression that he is a veritable lunatic. He is a reasoning melancholiac, morbidly changed from his former state of thought, feeling, and conduct. He has "foregone all custom of exercise," and longs to commit suicide, but dares not. Yet, like the melancholiacs described by Burton, he is "of profound judgment in some things, excellent apprehensions, judicious, wise, and witty ; for melancholy advanceth men's conceits more than any humour whatever." He is in a state which thousands pass through without becoming truly insane, but which in hundreds does pass into actual madness. It is the state of incubation of disease, "in which his melancholy sits on brood," and which, according to the turn of events or the constitution of the brain, may hatch insanity, or terminate in restored health.

There is an apparent inconsistency between the sombre melancholy of Hamlet's solitary thoughts and the jesting levity of his conversation, even when he

seeks least to put on the guise of antic behaviour;
an inconsistency apparent only, for in truth this
gloomy reverie, which in solitude "runs darkling down
the stream of fate," is thoroughly coherent in nature
with the careless mocking spirit playing in derisive
contempt with the foibles of others. The weeping
and the mocking philosopher are not usually divided
as of old, but are united in one, whose laugh is be-
stowed on the vanity of human wishes as observed in
the world around, while the earnest tear is reserved
for the more deeply felt miseries of his own destiny.
The historian of melancholy himself was a philosopher
of this complexion. Deeply imbued with melancholy
when his mental gaze was introverted, when employed
upon others it was more mocking than serious, more
minute than profound. Thence came the charming
and learned gossip of the *Anatomy;* thence also the
curious habit recorded of him, that for days together
he would sit on a post by the river-side, listening and
laughing at the oaths and jeers of the boatmen, and
thus finding a strange solace for his own profound
melancholy. Here is his own evidence:

" Humorous they (melancholiacs) are beyond measure;
sometimes profusely laughing, extraordinary merry, and then
again weeping without a cause; groaning, sighing, pensive,
sad, almost distracted, restless in their thoughts and actions,
continually meditating.
                    Velut ægri somnia, vanæ
                Finguntur species;
more like dreamers than men awake, they feign a company
of antick fantastical conceits."

There is an intimate relationship between melancholy and humour. The fact is finely touched in the Yorick of Lawrence Sterne, and, what is more to the purpose, in the real history of many of the most celebrated humourists; and the truth even descends to those humourists of action, theatrical clowns. Who has not heard the story of one of the most celebrated of these applying incognito to a physician for the relief of melancholy, and being referred for a remedy to his own laughter-moving antics? Not that humour is always attended by any tinge or tendency to melancholy, as the plenitude of this faculty exhibited by jolly Sir John fully proves. Still there is this in common to the roystering humour of Falstaff, the melancholy humour of Jacques, and the sarcastic humour of Hamlet, that they have each a perverse ingenuity in contemplating the weakness and selfishness of human motive. Wit deals with ideas and their verbal representations; humour with motives and emotions; and that melancholy cast of thought, which tends to exhibit our own motives in an unfavourable light, is apt to probe the motives of others with searching insight, and to represent them in those unexpected contrasts and those true but unusual colours which tickle the intelligence with their novelty and strangeness.

The character of Hamlet presents another contrast, which, if not more obvious than the above, has at least attracted more attention, perhaps because he himself

K

comments upon it, and because it is a main point upon which the drama turns. It is the contrast between his vivid intellectual activity, and the inertness of his conduct. To say that this depends upon a want of the power of will to transmute thought into action, is to do no more than to change one formula of words into another. There must be some better explanation for the unquestionable fact that one man of great intellectual vigour becomes a thinker only, and another a man of vehement action. That activity of intellect is in itself adverse to decisiveness of conduct, is abundantly contradicted by biography. That activity of intellect may exist with the utmost powerlessness, or even perversity of conduct, is equally proved by the well-known biographies of many men, "who never said a foolish thing, and never did a wise one." The essential difference of men who are content to rest in thought, and those who transmute it into action, appears not to consist in the presence or absence of that incomprehensible function, that unknown quantity of the mind, the *will;* but in the presence or absence of clearly-defined and strongly-felt *desire,* and in that power of movement which can only be derived from the exercise of power, that is, from the habit of action. It is conceivable, as Sir James Mackintosh has well pointed out, that an intellectual being might exist examining all things, comparing all things, knowing all things, but desiring and doing nothing. It is equally conceivable that a being might exist with two strong desires, so equally poised that the result should be complete neutralization of each other, and a state of inaction as if no emotional spring to conduct whatever existed. Hence, inaction may arise from want of desire, or from equipoise of desire.

It is, moreover, conceivable that an intellectual being might exist, in whom desires were neither absent nor equipoised, but in whom the habit of putting desires into action had never been formed. We are indeed so constituted, that clearly-formed desires tend naturally to transmute themselves into action, and the idea of a being at once intellectual and emotional, in whom circumstances have entirely prevented the development of the habit of action, has more the character of a metaphysical speculation than of a possible reality. Still the immense influence of habit upon the power of action is unquestionable, and the want of this habit appears to have been one chief cause of Hamlet's inert and dilatory conduct, and of the contention between that meditative cast of thought which he in vain strove to screw up to the point of action, and the desire to discharge that repulsive duty which his uncle's villanies had laid upon him. That the time was out of joint would have been for him a subject of painful reflection only, but for the accursed spite which had laid it upon him to set it right, and which was the cause of that fierce moral strife between duty and disposition which forms

the innermost web of the piece. The rash execution
of an unpremeditated action is entirely consistent with
this sensitive motive-weighing inability to act upon
mature resolve. The least resolute men are often the
most rash ; as quick spasm in feeble muscles is substituted for healthy, regular, and prolonged exertion.
Hamlet praises rashness in the instance in which it
served him, but he would scarcely have been able
to have done so when it led him to slay Polonius
in mistake for the King ; and the incidents of the
drama, no more than the incidents of real life, justify
us in rough-hewing our purposes with rashness, though
the Divinity may shape the ends even of our most
politic arrangements.

This reasoning melancholiac, disgusted with the
world, and especially disgusted with the repulsive
duty which a hard fate has laid upon him, is not less
different to the Hamlet of the past, to him who had
been

> "The expectancy and rose of the fair state,"

to him who, as a soldier,

> "was likely, had he been put on,
> To have proved most royally,"

than he is the good feeble young gentleman whom
Goëthe describes, and whose "mind is too feeble for
the accomplishment" of "the great action imposed
as a duty." "Here is an oak planted in a vase ;
proper only to receive the most delicate flowers.

The roots strike out, the vessel flies to pieces. A pure, noble, highly moral disposition, but without that energy of soul which constitutes a hero, sinks under a load which it can neither support nor abandon altogether." "Observe how he shifts, hesitates, advances, and recedes!" Goëthe's simile however, beautiful though it be, appears to halt on both feet, for the great action, which is the oak, does not strike out its roots, does not increase in magnitude or responsibility; nor does the Prince deserve to be compared to a vase, senseless and inert, which cannot expand or "shift"; and, moreover, it is not the greatness of the action which is above the energy of his soul, but the nature of it which is repulsive to its nobility. If Hamlet must be compared to a vase, let it not be to a flower-pot, but to that kingly drinking-cup, whose property it was to fly to pieces when poison was poured into it.

In addition to the above, there are other causes of turmoil in Hamlet's mind less plainly stated, but traceable enough throughout the piece. One of these is the contention between his religious sentiments and his sceptical philosophy. His mind constantly wavers between belief and unbelief; between confidence in an overruling Providence, who shapes all our ends to wise purposes, and even permits its angels and ministers of grace to attend unseen on our hours of trial; between this reverential faith and that scepticism which sees in man but so much animated dust, and looks upon death as annihilation. The pain of

this same doubt has been finely expressed by him,
whom future centuries will regard as the great lyric
of the nation, even as Shakespeare is for aye its great
dramatist :

> "I trust I have not wasted breath :
>   I think we are not wholly brain,
>   Magnetic mockeries ; not in vain,
> Like Paul with beasts, I fought with Death :
>
> Not only cunning casts in clay :
>   Let Science prove we are, and then
>   What matters Science unto men—
> At least, to me ?   I would not stay."
>
>   "And he, shall he
> Who loved, who suffered countless ills,
>   Who battled for the true and just,
>   Be blown about the desert dust,
> Or sealed within the iron hills ?"

Indeed, the manifold points of resemblance between
Hamlet and *In Memoriam* are remarkable.   In each
the great questions of eternal interest are debated by
a mind to whom profound grief makes this world
a sterile promontory.   The unknowable future absorbs all interest.   The lyric bard, however, fights his
way to more light than the dramatist attains.   The
fear of annihilation oppresses, but does not conquer
him.   He rebukes Lazarus for holding his peace on
that which afflicts the doubting soul, but for himself
he fights his way to faith.

> "He fought his doubts, and gathered strength ;
>   He would not make his judgment blind ;
>   He faced the spectres of the mind,
> And laid them."

It is not easy to estimate the amount of emotional
disturbance for which Love is answerable in Hamlet's
mind. Probably, if other matters had gone well with
him, Ophelia's forced unkindness would easily have
been seen through and overcome ; but, with a mind
pre-occupied with the dread mission of his father's
revenge, it is likely that he would not question the
earnestness of Ophelia's rejection, and that "to the
pangs of despised love" he might well attribute one
of the most poignant ills that flesh is heir to. His
demeanour to Ophelia, when he first puts on his antic
disposition, and which she so graphically describes,
not less than his own avowal at her grave, that
"twenty thousand brothers could not make up his
sum of love," point to the existence, not of "trivial
fond records," but of a passion for her both deep and
constant ; a passion thrust rudely into the back-
ground indeed, but not extinguished or even weakened, by the more urgent emotions of revenge for his
father, of shame for his mother, of scorn and hatred
for his uncle. The character of Hamlet would have
been incomplete if the element of love had been forgotten in its composition. Harshly as he may seem
to treat his mistress, this element adds a warm sienna
tint to the portraiture, without which it would have
been not only cold and hard, but less true to the
nature of the melancholy sensitive being delineated.

There is little trace of ambition in his character ;
for, although he makes the King's having stepped

between the election and his hopes one in the list of
his injuries, his comments upon the manner in which
this was done savour of contempt for his uncle's
ignoble means of success, for the manner in which he
filched the crown, and was "a cutpurse of the empire
and the rule," rather than of any profound disappointment that the election had not fallen upon himself.
Indeed, this character has been painted in dimensions
far exceeding those of the sceptred rulers of the earth.
Ambition would have dwarfed him to the type of
a class; he stands forth the mighty poetical type of
the race.

It is this universal humanity of the character which
lies at the root of its wonderful reality and familiarity.
Hamlet seems known to us like an old friend. "This
is that Hamlet the Dane," says Hazlitt, "whom we
read of in our youth, and whom we seem almost to
remember in our after years." "Hamlet is a name:
his speeches and sayings but the idle coinage of the
poet's brain. What, then, are they not real? They
are as real as our own thoughts. Their reality is in
the reader's mind. It is *we* who are Hamlet. This
play has a prophetic truth which is above that of
history." Are we then wrong in treating Hamlet as
a reality, and in debating the state of his mind with
more care than we would choose to bestow upon the
insane vagaries of an Emperor Paul or a Frederick
Wilhelm? Have we not more sure data upon which
to exercise judgment than upon the uncertain truth

of history? Buckle, in his *History of Civilization*, has elaborately argued the madness of Burke; a domestic grief, a change of temper, and above all, a change of political opinions from those which the historian thinks true to those which he thinks false, being held sufficient to establish the confirmed insanity of the great statesman. Those who read the ingenious argument will feel convinced at least of this, that history rarely or never leaves grounds relative enough to solve such a question. Nay, when we are close upon the footsteps of a man's life, when the question is not one of learned trifling, like that of the insanity of Socrates, but the practical one of whether a man just dead was competent to devise his property, when his papers and letters are ransacked, his daily life minutely examined, when scores of men who knew him intimately bear testimony to their knowledge, we often find the balance of probability so even, that it is impossible to say to which side it inclines, and the feelings of the jury as often as not fabricate the will. But when the great mind of mind speaks out as in Hamlet, it is not so. Then it is as in the justice of Heaven, then the "action lies in its true nature," which neither ignorance can obscure nor sophistry pervert.

It is by this great faculty that Shakespeare unfolds to our view the book of the mind, and shews alike its fairest and most blotted pages, and leaves in us a thirst not for more light, but for more power to read.

If familiarity and fellow-feeling compel us at one
time to regard Hamlet as a reality, reflection and
curious admiration compel us at others to wonder at
it as a work of man's creative power; and it has ever
been to us a question of intense interest to speculate
upon the manner it was worked out.   There appears
this great distinction between Hamlet and all other
characters of Shakespeare in which real or feigned
insanity is represented, that, while they are evidently
all drawn from the life, it could scarcely have been
drawn from observation.   Ophelia, for instance, is the
very type of a class of cases by no means uncommon.
Every mental physician of moderately extensive experience must have seen many Ophelias.   It is a copy
from nature, after the fashion of the pre-Raphaelite
school, in which the veins of the leaves are painted.
Hamlet however is not pre-Raphaelite, but Raphael-
ite; like the Transfiguration, it is a glorious reflex
from the mind of the author, but not a copy of aught
which may be seen by other eyes.   It is drawn, indeed, in accordance with the truth of nature, just as
Raphael made use of anatomical knowledge in painting the Transfiguration; but there is something beyond and above that which any external observation
can supply.   From whence did this come?   Without
doubt, from within.   Shakespeare has here described
a broad phase of his own mind; has reflected the
depth of his own great soul; has set up a glass in
which the ages will read the inmost part of him; how

he thought of death and suicide ; how he doubted of
the future, and felt of the present,

"That this huge state presenteth naught but shows ;"

how he looked inwards until fair nature became dark,
and spun

"A veil of thought, to hide him from the sun."

Hallam, the most learned and just of English critics,
has recognised this inner reflection of the soul in this
and some others of the great bard's sombre characters.

"There seems to have been a period of Shakespeare's
life when his heart was ill at ease, and ill-content with the
world or his own conscience ; the memory of hours misspent,
the pang of affection misplaced or unrequited, the experience of man's worser nature, which intercourse with ill-
chosen associates, by choice or circumstance, peculiarly
teaches ; these, as they sank down into the depths of his
great mind, seem not only to have inspired into it the
conception of Lear and Timon, but that of one primary
character, the censurer of mankind. This type is first seen
in the philosophic melancholy of Jacques, gazing with un-
diminished serenity, and with a gaiety of fancy though not
of manners, on the follies of the world. It assumes a graver
cast in the exiled Duke of the same play, and next one
rather more severe in the Duke of *Measure for Measure.* In
all these, however, it is merely contemplative philosophy.
In Hamlet this is mingled with the impulses of a perturbed
heart, under the pressure of extraordinary circumstances ; it
shines no longer as in the former characters, with a steady
light, but plays in fitful corruscations amid feigned gaiety
and extravagance. In Lear it is the flash of sudden inspiration across the incongruous imagery of madness ; in Timon
it is obscured by the exaggerations of misanthropy."

However true this may be in the main, we can
scarcely agree to recognise any part of our own ideal

of Shakespeare's individuality in any of these characters, except in Hamlet and in Jacques. Doubtless
there was melancholy and cynicism enough in the
great bard, but there could have been no real misanthropy, no mad fury, no stern congelation of feeling,
as in Timon, Lear, and the Duke; nor is there any
of these in Hamlet or Jacques, or in the real heart
history as it is written in the Sonnets.

Misanthropy and cynicism appear to have been
very generally confounded. Doubtless they are often
found together; yet is there a wide difference between the two in their real nature. The cynic may
even carp and sneer at the faults of his brother men
from the depth of his human love, and thus be at
quite the opposite pole of feeling to him who avows
" I am misanthropos, and hate mankind." The author
of Rasselas, that prosaic reflection of Hamlet, was
eminently a cynic; yet a more tender and pitiful
soul never animated human clay, than that which
dwelt in the burly Diogenes of Fleet Street. He
of Sinope so zealously inculcated virtue as to derive
from Plato the nickname of the mad Socrates.
Though he lived in a tub he loved mankind, and
rudely taught them at how cheap a rate they might
obtain happiness. But misanthropy is quite a different thing, either from melancholic dissatisfaction
or cynical content. It is a perversion of all human
sympathy, incompatible with all nobility of soul, and,
most of all, with that sympathetic touchstone of

human emotions, the soul of the true poet. We recognise this in Swift, who was a misanthropist *pur sang*, and whose vast intellectual powers might have placed him among the first of his country's poets, had not his sympathies been utterly out of unison with those of his kind. The true expression of universal hatred is not that of exalted passion, but that of the heartless sneer which is utterly anti-pathetic. Goëthe touches the point when he makes the man-hating demon excuse himself in the heavenly court from the use of pathetic speech.

> " Verzeih, ich kann nicht hohe Worte machen,
>   Mein Pathos brachte dich gewiss zum Lachen."

The poetic soul of Faust, on the contrary, swells with wide and warm human sympathy ; although in despairing rage he curses all human desires, all hope, all faith, and, above all, all patience. In one of these characters we have true misanthropy serving as a foil to the other, to whom, as in Hamlet, not man but man's position is hateful, and whose human sympathies are passionate, even in the despair which cries out in the life-weary agony, and almost in the words of Hamlet :

> " Und so ist mir das Daseyn eine Last
>   Der Tod erwünscht, das Leben mir verhasst."

An enquiry into the mental pathology of this character may aptly conclude with a quotation from the writings of a kindred and cotemporary mind to that of the great dramatist, namely, those of Michael de Montaigne. Coleridge, in his truly beautiful lectures, which have been so happily preserved by the notes of Mr. Payne Collier, admits that "such a mind as Hamlet's is near akin to madness" from its "greatness of genius," which is the sense in which Dryden used the word "wit" in the line—

"Great wit to madness nearly is allied."

Montaigne actually saw the saddest exemplification of this truth in one of the greatest "wits" of the age —the immortal Tasso. His comments on the sad spectacle are less harsh than they seem ; for although very far from being deficient in human sympathy and pity, he also had a strong dash of the cynic in him, cynicism without misanthropy.

"What puts the soul beside itself, and more usually throws it into madness, but her own promptness, vigour, and agility, and finally her own proper force? Of what is the most subtle folly made, but of the most subtle wisdom? As great friendships spring from great enmities, and vigorous health from mortal diseases, so from the rare and vivid agitations of our souls proceed the most wonderful and most distracted frenzies ; 'tis but half a turn of the toe from the one to the other. In the actions of madmen we see how infinitely madness resembles the most vigorous operations of the soul. Who does not know how indescribable the difference is betwixt folly and the sprightly aspirations of a free soul, and the effects of a supreme and extraordinary virtue? Plato says that melancholy persons are the most capable of discipline, and the most excellent ; and accordingly in none is there so great a propension to madness. Great wits are ruined by their own proper force and pliability : into what a condition, through his own agitation and promptness of fancy, is one of the most judicious, ingenious,

and nearest formed of any other Italian poet to the air of
the ancient and true poesy, lately fallen? Has he not vast
obligation to this vivacity that has destroyed him? to this
light that has blinded him? to this exact and subtle apprehension of reason that has put him beside his own? to
this curious and laborious search after sciences, that has reduced him to imbecility? and to this rare aptitude to the
exercises of the soul, that has rendered him without exercise
and without soul? I was more angry, if possible, than compassionate, to see him at Ferrara in so pitiful a condition,
surviving himself, forgetting both himself and his works,
which, without his knowledge, though before his face, have
been published unformed and incorrect.

"Would you have a man healthy, would you have him
regular, and in a steady and secure posture? Muffle him
upon the shades of stupidity and sloth. We must be made
beasts to be made wise, and hoodwinked before we are fit
to be led. And if one shall tell me that the advantage of
having a dull sense of pain and other evils brings this dis-
advantage along with it, to render us consequently less
sensible also in the fruition of good and pleasure, this is
true; but the misery of our condition is such, that we have
not so much to enjoy as to avoid, and that the extremest
pleasure does not affect us to the degree that a light grief
does: 'Segnius homines bona quam mala sentiunt.' 'We
are not so sensible of the most perfect health as we are of
the least sickness.'

"Pungit
In cute vix summa violatum plagula corpus;
Quando valere nihil quemquam movet. Hoc juvat unum,
Quod me non torquet latus, aut pes: Cætera quisquam
Vix queat aut sanum sese, aut sentire valentem."

OPHELIA.

"Che per amor venne in furore e matto."

OPHELIA, so simple, so beautiful, so pitiful! The exquisite creation is so perfect, yet so delicate, that we fear to approach it with the rough touch of critical remark. Child of nature in simplicity and innocence —without guile, without suspicion—and therefore without reserve, or that deceit which often simulates a modesty more dainty than the modesty of innocence. And yet, not ignorant though innocent; but with quick native intellect, which appreciated the selfishness and rebuked the fears of her brother's caution; which still more fully appreciated, and was able most eloquently to describe the noble qualities of her princely lover, "the glass of fashion and the mould of form;" simple, yet not obtuse; but possessing quick sentiment and lively fancy to a degree which made her most impressible to all generous emotion; sensitive, but yet reticent; thrilling through every fibre of the soul to the touch of love and the anguish of despair; yet allowing no confession to be extorted, and no cry to escape, until she sees her lover "quite, quite down;" when, with unselfish grief lamenting his fall, she allies her fate with his, and cries aloud in the agony of woe,—"and I of ladies most deject and wretched." It is strange how thoroughly we seem to know Ophelia, notwithstanding her taciturnity and reserve. She says nothing of herself, and yet we seem to look into the very recesses of her clear soul; thus presenting one form of contrast to the being with whose fate her own was entwined, who constantly soliloquising and self-analysing, nevertheless leaves upon us the impression that we know the vast amplitude of his thoughts and feelings but dimly and in part. The one is the translucent and limpid fountain, reflecting but one image ; the other, the ever-varying river, with rapids, and smooth reaches, and profound depths, reflecting and representing the varied features of earth and heaven.

Ophelia is passive, but not impassive ; her very reticence is eloquent of feeling. Her love, like that of Imogen and Desdemona, has more of sentiment than of passion in it. It does not vent itself in strong expressions, like the passions of Juliet and Cleopatra. It is imaginative, retiring, sensitive, fearful of itself, and yet without one particle of selfishness. In this, also, it is unlike the *amour passion*, which is essentially selfish. Not that Ophelia is wholly without passion ; for love without passion cannot exist, except as a mere dream. But the constituents, sentiment and passion, which are in all love, though in infinitely varying degrees, appear in Ophelia to exist

L

in the greatest possible amount of the former, and the least of the latter.

Sensitive, and imaginative, and devoted, the poor girl was endowed with all the faculties of moral suffering. That she should suffer greatly, undeservedly, irremediably, was needful, in order to make her the object of that intense pity which the character excites, and which was certainly wanted in the drama to perfect it as a tragedy. The character is not very prominent, but it so entirely seizes upon our sympathy and pity, that, in this respect, it leavens our regard for the whole play. Ulrici has called Hamlet a "Gedankentrauerspiël," or, tragedy of thought; as if there could be any tragic emotion excited by thought alone, whose unmodified influence is to cause assent or dissent? Yet, if the character of Ophelia were wanting, there would be so much justice in the epithet which this critic has applied to the drama, it would appeal so much to thoughts and opinions, and so little to sentiment, that it would be too much a drama of thought and opinion to take the rank it does in the most sacred shrine of the tragic muse.

Pity, soft-eyed mother of the virtues, ever assuaging the severe aspect of their male parent, justice; pity, most unselfish of all the emotions, although in truth but one form of self-suffering; pity, that appreciation of evil which we understand and sympathize with, and therefore suffer with or compassionate when we behold others under the weight of its affliction;

pity, whose Heavenly influence it is the highest aim
and object of the tragic muse to invoke, is the sentiment which the character of Ophelia more powerfully
elicits than that of any other of Shakespeare's female
characters. For if Imogen was at one time as
wretched, her misery was changed into joy; and if
Desdemona was equally innocent, her agony was
more brief and less intense. The sufferings of Cordelia were alleviated by active resistance against the
evil power by which they were occasioned. In Lear,
the king of sorrows, and in Othello, the lion poisoned
by a villain's hand, are characters which excite pity
as intense, though not as unmixed; for in neither is
the agony felt to be quite undeserved or quite unavoidable. For it is to be remarked, that to excite
the pure sentiment of pity—First, it is needful the
suffering reflected from the consciousness of another
upon our own sensibility should be such as we can
appreciate, and bring home as it were to ourselves:

"Haud ignara mali miseris succurrere disco."

Secondly, that the sufferings should be great. We do
not pity the petty miseries of life; and although a
man's happiness may be stung to death by poisonous
insects as certainly as it can be torn by the fangs of
a savage monster, we are not revolted at wounds
which we cannot see. Thirdly, unmixed pity can
only be excited by suffering, which is undeserved and
unavoidable. When a man brings upon himself only

so much suffering as he deserves to endure; or when, through wilfulness or obstinacy, he endures suffering which he can avoid, justice holds up the stern finger and forbids pity to interfere. But avoidability of suffering and desert of suffering are so relative and varied with circumstance, that some amount of obstinacy or demerit is readily overlooked by the tender eyes of compassion. "Treat us all according to our merits," says Hamlet, "and who shall escape whipping?" Feel for us all according to our merits, and who shall deserve pity?

Yet justice modifies pity, nay, sometimes forbids it—even where suffering is greatest. The agonies of hell, as they are painted on the broad canvas of Milton, do not excite pity, because they are felt to be justly endured.

Ophelia is, from the first moment of her appearance, suffering the anguish of doubt and wounded love. Unlike Desdemona and Imogen, there is no bright period of the character. There is gentle but real sorrow in her first words, "No more but so?" Must she consider herself merely the toy of her princely lover? "The perfume and suppliance of the minute?" Has he been trifling with her love? and his own, is it nothing but youthful lust, dishonourable to himself and dangerous to her? "No more but so?" She does not believe it; her brother sees that she does not believe it, and he gives more credit to Hamlet's earnestness. "Perhaps he loves

you now"; but he may not marry where he chooses;
he may not carve for himself; therefore it behoves
poor Ophelia to exercise her wisdom where wisdom is
rarely exercised, and to believe Hamlet's love only so
far as the probability of an honourable marriage may
justify her faith. Match-making probabilities, which
the poor girl was far enough from being able to
estimate! Laertes does not advise his sister according to the truth of the saying, that "the woman who
hesitates is lost." He advises her to believe in Hamlet's love to a certain extent, but not to give *too*
credent an ear:

> "Be wary then, best safety lies in *fear;*
> Youth to itself rebels, though none else near."

Polonius knows that best safety lies in *flight;* he in-
sists upon no half measures. The not very delicate
warning of Ophelia's disagreeable brother, that she is
likely to lose her honour to Hamlet's unmastered importunity, is evidently distasteful to the poor girl, and
gives occasion to the only sparkle of displeasure which
the gentle creature ever shows, in that quick witted
retaliation of advice:

> "But, good my brother,
> Do not, as some ungracious pastors do,
> Show me the steep and thorny way to heaven;
> Whiles, like a puff'd and reckless libertine,
> Himself the primrose path of dalliance treads,
> And recks not his own rede."

Ophelia's reference to the primrose path of dalliance
which her libertine brother was likely to lead, shows

from the first that her purity of mind is not the result of ignorance. She seems young and ardent—her brother fears for her honour not more on account of Hamlet's importunity, than on account of her own youth, which is likely to rebel against the dictates of prudence, though unsolicited, "though none else near."

What the old father has to say takes a much more straightforward and decisive form than the advice of Laertes, who feels that he is treading on tender ground, and who gets repaid by counter advice. Polonius reproaches his daughter that she has been "most free and bounteous of her audience with Hamlet"; and he tells her downright, "you do not understand yourself so clearly, as it behoves my daughter, and your honour." To the demand that she should give up the truth to him, the poor frightened girl at once acknowledges Hamlet's suit, but carefully conceals the state of her own heart.

"*Ophelia.* He hath, my lord, of late made many tenders
Of his affection to me.
Polonius. Affection! pooh! you speak like a green girl,
Unsifted in such perilous circumstance.
Do you believe his tenders, as you call them?
Oph. I do not know, my lord, what I should think.
Pol. Marry, I'll teach you: think yourself a baby:
That you have ta'en these tenders for true pay,
Which are not sterling. Tender yourself more dearly;
Or—not to crack the wind of the poor phrase,
Wronging it thus—you'll tender me a fool.
Oph. My lord, he hath importuned me with love,
In honourable fashion.

Pol. Ay, fashion you may call it; go to, go to.
Oph. And hath given countenance to his speech, my lord,
With almost all the holy vows of heaven.
Pol. Ay, springes to catch woodcocks."

A green girl, indeed; a baby in the perils of court
amours, having the credulity of innocence, but not
that of stupidity. A sensitive unsophisticated maiden
for the first time in love, wondering at the new and
strange sensation, scarcely confessing it to herself,
unable to distinguish the traits of the mysterious
tyrant who has set up his throne in her young heart.
The father and the brother fear for her chastity; and
these fears may have been well founded, for she appears the very prototype of Margaret in Faust, who,
in the spirit of unselfish devotion, could refuse her
lover nothing. But they need not have feared for
her modesty, or for that precious quality in women
which the cold word modesty, or moral moderation,
does not express, the shamefacedness of love *(pudi-
citia, pudeur, Keuscheit),* at once the effect and the
proof of moral purity. Had Ophelia been capable of
measuring and moderating her love in accordance
with the advice of her worldly brother, of yielding to
Hamlet so far as the probability of the voice of the
nation assenting to his marriage might justify her,
her chastity might have been perfectly safe; but it is
certain that the true modesty of her love would have
been lost. There are such beings as brazen prudes.
There are also those who have fallen and are pure.
Rousseau well says, "Le vice a beau se cacher dans

l'obscurité, son empreinte est sur les fronts coupables ;
l'audace d'une femme est le signe assuré de sa honte ;
c'est pour avoir trop à rougir qu'elle ne rougit plus,
et si quelquefois la pudeur survit à la chastité, que
doit on penser de la chastité quand la pudeur même
est éteinte ?"

Between this scene and the next one in which
Ophelia appears, time must have elapsed during
which Hamlet has pursued his suit ; since Ophelia,
in obedience to her father's command, has repelled
his letters and denied access. These letters would
scarcely have been written by Hamlet, subsequently
to his interview with the ghost and his vow to erase
all trivial fond records from the table of his memory.
According to the progress of the love story, therefore,
the last scene of the first act would appear to belong
to the second act ; which would leave Hamlet's mad
appearance in Ophelia's closet as the first and immediate consequence of his resolve " to put an antick
disposition on." This it is which changes the old
courtier's fear that Hamlet intended to wreck his
daughter's honour, into the belief in his sincerity and
consequent madness ; and thus arises his regret that
he had not noted him with better heed and judgment.

Ophelia's plasticity and yieldingness of character,
rather than her depth of filial affection, appear manifested in the readiness with which she first obeys the
old man's orders to reject Hamlet's addresses, and
with which she subsequently lends herself to the

deceit which is practised upon her lover, to test and demonstrate his state of mind, and especially, whether, as Polonius maintained, and the Queen finely expressed, that her "good beauties be the happy cause of Hamlet's wildness." The arranged meeting of Hamlet and Ophelia, "as 'twere by accident," and the pretence of the maiden to read a book as a colour to her loneliness, was a species of conduct inconsistent with her ingenuousness of character, and to which she appears to have lent herself in sorrowful unquestioning obedience. The dialogue which follows is a terrible punishment for any fault she may almost unconsciously have committed. Her lover sees the snare laid for him, and recognizes the deceitful part she is taking. She has not seen him "for this many a day," and longs to re-deliver his remembrances formerly so precious to her, now become so poor since he has proved unkind. How much she expresses in how few words. What simplicity and faith in his love—"Indeed, my lord, you made me believe so." What patient anguish at his denial of his love—"I was the more deceived." What unselfish forgetfulness of her own deep sorrow, to which the word forgiveness would be misapplied, since the slightest notion of resentment never seems to have entered her gentle soul. When she recognizes in his disdainful vituperation the incoherence of insanity, she cries, "O, help him, ye sweet heavens!"—not herself, but him. Not because she is deceived and rejected, but because he

is quite, quite down, is she of ladies most deject and
wretched. Not for her own blighted hopes, but because his unmatched form is blasted with ecstacy,
does she raise that cry of anguish—

> " O, woe is me,
> To have seen what I have seen, see what I see !"

In the whole of the play there is not a more exquisite
passage than this lamentation of the desolate maid
over the supposed ruin of her lover's intellect.

Ophelia appears once more as one of the audience
before the players, before her own mind is "as sweet
bells jangled out of tune ;" but it is to be remarked
that she never makes a consecutive speech again.
To Hamlet's indelicate banter she makes the curtest
replies, scarcely sufficient to defend her outraged
modesty. She is concealing, and, as well as may be,
bearing up against the anguish gnawing at her heart.
But fancy and intellect are benumbed by sorrow, only
to display themselves at a later date, again active,
though perverted, under the stimulus of disease.

It is left in some doubt to what extent grief at
the death of Polonius concurred, with pining sorrow
at the blight of her love, in giving rise to Ophelia's
distraction. The King and Queen, and Laertes,
evidently refer it to the former cause ; yet although
in her gentle ravings she constantly refers to her
father's death, and never directly to her lover's unkindness, we are inclined to consider the latter as by
far the most potent, though it may, perhaps, not be

the sole cause of her distraction. This opinion founds itself upon the form of insanity which is depicted, namely, mania with prevalent ideas of the sentiment of love, or erotomania, as it is learnedly called. " In medicine," says Ferriar, "we have fine names at least, for every species of disease," and erotomania is the fine name for that form of insanity in which the sentiment of love is prominent, as nymphomania is the fine name for an allied but sufficiently distinct variety in which the instinct is excessive.

We have somewhere read that Ophelia's snatches of song were culled from the street ballads of the day, and that Shakespeare thus obtained an easy theatrical effect. This, however, seems probable only with reference to the two longer and more indelicate effusions beginning, " Good morrow, 'tis St. Valentine's day," and " By Gis and by Saint Charity." The snatches of song which precede having reference to her own circumstances, seem impromptu, strung together at the time :

> " How should I your true love know
> From another one ?
> By his cockle hat and staff,
> And his sandal shoon ?
>
> " He is dead and gone, lady,
> He is dead and gone ;
> At his head a grass-green turf,
> At his heels a stone."
>
> " White his shroud as the mountain snow,
> Larded all with sweet flowers ;
> Which bewept to the grave did go,
> With true-love showers."

They well express the confused connection in the
poor head between the death of her father and the
loss of her lover ; the one is foremost on her lips,
but it is not difficult to see that the latter is upper-
most in her thoughts. The same confusion between
the two sources of her sorrow is manifested in all she
says. In the lines—

> " They bore him barefaced on the bier ;
>   And in his grave rain'd many a tear ;—
> Fare you well, my dove !"—

the two first lines seem to go for the loss of her father
—the last for her lover. The same lucid confusion
and imperfect concealment are still more obvious in
her distribution of flowers.

> "*Ophelia.* There's rosemary, that's for remembrance ;
> pray, love, remember : and there is pansies, that's for
> thoughts. There's fennel for you, and columbines : there's
> rue for you ; and here's some for me : we may call it herb-
> grace o' Sundays : O, you must wear your rue with a dif-
> ference. There's a daisy : I would give you some violets,
> but they withered all when my father died : they say he
> made a good end."

Well might her passionate brother, softened for
a moment by her grief and sweetness, exclaim—

> " Thought and affliction, passion, hell itself,
>   She turns to favour and to prettiness."

for never was sentimental mania more truly and
more exquisitely depicted than in this effusion of
mad song.

"Sie wiegte Schmerz und Sehnsucht
Und jeden Wunsch mit leisen Tönen ein.
Da wurde Leiden oft Genuss, und selbst
Das traurige Gefühl zur Harmonie."—Goëthe's *Tasso.*

It seems impossible that Shakespeare could have
done otherwise than drawn from the life in this character. He has in truth and in deed verified the in-
troductory observation that her mood will needs be
pitied, for gentleness and goodness, struggling in the
deepest affliction of which human nature is capable,
have never been more finely drawn; and yet not
overdrawn, for in the vivid reality of the picture there
is not one touch of mawkishness. Compare, in this
respect, the love-lorn maiden of Sterne, poor Maria,
who allowed the stranger to wipe away the tears which
trickled down her cheeks with his handkerchief, which
he then steeped in his own tears, and then in hers,
then in his own, until it was steeped too much to be
of any further use. "And where will you dry it,
Maria?" said I. "I will dry it in my bosom," said
she, "it will do me good." One never meets with
such bathos of sentiment as this in the real insane,
nor in the insane characters of the great master.
Ophelia's prettinesses are as natural as they are touching. The freshness of reality encircles her head like
the wild flowers with which she weaves her garlands.
This fantastical dress of straws and flowers is a common habit of the insane, but it seems more natural
in Ophelia than in the angry and raging madness of

old Lear, in whom it is also represented. The picture
of her insanity is perfected by many other touches as
natural and true. She

> "Spurns enviously at straws ; speaks things in doubt,
>   That carry but half sense."

She winks, and nods, and makes gestures, which have
the double effect of breeding dangerous conjectures
in the minds of the people, and of delineating with
exactness the habits and practices of gentle but
general mania. There is no consistency in her talk,
or rather, there is only the consistency of incoherence,
with two prominent ideas, the loss of her lover, and
her father's death.

> "Well, God 'ield you ! they say the owl was a baker's
> daughter. Lord, we know what we are, but know not what
> we may be. God be at your table !"

> "You must sing, *Down a-down, an you call him a-down-a.*
> O, how the wheel becomes it ! It is the false steward, that
> stole his master's daughter."

Compare this perfect incoherence with the apparent
incoherence of Hamlet, whose replies, as Polonius observes, are often more pregnant of indirect meaning
than reason and sanity could be. There is no hidden
meaning in aught that poor Ophelia says. When for
a moment she wanders from her leading train of
thought, the sequence of ideas is utterly lost. Even
at the last, when she has fallen into the weeping
brook, she has no appreciation of her danger.

> " Her clothes spread wide ;
> And, mermaid-like, awhile they bore her up :
> Which time she chanted snatches of old tunes,
> As one incapable of her own distress."

Utterly lost, except to the insane train of ideas, she is as insensible to danger as a somnambulist ; and singing her life away, she passes from the melody of madness to the silence of the grave. O rose of May! too soon blighted ! but whose perfume shall endure in a monument of immortal words, when the tombs of Egyptian kings shall have crumbled into the desert dust !

KING LEAR.

AYE, every inch a king, in all his pompous vanity,
his reckless passion, his unstable judgment, a thorough
king, whom even madness could not dethrone from
the royal habits of authority, of strenuous will, and
of proud predominance. As the highest mountain
summit becomes the fearful beacon of volcanic flame,
testifying in lurid characters to the world's deep
heart-throes, so this kingliest of minds—he who in
his little world has been the summit and the cope
of things—becomes, in the creative hand of the poet,
the visible outlet of those forces which devastate the
soul. We stand by in reverential awe, despairing,
with our small gauge of criticism, to estimate the
forces of this human Enceladus. Oppressed by the
power and magnitude of the passions, as depicted in
this most sublime and awful of poetic creations, it is
only after the senses have become accustomed to the
roar and turmoil that we throw off the stupor, and
dare to look down upon the throes of the Titan, and
begin to recognize the distinctive features of the fierce
commotion. Even then we must stand afar off; for
not in Lear, as in others of the poet's great characters,
can one for a single moment perform the act of mental

transmutation. In Hamlet, for instance, the most
complex of all, many a man may see reflected the
depths of his own soul. But Lear is more or less
than human in its isolated grandeur, in the force and
depth of its passions, in its abstraction from accidental
qualities. In the breadth of his strength and weakness he is painted like one of those old gods, older
and greater than the heathen representatives of small
virtues and vices—the usurping vulgarities of poly-
theism. The true divinities of Lear were old, like
himself very old and kingly—Saturn and Rhea, the
autochthones of the heavens; even as his qualities
are laid upon the dark and far off, yet solid and deep
foundations of moral personality. Well might this
king of sorrows exclaim, in the words of the World-
spirit, to those who attempt to tear his passions to
tatters before the footlights, yea, even to the more
reverent efforts of critics—

> "Du gleichst dem Geist den du begreifst,
> Nicht mir !"

Essayists upon this drama have followed each
other in giving an account of the development of
Lear's character and madness, which we cannot but
regard as derogatory to the one and erroneous in
relation to the other. They have described Lear as
an old man, who resolves upon abdication, and the
partition of his kingdom, while he is of sane mind,
and fully capable of appreciating the nature of the
act. Thence it becomes necessary to view the original

M

character of Lear as that of a vain weak old man ;
thence it becomes necessary to discuss the point when
the faculties first give way ; thence it becomes necessary to view the first acts of the drama as a gross
improbability. " Lear is the only serious performance
of Shakespeare," says Coleridge, "the interest and
situations of which are derived from the assumption
of a gross improbability." Such undoubtedly they
would be, if they were the acts of a sane mind ; but
if, on the contrary, it be accepted that the mind of
the old king has, from the first, entered upon the
actual domain of unsoundness, the gross improbability
at once vanishes, and the whole structure of the drama
is seen to be founded, not more upon " an old story
rooted in the popular faith," than upon the verisimilitude of nature. The accepted explanation of
Lear's mental history, that he is at first a man of
sound mind, but of extreme vanity and feeble power
of judgment, and that, under the stimulus of subsequent insanity, this weak and shallow mind develops
into the fierce Titan of passion, with clear insight into
the heart of man, with vast stores of life science,
with large grasp of morals and polity, with terrible
eloquence making known as with the voice of inspiration the heights and depths of human nature ; that
all this, under the spur of disease, should be developed
within the sterile mind of a weak and vain old man ;
this, indeed, is a gross improbability, in which we see
no clue to explanation.

Gross improbabilities of circumstance are not rare in Shakespeare. The weird sisters in Macbeth, and the ghost in Hamlet, are certainly not more probable as events, than the partition of Lear's kingdom. But there is one kind of improbability which is not to be found in Shakespeare—the systematic development of goodness from badness, of strength from weakness; the union of that which, either in the region of feeling or of intellect, is antagonistic and incompatible. Even in depicting the mere creatures of the imagination, Shakespeare is consistent; we feel the fairy to be a fairy, the ghost to be a ghost; and even those foul tempters in woman's form,

> " Who look not like the inhabitants of the earth
>   And yet are on it,"

are distinct, special, clear-cut creations of the poet's brain, consistent in every characteristic with themselves: Ariel is all aerial, and Caliban all earthly. In Shakespeare's characters there is no monstrous union of fair with foul, and foul with fair, as in those phantasms who opposed Ruggier in the island of Alcina:

> " Alcun' dal collo in giù d'uomini han forma,
>   Col viso altri di simie, altri di gatti ;
>   Stampano alcun' con piè caprigni l'orma ;
>   Alcun son centauri agili et atti ;
>   Son gioveni impudenti, e vecchi stolti,
>   Chi nudi, e chi di strane pelli involti."

There is nothing of this in the works of the Supreme Mind, whose poem is created nature. There is no-

thing of this in the works of that human mind, who,
in the consistency and power of his work, has attained the nearest approximation to his great Author.
Neither in nature, that is, in the works of God, nor
in high art, that is, in truthful imitation of nature, is
any such monster to be found as a vain and weak old
man developing into the strength and grandeur of
a prophet; the voice of Isaiah in the mouth of an
imbecile.

Hallam expresses unreservedly the opinion that
Lear's wondrous intellectual vigour and eloquence
are the result of his madness, and that the foundation
of his character is that of a mere "headstrong, feeble,
and selfish being."

"In preparing us for the most intense sympathy with
this old man, he first abases him to the ground; it is not
Œdipus, against whose respected age the gods themselves
have conspired; it is not Orestes, noble minded and affectionate, whose crime has been virtue; it is a headstrong,
feeble, and selfish being; whom, in the first act of the
tragedy, nothing seems capable of redeeming in our eyes;
nothing but what follows—intense woe, unnatural wrong.
Then comes on that splendid madness, not absurdly sudden
as in some tragedies, but in which the strings, that keep his
reasoning powers together, give way, one after the other, in
the frenzy of rage and grief. Then it is that we find, what
in life may sometimes be seen, the intellectual energies grow
stronger in calamity, and especially under wrong. An awful
eloquence belongs to unmerited suffering. Thoughts burst
out more profound than Lear, in his prosperous hour, could
ever have conceived; inconsequent, for such is the condition of madness, but in themselves fragments of coherent
truth, the reason of an unreasonable mind."

If this great and sound critic had possessed any

practical knowledge of mental pathology, he could
not have taken this view of the development of the
character. Intellectual energy may, indeed, sometimes be seen to grow stronger under the greatest
trials of life, but never when the result of these trials
is mental disease. So far as eloquence is the result
of passion, excitement of passion may stimulate its
display; and it is remarkable that so long as Lear
retains the least control over his passion, his imagination remains comparatively dull, his eloquence tame.
It is only when emotional expression is unbridled,
that the majestic flow of burning words finds vent.
It is only when all the barriers of conventional restraint are broken down, that the native and naked
force of the soul displays itself. The display arises
from the absence of restraint, and not from the
stimulus of disease.

The consistency of Shakespeare is in no characters
more close and true, than in those most difficult ones
wherein he pourtrays the development of mental unsoundness, as in Hamlet, Macbeth, and Lear; into
these he throws the whole force of his genius; in
these he transcends, not only all that other poets
have effected before him, but all that he has ever
done himself. The border country between sanity
and insanity—that awful region of doubt and fear,
where the distorted shadows of realities, and the
chimeras dire of the brain, are distinguishable in the
sunless gloom of our unreason by flickering corrusca-

tions of the fancy, by fog meteors of humour, and by lightning flashes of passion—this region his bold and fearless mind delights to explore, and to lead those who can follow him, even as Virgil led Dante through the circles of hell. He delights to observe and to explore it, and with his own clear light of genius to look down upon it and through it, and to trace the wanderings and the falls of the erring, misled, spirit; but never, for one moment, does he lose his own sharp and accurate faculty of distinguishing realities and moral probabilities. In his hands the development of an insane character is as strictly amenable to law, as that of the most matter-of-fact and common-place sanity. In his hands the laws of mental aberration are as sure as those of the most regular development; nay, they often tend to illustrate the latter, as in the hands of a botanist a green petal proves the development of the flower from the leaf. It is on the development of insanity, the gradual loosening of the mind from the props and supports of reason and of fact, the gradual transition of the feelings from their old habitudes and relations to morbid and perverted excess, the gradual exaggeration of some feelings and the extinction of others and the utter loss of mental balance resulting therefrom; it is in this passage from the state of man when reason is on its throne to a state when the royal insignia of his preeminence among God's creatures are defaced, that the great dramatist delights to dwell.

Cervantes, indeed, has painted with exquisite skill the half-lights of one form of insanity; but Shakespeare alone has described the transition period and the state of resistance. It is remarkable within how small a compass all that Shakespeare has written on perfected madness may be brought; namely, one short scene of Ophelia's madness, and three scenes of the madness of Lear.

The persistency with which critics have refused to see the symptoms of insanity in Lear, until the reasoning power itself has become undeniably alienated, is founded upon that view of mental disease which has, until recently, been entertained even by physicians, and which is still maintained in courts of law, namely, that insanity is an affection of the intellectual, and not of the emotional part of man's nature. The author of these essays was among the first to raise the standard of revolt against this theory, in two articles on the "Law and Theory of Insanity," in the 24th and 25th numbers of the *Medico-Chirurgical Review*. The veteran Guislain had already fully recognized the immense influence of emotional suffering in the causation of insanity; but the wider and still more important principle, that morbid emotion is an essential part of mental disorder, still remained a novel doctrine. Any detailed exposition of the metaphysical and psychological arguments, by which the author has endeavoured to maintain the validity of this doctrine, would here be out of place. It must suffice to state, that with the exception of those cases of insanity which arise from injuries, blood poisons, sympathetic irritations, and other sources of an unquestionably physical nature, the common causes of insanity are such as produce emotional changes, either in the form of violent agitation of the passions, or that of a chronic state of abnormal emotion, which pronounces itself in the habitually exaggerated force of some one passion or desire, whereby the healthy balance of the mind is at length destroyed. From these and other reasons founded upon the symptomatology and treatment of insanity, upon the definite operation of the reasoning faculties, and their obvious inability to become motives for conduct without the intervention of emotional influence, and also from the wide chasm which intervenes, and must intervene, between all the legal and medical definitions of insanity founded upon the intellectual theory and the facts as they are observed in the broad field of nature, the conclusion appears inevitable, that no state of the reasoning faculty can, by itself, be the cause or condition of madness; congenital idiocy and acquired dementia being alone excepted. The corollary of this is, that emotional disturbance is the cause and condition of insanity. This is especially obvious in the periods during which the disease is developing; "in the prodromic period of the disorder the emotions are always perverted while the reason remains intact." Disorders of the intellectual faculties are secondary; they are often, indeed, to be recognized as the morbid emotions transformed into perverted action of the reason; but in no cases are they primary and essential.

How completely is this theory supported by the development of insanity, as it is pourtrayed in Lear! Shakespeare, who painted from vast observation of nature, as he saw it without and felt it within, places this great fact broadly and unmistakably before us. It has, indeed, been long ignored by the exponents of medical and legal science, at the cost of ever futile attempts to define insanity by its accidents and not by its essence; and, following this guidance, the literary critics of Shakespeare have completely over-looked the early symptoms of Lear's insanity; and, according to the custom of the world, have postponed its recognition until he is running about a frantic, raving, madman.

Lear is king at a time when kings are kings. Upon his will has hung the life and wealth, the being and the having, of all around. Law exists indeed; the reverend man of justice and his yoke-fellow of equity are benched high in the land, but he is the little godhead below.

> "Aye, every inch a king.
> When I do stare, see how the subject quakes!"

Perilous height, too giddy for the poor human brain! Uneasy lies the head which wears a crown! Unsafely thinks the head which wears a crown! The

very first king by divine appointment went mad.
What are the statistics of insanity among crowned
heads? Who can tell? About half a century ago,
one fourth of the crowned heads of Europe were
insane, those of Portugal, Denmark, Sweden, Russia,
and England. But often the chariot of government
may be kept in the ruts of routine long after the
guiding mind is obscured. With trembling hands,
royal servants and kinsfolk hold a veil before the
piteous spectacle. Not as of old does Nebuchadnezzar
wear his chains in public. The wide purple hides all,
until the service becomes too dangerous ; and then
perchance the sharp remedy of the assassin's scarf
has been applied round Paul's imperial neck.

Or the madness may not be quite so extreme, nor
the remedy so conclusive. It may be disguisable and
tolerable until it abates, and the poor patient emerges
to become one of Mr. Carlyle's hero-kings. It may
display itself, as in Frederick Wilhelm of Prussia,
only in violence of language and conduct towards his
children, in beatings and kickings, in restless frightened nights and wanderings from chamber to chamber,
in terrors of assassination with loaded pistols under
the pillow, and yet the government machine be guided
by the frantic hand in an altogether admirable manner,
according to Mr. Carlyle, and those who bow down in
pious worship before power in high places, be it ever
so wild.

And why should not Mr. Carlyle make a hero of

his mad king, who is also a dumb poet polishing to perfection practical unspoken stanzas, as that of his giant regiment, which might irreverently be called one of his delusions? Why not? since Schiller has made a beautiful, all perfect hero from the materials of an insane prince : Don Carlos, who in this country and in private station, might have found his way to the criminal wards at Bethlem, to whom, in fact, the sharp remedy of assassination had to be applied, as to Muscovite Paul. Why not? except that poetry and history are rather different things.

This fact of royalty in Lear; that he has been eighty years and more a prince and king, that he is not only despotic in authority but in disposition, that his will can tolerate no question, no hindrance; this, if not the primary cause of his lunacy, gives colour and form to it. He strives to abdicate, but cannot ; even madness cannot dethrone him ; authority is stamped legibly on his brow ; he is not alone a mad man but a mad king.

Unhappy king, what was his preparation for his crown of sorrows, his sceptre of woe! Unlimited authority ; that is, isolation. To have no equals, that is to say, no friends. To be flattered to the face, and told that there were grey hairs in the beard before the black ones were there ; plied with lies from early youth (for this teaches that Lear was a king before he wore a beard), and therefore to be set on a pedestal apart from his kind, even from his own flesh and blood, until all capacity to distinguish truth from falsehood, affection from hypocrisy, is lost; this was his preparation.

Half a century of despotic power, yielded by a mortal of rash and headstrong temper, and with vivid poetic imagination, may well produce habitudes of mind to which any opposition will appear unnatural and monstrous as if the laws of nature were reversed, to which the incredible fact of opposition can be accepted only with astonishment and rage.

But Lear's mind is conditioned by extreme age as well as by despotism; age which too often makes men selfish, unsympathising, and unimpressible; age, which in some "hardens the heart as the blood ceases to run, and the cold snow strikes down from the head and checks the glow of feeling," in others, is the occasion of stronger passion and hotter temper; a sad state, one of labour and sorrow, and dangerous to happiness, honour, and sanity. The natural state of old age is, that the judgment matures as the passions cool; but a tendency of equal force is, that the prevailing habitudes of the mind strengthen as years advance; and a man who, in "the best and soundest of his time hath been but rash," feels himself, and makes those around him feel, "not alone the imperfections of engrafted condition, but therewithal the unruly waywardness that infirm and choleric years bring with them;" a maxim not less true because it is the heartless observation of a thankless child,

and one capable of being extended to almost all the
prevailing emotions and tendencies of man. In old
age, the greedy man becomes a miser; in old age,
the immoral man becomes the shameless reprobate;
in old age, the unchecked passions of manhood tend
to develop themselves into the exaggerated proportions of insanity. How stern a lesson is the folly,
the extravagance, and the vice of old men, that while
it is yet time, passion should be brought into subjection, and the proportions and balance of the mind
habitually submitted to the ordinances of the moral
law!

It is worthy of remark that Lear's age is physically
strong and vigorous. He has been a warrior as well
as a king.

> "I've seen the day with my good biting falchion
> I would have made them skip."

Even at the last he has vigour enough to kill the
slave who is hanging Cordelia. He is a keen hardy
huntsman, and he rides from the house of one daughter
to that of another with such speed, that his strong
willing messenger can scarcely arrive before him by
riding night and day. Physically, therefore, he is
a strong, hale, vigorous man; and the desire he expresses to confer his cares on younger strengths, that
he may "unburthened crawl towards death," is either
a specious reason for his abdication, or one which has
sole reference to the consciousness of that failing judgment which is obvious to others, and probably not

unfelt by himself; and which his daughter so cruelly insinuates when he claims her gratitude.

This state of hale bodily strength in senile mania is true to nature ; it is observed, both in second childhood, that is, in the dementia of old age, and in the insanity of old age, that the physical powers are commonly great—the body outlives the mind—or to speak more physiologically and truthfully, some functions of the body remain regular and vigorous, while others suffer morbid excitement or decay ; general nutrition retains its power, while the nutrition of the brain becomes irregular or defective.

Coleridge justly observes, that "it was not without forethought, nor is it without its due significance, that the division of Lear's kingdom is, in the first six lines of the play, stated as a thing determined in all its particulars previously to the trial of professions, as the relative rewards of which the daughters were to be made to consider their several portions." "They let us know that the trial is a silly trick, and that the grossness of the old king's rage is in part the result of a silly trick suddenly and most unexpectedly baffled and disappointed."

That the trial is a mere trick is unquestionable ; but is not the significance of this fact greater than Coleridge suspected? Does it not lead us to conclude, that from the first the king's mind is off its balance ; that the partition of his kingdom, involving inevitable feuds and wars, is the first act of his developing insanity; and that the manner of its partition, the mock-trial of his daughters' affections, and its tragical denouement, is the second, and but the second act of his madness? The great mind, so vigorous in its mad ravings, with such clear insight into the heart of man that all the petty coverings of pretence are stripped off in its wild eloquence, not only is unable to distinguish between the most forced and fulsome flattery and the genuineness of deep and silent love; it cannot even see the folly of assuming to apportion the three exact and predetermined thirds of the kingdom according to the professions made in answer to the "silly trick;" cannot even see that after giving away two-thirds, the remainder is a fixed quantity which cannot be more or less according to the warmth of the professions of his youngest and favorite daughter; a confusion not unlike the account he subsequently gives of his own age—"four score and upwards; not an hour more or less."

With what courtly smoothness of pretence goes on the mocking scene, until Cordelia's real love, and obstinate temper, and disgust at her sister's hypocrisy, and repugnance perhaps at the trick she may see through, interrupt the old king's complacent vanity; and then the astonishment, the retained breath, the short sentences, the silence before the storm! and then the outbreak of unbridled rage, in that terrible curse in which he makes his darling daughter—her whom he loved best, whom he looked to as the nurse of his age—for ever a stranger to his heart! It is madness or it is nothing. Not indeed raving, incoherent, formed mania, as it subsequently displays itself; but exaggerated passion, perverted affection, enfeebled judgment, combining to form a state of mental disease—incipient indeed, but still disease—in which man, though he may be paying for past errors, is during the present irresponsible.

The language in which is couched the expostulations of the noble-minded Kent collected and even-tempered in all his devoted loyalty and self-sacrifice, shews the impression which this conduct makes upon the best and boldest mind present:

> "Be Kent unmannerly
> When Lear is *mad*."

> "With better judgment check
> This hideous rashness."

> "Kill thy physician, and thy fee bestow
> Upon the foul disease."

Lear's treatment of Kent; his ready threat in reply to Kent's deferential address, which, in the words of true devotion, only looks like the announcement of an expostulation; his passionate interruptions and reproaches; his attempted violence, checked by Albany and Cornwall; and finally the cruel sentence of banishment, cruelly expressed; all these are the acts of a man in whom passion has become disease. In the interview with France and Burgundy the seething passion is with difficulty suppressed by the rules of decorum and kingly courtesy. To Cordelia's entreaty that Lear would let the King of France know the simple truth of his displeasure, only the savage reply is given—

> "Better thou
> Hadst not been born than not to have pleased me better;"

and he casts out his once loved daughter—the darling of his heart, the hope of his age—without his grace, his love, his benison.

All this is exaggerated passion, perverted affection, weakened judgment; all the elements, in fact, of madness, except incoherence and delusion. These are added later, but they are not essential to madness; and as we read the play, the mind of Lear is, from the first, in a state of actual unsoundness, or, to speak more precisely, of disease. The conference between Regan and Goneril, which ends the scene, seems to prove this view correct; for, although they attribute their father's outrageous conduct to the infirmity of age, it is evident it has surprised and alarmed them. His sudden changes, unguarded by any judgment, are evidently a new thing to these selfish and clear-sighted observers; although, indeed, they may be but the exaggerated results of long habits of rashness, matured into a state which renders him unfit for the exercise of authority.

"*Goneril.* You see how full of changes his age is; the observation we have made of it hath not been little: he always loved our sister most; and with what poor judgment he hath now cast her off appears too grossly.

N

Regan. 'Tis the infirmity of his age : yet he hath ever but slenderly known himself.

Gon. The best and soundest of his time hath been but rash ; then must we look to receive from his age, not alone the imperfections of long-engraffed condition, but therewithal the unruly waywardness that infirm and choleric years bring with them.

Reg. Such inconstant starts are we like to have from him as this of Kent's banishment.

Gon. There is further compliment of leave-taking between France and him.   Pray you, let's hit together : if our father carry authority with such disposition as he bears, this last surrender of his will but offend us.

Reg. We shall further think on 't.

Gon. We must do something, and i' the heat."

Goneril speedily finds that such authority as her old father chooses to exercise does offend her.   He strikes her gentleman for chiding his fool ; wrongs her, as she thinks, by day and night ; every hour he flashes, as she thinks, into one gross crime or other ; he upbraids her on every trifle.   She'll not endure it. She has no love for the old man, and little patience for his infirmities, whether they be those of native disposition, of dotage, or of disease :

> " Idle old man,
> That still would manage those authorities
> That he hath given away !   Now, by my life,
> Old fools are babes again ; and must be used
> With checks as flatteries,—when they are seen abused."

Strong as her language has been on her father's constant wrongs to her, and his 'gross crimes,' Goneril attributes them to the effects of dotage, and appears to entertain no suspicion that real madness is threatening. It is not till long after—in the third act, when Glo'ster is "tied to the stake"—that the old king's insanity is recognized by one of his ungrateful daughters ; Regan asking—

"To whose hands have you sent the lunatic king?"

Soon after Goneril's exposition of the terrain, Lear enters from hunting, hungry and impatient—

"Let me not stay a jot for dinner, go get it ready."

A collected conversation with disguised Kent follows, and then the steward appears to put upon him the predetermined insolent negligence, which his mistress had given him instructions for. Lear, in his magnanimity, does but half see it, and requires to have his attention directed to it by the knight, whose keener observation has remarked the great abatement of kindness and lack of ceremonious attention which has been latterly shewn to his master. The king has seen it too, but had rather blamed his own jealous curiosity, than permitted himself to think the unkindness was intentional. Even now he throws off the thought lightly and calls eagerly for that strange being, that wonderful medley of wit and philosophy, of real affection and artificial folly, "my fool!" whom he loves none the less for his attachment to disgraced Cordelia.

"*Knight.* Since my young lady's going into France, sir, the fool hath much pined away.
Lear. No more of that, I have noted it well."

Silent repentance for his rash and cruel treatment of this well-loved daughter hath already touched the old man's heart. But the transitions of feeling are more rapid than the changes of sunshine and shade in an April day. In the next sentence, he is in unmeasured rage with the steward for his insolent reply, and has no control over his tongue or his hands:

"My lady's father! my lord's knave: you whoreson dog! you slave! you cur!" "Do you bandy looks with me, you rascal? [*Striking him.*]"

Enough of Lear's violence, both in language and conduct is manifested, to confirm the truth of Goneril's harsh accusations. It must be owned that the old king has a terrible tongue, and a quick and heavy hand. The slightest opposition throws him into violent and outrageous speech and behaviour, little likely to be endured with patience, except by those who have strong motives for it in love or duty or interest. It is strange, however, with what patience he endures the bitter taunts and sarcasm of his fool. They seem only to pique his curiosity, and to excite his interest in the gladiatorial display of wit and folly. The fool, indeed, is "a bitter fool," "a pestilent gall," but his taunts are elicited, not repressed; and the "all-licensed fool" says to his master's face, and without a word of reproof, fifty times more than had brought upon Kent his cruel sentence of banishment. But the talk with the fool is only a lull in the storm. Goneril enters with a frontlet of frowns, and in a set speech—harsh in its rythm even, and crabbed in its diction—she accuses her old father of the rank and not to be endured riots of his insolent retinue; charges him with allowing and protecting them, and threatens to apply instant redress, whether it offend him or not. Too much astonished to be angry, he exclaims, "Are you our daughter?" She retorts with accusations personal to himself, forcibly conveying the impression of Lear's changed state at this period; a point important to the view here maintained, that from the first the old king's mind is off its balance.

. "*Goneril.* I would you would make use of your good wisdom,
Whereof I know you are fraught; and put away
These dispositions, which of late transform you
From what you rightly are."

The altercation becomes warmer, the daughter's accusations more pointed and offensive. Her father's changed dispositions are "new pranks," his knights, "debosh'd and bold," infecting the court with their lewd and riotous manners. The king is commanded, rather than requested, to apply the remedy by diminishing and reforming his train. If he does not, Goneril will do it herself—"will take the things she begs." The impression left on the mind is, that Goneril's accusations are well founded; urged, indeed, without affection or sense of gratitude or duty, or even of that decent forbearance towards the failings of the old king, which a good woman would have felt had she not been his daughter. Hitherto only the hard selfishness of Goneril's character has been developed; its dark malignancy is unfolded by future events. However, she has struck her old father on the heart with harsh and bitter words, and his changing moods are now fixed into one master-passion. Delusion and incoherency and other features of insanity are added as the disease subsequently develops itself; but incontrollable rage is nowhere more strongly expressed than in the execrations and curses which Lear now hurls against his daughter. Eloquent as his terrible curses are, they are without measure and frantic. He beats his head,

> "Oh, Lear, Lear, Lear!
> Beat at this gate, that let thy folly in,
> And thy dear judgment out !"

He weeps, and is ashamed at the hot tears; he weeps for rage, and curses through his tears. He threatens to resume his kingly power, and adds to Goneril's other selfishness, that of alarm. There cannot be a doubt that at this time his conduct is thoroughly beyond his control. He is beside himself and insane.

Lear, who never appears more tranquil than when the butt of the fool's jests, is diverted by them for a few moments, and consents to laugh at his own folly; but his thoughts run upon his injury to Cordelia, and the one he has himself received:

> "I did her wrong.
> To take it again perforce !   Monster ingratitude !"

He is conscious of his mental state, and even of its cause. He feels the goad of madness already urging him, and struggles and prays against it, and strives to push it aside. He knows its cause to be unbounded passion, and that to be kept in temper would avert it.

> " O, let me not be mad, not mad, sweet heaven !
>   Keep me in temper : I would not be mad !"

This self consciousness of gathering madness is common in various forms of the disease. It has recently been pointed to by an able French author as a frequent symptom in that form of insanity accompanied by general paralysis. According to the observation of the author, it is a far more common symptom in that form of mania which developes gradually from exaggeration of the natural character. A most remarkable instance of this was presented in the case of a patient, whose passionate but generous temper became morbidly exaggerated after a blow upon the head. His constantly expressed fear was that of impending madness ; and when the calamity he so much dreaded had actually arrived, and he raved incessantly and incoherently, one frequently heard the very words of Lear proceeding from his lips : " Oh, let me not be mad !"

Lear struggles against this temper, which he feels is leading towards madness ; and even against the plain evidence of his daughter's ingratitude, which inflames the temper. He will not understand Goneril's accusations and threats, until they are expressed in language too gross and cruel to be mistaken. In the same manner he will not believe that Regan and Cornwall have placed his messenger in the stocks. To Kent's blunt assertion, it is both he and she—your son and daughter—he reiterates denial, and swears by Jupiter it is not so :

> "They durst not do't ;
> They could not, would not do't ; 'tis worse than murder,
> To do upon respect such violent outrage ;"

and when conviction follows upon Kent's plain narrative of his treatment and its occasion, rage almost chokes the utterance. At first he struggles to repress its expression :

> "*Lear.* O, how this mother swells up towards my heart !
> *Hysterica passio*, down, thou climbing sorrow,
> Thy element 's below !"

He does not succeed long, and when denied access to his child, under the pretence of sickness, which he well recognizes as the image of revolt and flying off, and when reminded, inopportunely enough, "of the fiery quality of the duke," the climbing sorrow will not be repressed :

> "*Lear.* Vengeance ! plague ! death ! confusion !
> Fiery? what quality? Why, Gloucester, Gloucester,
> I'll speak with the duke of Cornwall and his wife.
> *Gloucester.* Well, my good lord, I have inform'd them so.
> *Lear.* Inform'd them ! Dost thou understand me, man ?
> *Glo.* Ay, my good lord.
> *Lear.* The king would speak with Cornwall; the dear father
> Would with his daughter speak, commands her service :

Are they inform'd of this? My breath and blood!
Fiery? the fiery duke? Tell the hot duke that—
No, but not yet: may be he is not well:
Infirmity doth still neglect all office
Whereto our health is bound; we are not ourselves
When nature, being oppress'd, commands the mind
To suffer with the body: I'll forbear;
And am fall'n out with my more headier will,
To take the indisposed and sickly fit
For the sound man. Death on my state! wherefore
Should he sit here? This act persuades me
That this remotion of the duke and her
Is practice only. Give me my servant forth.
Go tell the duke and 's wife, I'ld speak with them,
Now, presently: bid them come forth and hear me,
Or at their chamber-door I'll beat the drum,
Till it cry *sleep to death.*
    Glo. I would have all well betwixt you.
    Lear. O me, my heart, my rising heart! but, down!"

The first indication of commencing incoherence is seen
in this most affecting expression of the conflict within:
—"commands, tends, service;"—unless it be that the
rapid flow of ideas only permits the expression of the
leading words, omitting the connecting ones which
would make sense of them. There is more of sorrow
than of haughty passion in this conflict of emotion;
the strong will resisting the stronger passion, and
attempting to palliate and explain the evidence of
that indignity, upon which it is too justly founded.
The Fool's philosophy, that absurd cruelty and absurd
kindness have the same origin, is well introduced at
this point; though little likely to attract his frantic
master's attention, whose unreasoning generosity to

his daughter is now replaced by unmeasured rage
and hatred.

> "*Fool.* Cry to it, nuncle, as the cockney did to the eels
> when she put 'em i' the paste alive; she knapp'd 'em o' the
> coxcombs with a stick, and cry'd, *Down, wantons, down!*
> 'Twas her brother that, in pure kindness to his horse,
> buttered his hay."

Lear is evidently more unwilling to quarrel with
Regan than with Goneril. He loves her better; and
indeed, if any difference can be marked between these
most bad women, the temper and disposition of Regan
are certainly far less repulsive than that of her fierce
sister. Black as her conduct undoubtedly is, viewed
by itself, it is but grey when brought into contrast
with that of her hellish sister—the adulteress, the
murderess-poisoner, and suicide. Lear himself acknowledges the difference between them:

> " No, Regan, thou shalt never have my curse :
> Thy tender-hefted nature shall not give
> Thee o'er to harshness : her eyes are fierce ; but thine
> Do comfort and not burn ;"

and it is remarkable that he does not curse Regan,
except in connection with her sister. His terrific
imprecations are heaped upon the head of Goneril
alone, as if, with the instinct of madness, he had
recognized the dark supremacy of her wickedness.
When Regan, whom he appears to have loved, joins
the old man, his heart is somewhat softened, and
grief, for a moment, takes the place of passion ; yet

it is passionate grief, choking its expression with its intensity :

> " Beloved Regan,
> Thy sister 's naught : O Regan, she hath tied
> Sharp-tooth'd unkindness, like a vulture, here :—
>   *[Points to his heart.*
> I can scarce speak to thee ; thou 'lt not believe
> With how deprav'd a quality—O Regan !"

He finds his convictions somewhat checked at this conjuncture ; he does not meet with that sympathy from Regan which he has made sure that his injuries will excite. She reasons with him, not accusingly and threateningly as Goneril, and yet not yielding a point of the question at issue. She tells him the truth without flinching, and strangely, without at first giving offence, as far as she is concerned :

> " O, sir, you are old ;
> Nature in you stands on the very verge
> Of her confine : you should be ruled and led
> By some discretion, that discerns your state
> Better than you yourself."

One cannot but perceive, that if Regan had been permitted to act without the bad interference of her fiend sister, she might have ruled and led the old king without seeming to do so, and have guided his madness in a less turbulent channel ; but she takes side with her sister, and suggests that the king should ask Goneril's forgiveness—the forgiveness of a daughter. The old king kneels, and adds the eloquence of action to his reproof—unsightly tricks, as Regan calls it—and certainly not dignified, nor consistent with the demeanour of a sane king; but adding terrible force to the mockery of the suggested forgiveness, and to the fierce imprecation which it calls forth; "You nimble lightnings," etc., during the utterance of which Lear probably remains on his knees, with hands extended, to call down "the stored vengeance of heaven," which he invokes.

He now returns to the outrage upon Kent. He will not believe that Regan knew on't, and is in a way, for the present, to be easily soothed, if it had suited the plans of the bad sisters to do so; but Goneril appears, and all goes wrong with him and with them:

"Who comes here? O heavens,
If you do love old men, if your sweet sway
Allow obedience, if you yourselves are old,
Make it your cause; send down, and take my part!"

Is there any passage more pathetic and sublime than this, even in Shakespeare?

Although Regan has immediately before defended the conduct of Goneril, Lear is astonished that she should take her by the hand; but the unison of the sisters, made patent to him by this act, recalls the cause of offence which he has with Regan herself, and which he has referred to and forgotten more than once:

"O sides, you are too tough!
Will you yet hold? How came my man i' the stocks?"

This flightiness of thought, this readiness to take up a subject strongly, and to lay it down again lightly, to run from one subject to another, and still more, from one temper to another, is a phase of mental disease approaching that which is called incoherency. At present, the sudden changes of thought and feeling are capable of being referred to some cause recognizable, although inadequate. In complete incoherency, the mind wanders from subject to subject without any clue being apparent by which the suggestion of thought by thought, or idea by idea, can be followed and explained. In the sane mind one idea follows another, according to laws of suggestion, which vary in individuals, but are subject to general principles ; so that a man, intimately acquainted with the mental peculiarities of another, might give a very probable opinion as to the succession of any ideas which had passed through the well known mind ; or, one idea being given, might guess the character of the one which suggested it, and the one which in turn it would suggest. But, in the mind of the insane, these general principles of the succession of ideas are abrogated. Doubtless there are rules of suggestion and succession if we knew them, but for the most part they are too strange and uncertain to be recognized ; the mode of suggestion of ideas in one madman being far more unlike that which exists in another madman, than the different modes which exist among sane people. Moreover, the genesis of thought differs greatly in the same insane mind, during different periods and phases of the malady. The idea of preaching, for instance, in the present phase of Lear's insanity, would probably have suggested some sublime expression of moral truth. At a later period it brought under his notice the make and material of his hat, and suggested cavalry shod with felt, and the surprise and slaughter of his enemies. The idea-chain of a sane mind is somewhat like the images in a moving panorama ; one can tell, if the country is known, what has preceded and what will follow any particular scene ; but the sequence of ideas in the insane mind is more like the arbitrary or accidental succession of grotesque images, which are thrown on the curtain of a magic lantern ; there is no apparent connection between them, and no certainty of sequence : it is as if ideas were suggested by the points and corners of those which precede, by the unessential parts, and not by their real nature and character. This, no doubt, is owing to the rapid flow of ideas which takes place in these phases of insanity ; an idea is not grasped in its entirety, it only touches the mind as it were, and suggests another. The *Ideen-jagd* of the Germans is a good descriptive term for a common form of incoherence.

Lear, however, is not yet incoherent ; he is only approaching that phase of the malady. He has entirely lost that obstinate resolve, which his heady and passionate will gave him at the commencement. He is flighty, even on subjects of the most dire moment to him. He takes up and lays down his determina-

tions with equal want of purpose. This is evident in
his hasty references to the treatment which Kent has
met with from the "fiery duke" and Regan. This
flightiness of thought is accompanied by a rapid and
undirected change of emotion, a still weightier evidence of the mind's profound malady. This is
strongly marked in the speech to Goneril, whom, in
eight lines, he addresses in four different tempers :
irritation ; sadness, with some memory of affection ;
followed by an outburst of rage and hate ; and again
by desire and effort to be patient :

> "*Lear.* I prithee, daughter, do not make me mad :
> I will not trouble thee, my child ; farewell :
> We'll no more meet, no more see one another :
> But yet thou art my flesh, my blood, my daughter ;
> Or rather a disease that 's in my flesh,
> Which I must needs call mine : thou art a boil,
> A plague-sore, an embossed carbuncle,
> In my corrupted blood. But I'll not chide thee ;
> Let shame come when it will, I do not call it :
> I do not bid the thunder-bearer shoot,
> Nor tell tales of thee to high-judging Jove."

This state of mind is further evident from the sudden
change of his resolution to return home and reside
with Goneril, because he believes that she will let him
have more attendants than her sister. He has just
before declared that he would rather "abjure all
roofs," or "knee the throne of France," or be "slave
and sumpter to this detested groom," than return
·with her ; and yet, because Regan entreats him to

bring but five-and-twenty followers, assigning as good reason :

> " How, in one house,
> Should many people, under two commands,
> Hold amity?   'Tis hard ; almost impossible ;"

he forgets all the comparisons he has drawn between her and Goneril, so unfavourable to the latter ; he forgets his deep-rooted hatred to Goneril, and proposes to return home with her :

> " I'll go with thee :
> Thy fifty yet doth double five-and-twenty,
> And thou art twice her love."

At this point the mind seems almost falling into fatuity ; yet it is but for a moment, for immediately after comes that outburst of eloquence : "O, reason not the need," etc., the grandeur of which it would be difficult to overmatch with any other passage from dramatic literature.   It concludes, not with expressions of noble anger, but with those of insane rage, at a loss for words to express itself.

> " No, you unnatural hags,
> I will have such revenges on you both,
> That all the world shall ——, I will do such things, ——
> What they are, yet I know not ; but they shall be
> The terrors of the earth.   You think I'll weep ;
> No, I'll not weep :
> I have full cause of weeping ; but this heart
> Shall break into a hundred thousand flaws,
> Or ere I'll weep.   O fool, I shall go mad !"

It is the climax of his intercourse with these daughters, who turn their backs on him and bar their doors. Not yet do they directly plot against his life. He rushes into the stormy night, such a night as nature seldom sees, such a storm that "man's nature cannot carry the affliction nor the fear." He escapes from the cruel presence of his daughters to the bare heath, where "for many miles about, there's scarce a bush." Here, in company with the fool, "who labours to out-jest his heart-struck injuries," in reckless, frantic rage, he "bids what will take all." On this scene Coleridge finely remarks,

"What a world's convention of agonies is here! All external nature in a storm, all moral nature convulsed,—the real madness of Lear, the feigned madness of Edgar, the babbling of the Fool, the desperate fidelity of Kent—surely such a scene was never conceived before or since! Take it but as a picture for the eye only, it is more terrific than any which a Michael Angelo, inspired by a Dante, could have conceived, and which none but a Michael Angelo could have executed. Or let it have been uttered to the blind, the howlings of nature would seem converted into the voice of conscious humanity. This scene ends with the *first* symptoms of positive derangement."

Hardly so ; it is but the climax of the disease, the catastrophy of the mind history. The malady, which has existed from the first, has increased and developed, until it is now completed. And yet writers generally agree with Coleridge in considering that Lear only becomes actually insane at this point, and some indeed have endeavoured to mark the precise expression which indicates the change from sanity to insanity. That which they (under the vulgar error that raving

O

madness, accompanied by delusion, is alone to be considered real insanity) take to be the first signs, must be considered the signs of the first crisis, or complete development of the disease.　It is to be remarked that Lear's first speeches in the storm, beginning

　　" Blow, winds, and crack your cheeks ! rage ! blow !"
　　" Rumble thy bellyfull.　Spit, fire ! spout, rain !"

and even his frantic demeanour as he contends unbonneted with the elements, are the same in character as his language and conduct have been hitherto. There is no difference in quality, although the altered circumstances make the language more inflated, and the conduct more wild.　He has, before this time, threatened, cursed, wept, knelt, beaten others, beaten his own head.　Under the exciting influence of exposure to a storm so terrible as to awe the bold Kent who never, since he was a man, remembers the like ; under this excitement, it is no wonder that the " poor, infirm, weak, and despised old man," should use the extremest emphasis of his eloquence.　These speeches, therefore, do not more appear the frantic rant of insanity than much which has preceded them.　Still less can be admitted as evidence of delusion, the accusation directed against the elements, that they are " servile ministers" of his " pernicious daughters." This seems but a trope of high-flown eloquence, consistent with the character and the circumstances.　The really critical point where delusion first shews itself ought to be placed a little further on, where Lear

for the first time sees Edgar, and infers, with the
veritable logic of delusion, that a state of misery so
extreme must have been the work of his unkind
daughters. Before this point, however, is reached,
an event occurs very notable, although likely to escape
notice ; than which there is nothing in this great case
from the poet's note book more remarkably illustrat-
ing his profound knowledge of mental disease, not
only in its symptomalology, but in its causation and
development. It is *the addition of a physical cause* to
those moral causes which have long been at work.

Lear's inflated speeches, which indicate resistance
to the warring elements, are followed by a moment
of resignation and of calm, as if he were beaten down
by them. He "will be a pattern of all patience." He
thinks of the crimes of other men, in that speech of
regal dignity : "Let the great gods find out their
enemies now." He is "a man more sinned against
than sinning." The energy of rage and of frantic
resistance has passed by. Calmer thought succeeds,
and then comes this remarkable admission :

> "My wits begin to turn.
> Come on, my boy : how dost, my boy? art cold?
> I'm cold myself. Where is this straw, my fellow?
> The art of our necessities is strange,
> That can make vile things precious. Come, your hovel.
> Poor fool and knave, I have one part in my heart
> That's sorry yet for thee."

The import of this must be weighed with a speech
in the last act, when Lear is incoherent and full of

delusion, but calmer than at this time, and with the reason and impertinency mixed of complete mania :

" When the rain came to wet me once, and the wind to make me chatter ; when the thunder would not peace at my bidding ; there I found 'em, there I smelt 'em out. Go to, they are not men o' their words ; they told me I was everything ; 'tis a lie, I am not ague-proof."

This is thoroughly true to nature. Insanity, arising from mental constitution, and moral causes, often continues in a certain state of imperfect development ; that state which has been somewhat miscalled by Prichard, moral insanity ; a state of exaggerated and perverted emotion, accompanied by violent and irregular conduct, but unconnected with intellectual aberration ; until some physical shock is incurred— bodily illness, or accident, or exposure to physical suffering ; and then the imperfect type of mental disease is converted into perfect lunacy, characterised by more or less profound affection of the intellect, by delusion or incoherence. This is evidently the case in Lear, and although we have never seen the point referred to by any writer, and have again and again read the play without perceiving it, we cannot doubt from the above quotations, and especially from the second, in which the poor madman's imperfect memory refers to his suffering in the storm, that Shakespeare contemplated this exposure and physical suffering as the cause of the first crisis in the malady. Our wonder at his profound knowledge of mental disease increases,

the more carefully we study his works ; here and elsewhere he displays with prolific carelessness a knowledge of principles, half of which would make the
reputation of a modern psychologist.

It is remarkable, that in the very scene where
Lear's madness is perfected, his first speeches are
peculiarly reasoning and consecutive. Shakespeare
had studied mental disease too closely not to have
observed the frequent concurrence of reason and un-
reason ; or the facile transition from one state to the
other. In Lear, his most perfect and elaborate representation of madness, he never represents the
mental power as utterly lost ; at no time is the intellectual aberration so complete that the old king is
incapable of wise and just remark. He is as a rudder-
less ship, which fills her sails from time to time, and
directs her course aright, and to the eye observing for
the moment only, her stately and well directed course
speaks of no want of guidance ; but inward bias or
outward force destroys the casual concurrence of circumstances to produce a right direction, and the next
moment she is tossing in the trough of the sea, with
sails a-back, drifting helpless, the sport of wind and
wave.

Lear's first speech in this scene contains a profound
psychological truth : Kent urges him to take shelter
in a hovel from the tyranny of the night, too rough
for nature to endure ; Lear objects that the outward
storm soothes that which rages within, by diverting

his attention from it. This he may well feel to be true, though the exposure and physical suffering are at the very time telling with fearful effect upon his excited, yet jaded condition. In the excitement of insanity physical injury is not perceived, for the same reason that a wound is not felt in the heat of battle. But the injury is not the less received, and the sanatory guardianship of pain being abrogated, is more likely to be endured to a fatal extent without resistance or avoidance. It is a cruel mistake, that the insane are not injured by hardships from which they do not appear to suffer. I have heard a barrister urge the argument to exonerate the most heartless and cruel neglect.

> "*Lear.* Thou think'st 'tis much that this contentious storm
> Invades us to the skin : so 'tis to thee ;
> But where the greater malady is fix'd,
> The lesser is scarce felt. Thou'ldst shun a bear ;
> But if thy flight lay toward the raging sea,
> Thou'ldst meet the bear i' the mouth. When the mind's free
> The body's delicate : the tempest in my mind
> Doth from my senses take all feeling else
> Save what beats there. Filial ingratitude !
>   *   *   *   *
> O, that way madness lies ; let me shun that ;
> No more of that."

This is the last speech of which there have been so many, expressing the consciousness of coming madness, which now yields to the actual presence of intellectual aberration ; the excited emotions of unsound mind giving place to the delusions and incoherence of mania. There is one more speech before delusion appears. Lear will not enter the hovel because the tempest will not give him leave to ponder on things which would hurt him more ; and yet he yields with meekness unnatural to him : he will go in, and then " I 'll pray and then I 'll sleep ;" and then comes that calm and pitiful exordium to houseless poverty, that royal appeal for " poor naked wretches," whose cause has been pleaded in these recent days with so much success by the great power which now acts in the place of despotic authority—the power of the press. What Lear thought, under the tyranny of the wild storm, the great and wealthy have recently felt under the newspaper appeals, which have so forcibly and successfully brought the cause of the houseless poor to their knowledge.

And now intellectual takes the place of moral disturbance. It is remarkable how comparatively passionless the old king is, after intellectual aberration has displayed itself. It is true, that even in his delusions he never loses the sense and memory of the filial ingratitude which has been the moral excitant of his madness ; but henceforth he ceases to call down imprecations upon his daughters ; or with confused sense of personal identity, he curses them, as the daughters of Edgar. It is as if in madness he has found a refuge from grief, a refuge which Gloucester even envies when he finds his own wretchedness " deprived that benefit to end itself by death :"

"*Gloucester.* The king is mad : how stiff is my vile sense,
That I stand up, and have ingenious feeling
Of my huge sorrows !	Better I were distract :
So should my thoughts be severed from my griefs ;
And woes, by strong imaginations lose
The knowledge of themselves."

To lose the sovereignty of reason is, indeed, to be degraded below humanity :

" A sight most pitiful in the meanest wretch ;
Past speaking of in a king !"

and yet, like the grave itself, it may be a refuge from intense agony. As the hand of mercy has placed a limit even to physical suffering in senseless exhaustion or forgetful delirium, so in madness it has raised a barrier against the continuance of the extreme agony of the soul. Madness may, as in acute melancholia, be the very climax of moral suffering ; but in other forms it may be, and often is, the suspension of misery —the refuge of incurable sorrow. This is finely shewn in Lear, who, from the time that his wits, that is, his intellects, unsettle, is not so much the subject as the object of moral pain. His condition is painful, past speaking of, to those who look upon it, but to himself it is one of comparative happiness, like the delirium which shortens the agony of a bed of pain. The second crisis, indeed, arrives—the crisis of recovery ; and then he experiences a second agony like that of a person reviving from the suspended animation of drowning.

The king recognizes, in Edgar's miserable state,

a reflection of his own ; and the intellect, now in every way prepared by the accumulation of moral suffering and physical shock, falls into delusion and confusion of personal identity :

> "*Lear.* Hast thou given all to thy two daughters?
> And art thou come to this?"

> "*Lear.* Now, all the plagues that in the pendulous air
> Hang fated o'er men's faults light on thy daughters !
> *Kent.* He hath no daughters, sir.
> *Lear.* Death, traitor ! nothing could have subdued nature
> To such a lowness but his unkind daughters.
> Is it the fashion, that discarded fathers
> Should have thus little mercy on their flesh?
> Judicious punishment ! 'twas this flesh begot
> Those pelican daughters."

The next speech is a wonderful example of reason and madness. He seizes, in Edgar's nakedness, upon the first suggestion of that train of thought which makes him the forerunner of Sartor Resartus.

> "*Lear.* Thou were better in thy grave than to answer with thy uncovered body this extremity of the skies. Is man no more than this? Consider him well. Thou owest the worm no silk, the beast no hide, the sheep no wool, the cat no perfume. Ha ! here's three on 's are sophisticated. Thou art the thing itself : unaccommodated man is no more but such a poor, bare, forked animal as thou art. Off, off, you lendings !—come, unbutton here. [*Tearing off his clothes.*"

Before this time he has placed a high value upon appearance and outward respect ; man's need must not be argued ; the gorgeous robes and appurtenance of royalty are of exaggerated value in his eyes ; but henceforth all is changed, and the spirit of that philosophy, which has found modern expression in the

grotesque and powerful work of Carlyle, pervades all
his rational speech.   He tears his clothes, not in the
common spirit of destructiveness, which instigated the
epileptic Orestes to the same act, and which is seen
in frequent operation where madmen are accumulated;
he tears off his clothes as disguises of the real man,
as he afterwards tears off the disguise of hypocritical
modesty from the simpering dame whose face presages
snow; as he afterwards tears off the disguises of un-
equal justice; and of the scurvy politician with glass
eyes; and of the gilded butterflies of court; and the
pretences of those who affect to look into the mys-
teries of things as if they were God's spies; the disguise, that is, of knowledge not possessed, the very
inmost rind of Teufelsdreck himself, the disguise of
philosophy.   This tendency of thought is the ground
of Lear's second delusion; he recognizes in Edgar,
a philosopher, one who has practically reduced man
to his elements; and he holds to the idea to the end
of the scene :

> " First let me talk with this philosopher :
>   What is the cause of thunder ?"

He is serious enough in the opinion :

> " Let me ask you one word in private."

He will not go into the shelter which Gloucester at
so much risk has provided, unless he is accompanied
by his "philosopher," his "good Athenian;" and
Gloucester and Kent are fain to permit the com-

panionship of the abject Edgar: "Let him take the fellow." But in the next scene in the farm house, this delusion has given way to a third: Edgar and the Fool are believed to be the high justiciaries of the kingdom, before whom Goneril and Regan shall be tried. This easy change of delusion is true to the form of insanity represented: acute mania, with rapid flow of ideas, and tendency to incoherence. In the more chronic forms of insanity, the delusions are more permanent; but in this form they arise and subside, giving place to others, with the rapidity thus faithfully represented.

At every stage the king recognizes his own madness. At this point, when the somewhat blind perceptions of Kent have only just recognized the fact, that "his wits begin to unsettle," Lear eagerly acknowledges the completed reality:

"*Fool.* Prithee, nuncle, tell me whether a madman be gentleman or a yeoman?
Lear. A king, a king!"

There never yet was an idea, sane or insane, which had not its origin in a sensation, physical or emotional, or in another idea. The laws of the genesis of thought are not abrogated in insanity: they only differ from those of the healthy mind, as the physical laws of pathology differ from those of physiology. Man's knowledge, indeed, of mental law, is far less precise than that of physical law, and he is far less able to trace its disturbed action. The means of making a probable conjecture at the genesis of Lear's delusions are, however, left us. The first, respecting Edgar's supposed daughters, is suggested by the lowness to which his nature is subdued, which could only be through his unkind daughters. The second is suggested by Edgar's naked, unaccommodated manhood. The third appears to have had its origin in a slighter suggestion, the sight of a pair of joint stools, hard and warped, whom the poor madman likens to his daughters, and for whose trial he suddenly extemporizes a court of justice:

"*Lear.* It shall be done, I will arraign them straight.
[*To Edgar.*] Come, sit thou here, most learned justicer.
[*To the Fool.*] Thou, sapient sir, sit here.   Now, you she
    foxes!   *   *   *   *
                         Bring in the evidence.
[*To Edgar.*] Thou robed man of justice, take thy place;
[*To the Fool.*] And thou, his yoke-fellow of equity,
Bench by his side: [*To Kent*] you are o' the commission,
Sit you too.
    Edgar. Let us deal justly.
          Sleepest or wakest thou, jolly shepherd?
            Thy sheep be in the corn;
            And for one blast of thy minikin mouth,
            Thy sheep shall take no harm.
Pur! the cat is grey.
    Lear. Arraign her first; 'tis Goneril.   I here take my oath before this honourable assembly, she kicked the poor king her father.
    Fool. Come hither, mistress.   Is your name Goneril?
    Lear. She cannot deny it.
    Fool. Cry you mercy, I took you for a joint-stool.
    Lear. And here's another, whose warp'd looks proclaim What store her heart is made on.   Stop her there! Arms, arms, sword, fire!   Corruption in the place! False justicer, why hast thou let her 'scape?"

Were it not for the comments of Kent and Edgar, this scene would read as if Lear threw some voluntary mockery into it ; but his amazed look which we learn from Kent, and the pity with which Edgar is overwhelmed, prove its sad earnestness. It would be most interesting could we know how this scene was actually played under the direction of Shakespeare. It does not seem probable that he wished to represent Lear as the subject of so extreme an hallucination as that his daughters were present, in their own figure and appearance, and that one of them escaped. It is more probable that he wished to represent them, personified by the excited imagination, in the form of the stools ; and that Kent or Edgar, seeing the bad effects which this vivid personification was working, snatched away one of the stools; and this produced the passionate explosion on Regan's supposed escape.

There is little indeed, which, in the features of madness, Shakespeare allowed to escape his observation. Here, thrown out with the carelessness of abundant wealth, is the knowledge that the accusations of the insane are worthless as evidence : " I here take my oath before this honourable assembly that she kicked the poor king her father." The honourable assembly, doubtless, did not believe the precision of this statement ; but assemblies more honourable, and real official persons, who, at least, ought to possess a larger knowledge of the peculiarities of the insane, have given credence to the accusations of lunatics, like to this of Lear's, except that they had no foundation in the reality of unkindness :

"'Tis the times' plague when madmen lead the blind."

In the speech, " Let them anatomize Regan," etc., passion has subsided into reflection ; the storm is past, the poor old heart is tranquillized by exhaustion, the senses are falling into the blessed oblivion of sleep :

"Make no noise, make no noise ; draw the curtains :
So, so, so.   We'll go to supper in the morning."

Even Kent now acknowledges that his dear master's wits are gone ; but trouble him not, he sleeps, and noble affection watches and hopes :

"*Kent.* Oppressed nature sleeps :
This rest might yet have balm'd thy broken senses,
Which, if convenience will not allow,
Stand in hard cure."

Hardly so, noble Kent.   The mind's malady is too deep-seated to be thus easily cured by nature's effort ; nature's sweet restorer will scarcely balm the wounds which have so long festered.   To use a surgical simile, there can be no union by first intention here ; sleep may terminate the brief and sudden insanity of delirium, but not this.   If, afterwards, his "untuned and jarring senses" are actually restored by the sweet influence of sleep, it is not by the brief and insufficient sleep of exhaustion, but by that of skilful and solicitous medication ; sleep, so long and profound, that it is needful to disturb it ; sleep, the crowning result of successful medical treatment conducted in the spirit of love and sympathy, whose final remedy hangs on the sweet lips of Cordelia. In mania, the broken sleep of mere exhaustion does but renew the strength of excitement; but the profound sleep, resulting from skilful treatment, is often the happy cause of restoration.

The excited babbling of the Fool, and the exaggerated absurdities of Edgar, are stated by Ulrici, and other critics, to exert a bad influence upon the king's mind. To persons unacquainted with the character of the insane, this opinion must seem, at least, to be highly probable, notwithstanding that the evidence of the drama itself is against it; for Lear is comparatively tranquil in conduct and language during the whole period of Edgar's mad companionship. It is only after the Fool has disappeared—gone to sleep at mid-day, as he says—and Edgar has left to be the guide of his blind father, that the king becomes absolutely wild and incoherent. The singular and undoubted fact was probably unknown to Ulrici, that few things tranquillize the insane more than the companionship of the insane. It is a fact not easily explicable, but it is one of which, either by the intuition of genius, or by the information of experience, Shakespeare appears to be aware. He not only represents the fact of Lear's tranquillity in the companionship of Edgar, of his sudden and close adherence to him, though drawn thereto, perhaps, by delusions; but he puts the very opinion in the mouth of Edgar, although applying it to his own griefs, and not to those of the king.

> " Who alone suffers suffers most i' the mind,
>   Leaving free things and happy shows behind ;
>   But then the mind much sufferance doth o'erskip,
>   When grief hath mates, and bearing fellowship."

Edgar's assumed madness presents a fine contrast to the reality of Lear's. It is devoid of reason and full of purpose. It has the fault, which to this day feigning maniacs almost invariably commit, of extreme exaggeration. It imposes upon the unskilful observation of Gloucester, Kent, and the others ; but could scarcely impose upon any experienced judgment. Had Edgar himself found any future need to repeat his deception, he might have taken lessons as to the truer phenomena of diseased mind from the poor old king, whom he observed from the covert of his disguise, and have represented that characteristic of true madness—"matter and impertinency mixed"—which he entirely fails to exhibit. Edgar's account of his motives for assuming this disguise to escape the hunt after his life, is a curious illustration of the manner in which the insane were permitted to roam the country, in the good old days :

> " Whiles I may 'scape,
> I will preserve myself : and am bethought
> To take the basest and most poorest shape
> That ever penury, in contempt of man,
> Brought near to beast : my face I'll grime with filth ;
> Blanket my loins ; elf all my hair in knots ;
> And with presented nakedness out-face

The winds and persecutions of the sky.
The country gives me proof and precedent
Of Bedlam beggars, who, with roaring voices,
Strike in their numb'd and mortified bare arms
Pins, wooden pricks, nails, sprigs of rosemary;
And with this horrible object, from low farms,
Poor pelting villages, sheep-cotes, and mills,
Sometime with lunatic bans, sometime with prayers,
Enforce their charity.   Poor Turlygod! poor Tom!
That's something yet: Edgar I nothing am."

In Disraeli's *Curiosities of Literature,* an interesting and learned account is given of the singular mendicants, known by the name of "Toms o' Bedlam." Bethlem, at the time when Shakespeare wrote, "was a contracted and penurious charity," with more patients than funds, and the governors were in the habit of relieving the establishment by discharging patients whose cure was very equivocal.   These discharged patients, thrown upon the world without a friend, wandered about the country chanting wild ditties, and wearing a fantastical dress to attract the notice and the alms of the charitable.   Sir Walter Scott suggested to Disraeli, "that these roving lunatics were out-door pensioners of Bedlam, sent about to live as well as they could on the pittance granted by the hospital."   In addition to the true "Tom," there was a counterfeit who assumed the grotesque rags, the staff, the knotted hair of the real one, to excite pity or alarm, and to enforce undeserved charity.   These men, who are described by Decker in his *English Villanies,* were called "Abram men," and hence the

P

phrase current to the present day, to "sham Abram."
They had a cant language, a silly, rambling "*maund,*"
or phrase of begging. The fullest source of information on this subject Disraeli found in a manuscript
note transcribed from some of Aubrey's papers, which
singularly elucidates a phrase which has been the
subject of some "perverse ingenuity" among the
critics—"Poor Tom, thy horn is dry!"

"Till the breaking out of the civil wars, *Toms of Bedlam*
did travel about the country; they had been poor, distracted
men, that had been put into Bedlam, where, recovering
some soberness, they were licentiated to go a begging, *i. e.*
they had on their left arm an armilla, or iron ring for the
arm, about four inches long, as printed in some works; they
could not get it off. They wore about their necks a great
horn of an ox, in a string or bawdry, which, when they came
to a house they did wind; and they put the drink given
them into this horn, whereto they put a stopple. Since the
wars I do not remember to have seen any one of them."

The whole description of these Toms o' Bedlam
and their counterfeits—"the progging Abram men,"
as they are given by Disraeli, from Decker and other
old authors—affords a curious illustration of the fidelity
of Shakespeare's delineation of character, even when
most grotesque and apparently unnatural. The assumed character of Edgar bears the most exact resemblance to the description of these beings, as it has
been dug out of the past by the researches of the
literary antiquarian.

"The wild ditties of these itinerant lunatics gave
rise," says this author, "to a class of poetry once

fashionable among the 'wits,' composed in the character of a Tom o' Bedlam." Purcel has set one of
them to very fine music. Percy has preserved six of
these mad songs, some of which, however, Disraeli
pronounces of too modern a date to have seen actual
service ; but he adds a fine one from a miscellany
published in 1661, and that not the first edition. It
concludes with the following stanza of wild imagery :

> " With a host of furious fancies,
>   Whereof I am commander :
>   With a burning spear,
>   And a horse of air,
>   To the wilderness I wander ;
> With a knight of ghosts and shadows,
>   Summoned am I to tournay :
>   Ten leagues beyond
>   The wide world's end ;
>   Methinks it is no journey !"

What can be said of the Fool ? What can be
thought of him ? Fool he was not, in the sense of
lack of wisdom or of knowledge. He is as individualized and unique as any character in Shakespeare.
He is Jacques with a cap.and bells, and a gay affectionate temper. He is a spiritualized and poetical
Sancho Panza, and, like him, adds to the sadness
of the tale by the introduction of ridiculous images :
for of Lear it may be said, as Byron said of Don
Quixote :

> " Of all tales 't is the saddest—and more sad
>   Because it makes us laugh."

Shakespeare represents his other fools as mere

ornaments and appendages to the tale, the grinning gurgoils of his structure : but the fool in Lear is an important character, a buttress of the tale. It is through him that Lear first gets into trouble with his dog-hearted daughter. Lear loves him, and he loves Cordelia, and thus there is a bond of affection which knits him to the two as part of the family. His reckless and all-licensed speeches serve the part of the Greek chorus in explaining many things which would not otherwise be so readily intelligible. Altogether, his child-like affection to Cordelia, his devoted attachment to the king, his daring contempt for the bad daughters, his insight into the motives of human action, cynical yet tempered by love, render him a most charming character, and give him an easy pre-eminence over all others who have philosophized in motley. Although called a boy, his great knowledge of the heart indicates his age to have been at least adult. So far from being in any degree imbecile, his native powers of intellect are of the finest order. His wayward rambling of thought may be partly natural, partly the result of his professed office, an office then held in no light esteem. In physique he is small and weak. His suffering from exposure to the inclement night excites Lear's tender compassion even in his wildest mood, and it does in effect extinguish his frail life. A waif of wayward unmuscular intellect in an age of iron ; an admirable union of faithful affection with daring universal cynicism ; he also illustrates the truth of the opinion, that the scoffer and the hater are different beings. The "comic sublime" of this character forms a grotesque counterpart and contrast to that of the king, and heightens the effect while it relieves the pain of the tragic development.

Ulrici has some excellent remarks on the supreme art of this contrast:

"Nowhere has Shakespeare pushed the comic into so close and direct proximity with the tragic, and with no one else has the great hazard of doing so succeeded as with him. Instead of thereby for one moment injuring the tragic effect, he has known how, by this means, wonderfully to exalt and strengthen it; not only does the wisdom of the Fool make, by contrast, the folly of the king and its tragic meaning more conspicuous; not only does he thus, on all occasions, hold up a mirror to the thoughts and acts of others, and through its reflex greatly strengthen the light of truth; but yet more, in the profound humour of the Fool a depth of intelligence conceals itself, upon which the tragic view of the world (Weltanschauung) generally rests. To this humour, the tragic art as it were allies itself, in order to place her deepest innermost centre nearer to the light. This genuine humour of the Fool plays, as it were, with the tragic; to him pleasure and pain, fortune and misfortune are synonymous; he jeers on the griping suffering and fate of earthly existence; death and annihilation are a jest to him. On this account he stands above the earthly existence and its tragic side; and he has already attained the aim of the tragic art, the elevation of the human spirit over the mere life of this world, with its sufferings and doings; this appears in him, as it were, personified. His very humour is in its conception, the comic sublime. Wonder has been expressed that the poet should confer such magnanimity and intelligence on one who has degraded himself to the position of a mere jester. I can only admire therein the profound wisdom of the master; for when life itself is nothing to a man, his own position in life will be nothing to him; and the lowliest lot will be preferred and selected, because it expresses most clearly our real elevation."

In Lear's next appearance a change has taken place both in his circumstances and in his state. He has arrived at Dover, and he

> "Sometime, in his better tune, remembers
> What we are come about, and by no means
> Will yield to see his daughter."

The memory of his own harsh and cruel conduct to this dear daughter, and the burning shame he feels, detain him from her. It appears from his subsequent interview with her, that apprehension of Cordelia's hatred affords another motive. "I know you do not love me." His old love for her indeed has returned, and he will take poison from her hands if she wills it; but the poor vexed mind cannot perceive that Cordelia differs from her sisters; differs so much as to lead Kent to declare that human disposition is the sport of fate, and not the result of law; that injuries cannot weaken her love, even as unbounded benefits could not secure theirs. Lear is no longer surrounded by the sympathizing but grotesque companions of his first maniacal hours. The dearly loved Fool has strangely disappeared; his frail existence ceasing without sign or comment. Edgar is transformed from mad Tom into the peasant guide of his blind father. Some dear cause must also wrap Kent in concealment until the catastrophe arrives ; he leaves an un-named gentleman to attend his master, and the poor mad-man escapes from the stranger's watch and guard, and roams in the fields alone, as Cordelia so touch-ingly describes :

"*Cordelia.* Alack, 'tis he : why, he was met even now
As mad as the vex'd sea ; singing aloud ;
Crown'd with rank fumiter and furrow-weeds,
With bur-docks, hemlock, nettles, cuckoo-flowers,
Darnel, and all the idle weeds that grow
In our sustaining corn. A century send forth ;
Search every acre in the high-grown field,
And bring him to our eye.   [*Exit an Officer.*
           What can man's wisdom do
In the restoring his bereaved sense ?
He that helps him take all my outward worth.
    Physician. There is means, madam :
Our foster-nurse of nature is repose,
The which he lacks ; that to provoke in him,
Are many simples operative, whose power
Will close the eye of anguish.
    Cor.   All blest secrets,
All you unpublish'd virtues of the earth,
Spring with my tears ! be aidant and remediate
In the good man's distress ! Seek, seek for him ;
Lest his ungovern'd rage dissolve the life
That wants the means to lead it."

The word rage seems here used not to designate passion, but the frenzy of maniacal excitement. At this time it is not passionate, but tending rather to gaiety. The first phase of mania was emphasized by the memory of recent injury; and although even then the passionate indignation was subdued from the in-tense bitterness which the first sense of his daughters' conduct occasioned, the emotional state was that of anger and sorrow. After the interval which has elapsed between Lear's sudden flight from the neighbourhood of these daughters who were plotting against his life, and his re-appearance at Dover with Cordelia's blessed succour nigh, the emotional state has changed into one less painful, yet indicating more profound disease. The proud and passionate king is now wild and gay, singing aloud, crowned with wild flowers ; his incoherence is sometimes complete, and no idea holds in his mind with sufficient tenacity to be called a delusion. This new phase of mania is as wonderfully and exactly true to nature as the one which it follows in consistent development. The more perfect incoherence is now dissociated from formal delusion. The emotional disposition natural to the man, and hitherto exaggerated by the wrongs he has suffered, is now completely lost and perverted by the progress of disease. Though he forgets that he is no longer a king, the regal deportment is altogether lost ; though he does not forget his daughters' injuries, and can compare their conduct with that of Gloucester's bastard, the fierceness of anger is quenched. The state of mind is one in which a delusion is suggested by a casual circumstance, just as a dream is suggested by casual sensations, in which the false idea thus originating is dwelt upon and examined in its various bearings as if it were the representative of truth in a sane mind, has given way to the one of more profound

injury called incoherence, in which false mental as-
sociations and false ideas arise and fade too easily,
too transiently to be called delusions. A dozen false
ideas chase each other in half as many minutes.
Strictly speaking, perhaps each of the false idea-
images of incoherence deserves the name of delusion,
although it is not usually given. The simple and
important fact may be stated with regard to Lear
thus: that in the first phase of his mania the false
ideas are few, and have some consistency and duration; in the present phase they are numerous, disjointed, and transitory.

"*Edgar.* The safer sense will ne'er accommodate
   His master thus.
   Lear. No, they cannot touch me for coining; I am the
king himself.
   Edg. O thou side-piercing sight!
   Lear. Nature's above art in that respect. There's your
press-money. That fellow handles his bow like a crow-
keeper: draw me a clothier's yard. Look, look, a mouse!
Peace, peace; this piece of toasted cheese will do 't.
There's my gauntlet; I'll prove it on a giant. Bring up
the brown bills. O, well flown, bird! i' the clout, i' the
clout: hewgh! Give the word.
   Edg. Sweet marjoram.
   Lear. Pass.
   Gloucester. I know that voice.
   Lear. Ha! Goneril, with a white beard! They flattered
me like a dog; and told me I had white hairs in my beard
ere the black ones were there. To say 'ay' and 'no' to
every thing I said!—'Ay' and 'no' too was no good divinity.
When the rain came to wet me once."   *   *

The withering denunciation of incontinency, "The
wren goes to 't," etc., and the grander one of injustice,

"Thou rascal beadle," etc., are too consecutively reasoned for the king's state of mind at this period. The apparent inconsistency is only to be accounted for by Lear's inherent grandeur of thought and natural eloquence, which even in frenzy rolls forth its magnificent volume. It is not common to see incoherence alternating with the precise expression of complex thought, but sometimes the phenomenon may be observed when the complex thoughts, so expressed, have formed a part of the hoarded treasures of the mind. And so it must be with Lear; the eloquence of his madness is partly the result of an imagination always vivid and now stimulated to excess, and of an involuntary display of oratorical power native to the man, and partly of profound knowledge of human nature acquired during an age of practical kingship. He speaks, as the bird sings, from inborn force, which neither anger, nor grief, nor madness, nor the pangs of approaching death, can subdue.

Blind Gloucester's reflection upon the ruin of such intellect is grand; for what is the inert world that it should outlast the spirit which dwelleth therein? What is the beauty of nature without eyes to behold it, or its harmony without mind to rejoice in it?

"*Gloucester.* O ruined piece of nature! This great world shall so wear out to nought. Dost thou know me?

Lear. I remember thine eyes well enough. Dost thou squiny at me? No, do thy worst, blind Cupid, I'll not love. Read thou this challenge; mark but the penning of it."

Stark madness again, instantly following reasoning eloquence ; the eyeless orbits of an old friend but the occasion of an incoherent jest. The thoughts are now the mere sport of the suggestive faculty. Any slight circumstance may give rise to the most earnest, any impressive object or terrible incident may give rise to the most trivial or wayward notions. His old friend's great calamity is lost in his own, and does but suggest absurd comparisons and empty quibbles.

The quibble on seeing without eyes induces the comments on the justice and thief, and the dog in office, beginning prosaically, rising into the grand poetic climax, and then ending in mere incoherence.

" None does offend, none, I say, none ; I'll able 'em :
Take that of me, my friend, who have the power
To seal the accuser's lips.   Get thee glass eyes ;
And, like a scurvy politician, seem
To see the things thou dost not.   Now, now, now, now :
Pull off my boots : harder, harder : so.
  Edgar. O, matter and impertinency mix'd !
Reason in madness !
  Lear. If thou wilt weep my fortunes, take my eyes.
I know thee well enough ; thy name is Gloucester :
Thou must be patient ; we came crying hither :
Thou know'st, the first time that we smell the air,
We wawl and cry.   I will preach to thee : mark.
  Gloucester. Alack, alack the day !
  Lear. When we are born, we cry that we are come
To this great stage of fools : this' a good block ;
It were a delicate stratagem, to shoe
A troop of horse with felt : I'll put 't in proof ;
And when I have stol'n upon these sons-in-law,
Then, kill, kill, kill, kill, kill, kill !"

Here is the inexpugnable notion of kingly power;
then the rambling "pull off my boots;" then tardy
pity for Gloucester, and consolation in the spirit of
the doctrine that we are born to trouble; then the
strange idea chain, that consolation shall be given in
the form of a religious discourse, which brings the hat
under observation, "a good block;" this the silent
cavalry and the stolen revenge. A more perfect representation of wandering intellect it is impossible to
conceive. Even his own pitiful recognition of his state
assumes a form of expression, half incoherent, half
poetical. He no longer distinguishes friends from
foes, and with other changed feelings he has become
susceptible of fear. When this is removed he perceives clearly enough that his personal liberty is not
secure even from his friends, and away he decamps,
poor old king, a veritable type of gay, incoherent
mania. Incoherency, the characteristic of rapid and
irregular idealization, is so far from being a definite
quality, like a clear-cut delusion, that its degree may
vary from the slight fault in the sequence and order
of ideas which may be observed in the earliest
stages of excitement from wine, to that ceaseless and
utterly unintelligible babble which is observed in some
chronic lunatics. Extreme degrees of incoherency
are invariably associated with advanced decay of the
mental powers. Perception and memory are greatly
enfeebled; the power of comparison is clean gone.
A ceaseless flow of shallow images ripples over the

mind, and continues ever after. All power of attention to new objects is lost; in some cases the babble of words appears to be continued, even after the mind has ceased to reflect the pale spectres of thought which they once represented. In Lear, incoherence, although the characteristic feature of his madness at this phase, has not attained this advanced degree. The force of the perceptions is uncertain, but they are not always weak: the memory still gives light, although it flickers: and the power of comparison is vigorous, although its exercise is vagrant. The incoherence arises more from the irregularity and strangeness of idea suggestion than from its want of power. The links of the chain of thought lie tumbled and confused, but are not broken. And what links they are! Some of gold, some of iron, some of earth! The finest poetry, the noblest sentiment, the strongest sense, held together by absurdity and grossness!

The ruins of this mind are grand and beauteous, even in their fragments. Breadth of imagination and loftiness of diction have never attained fuller development than in Lear's burning words. Wide as the scope of human nature in his passions, in his love and in his hate, in his sympathy and in his censure, he is a man to be dreaded, even in his fallen state, by such creatures as Goneril and Regan ; a man to be loved unto death by all good natures, however diverse from each other, by the blunt Kent, the rash Gloucester, the witty Fool, the firm, self-contained, yet devoted and gentle Cordelia. We see all his greatness reflected in the feelings he inspires.

The scene of Lear's restoration, touching and beautiful as it is, does not quite follow the probable course of mental change with the same exact and wondrous knowledge of insanity as that hitherto displayed. A long and profound sleep has been induced by the physician; this it is thought needful to interrupt, and, in order that the sensations on awaking may form a striking contrast to those which had preceded sleep, the patient must be awoke by music, and the first object on recovering consciousness must be that of his dear child:

> "*Physician.*   So please your majesty,
> That we may wake the king: he hath slept long.
>   *Cordelia.* Be govern'd by your knowledge, and proceed
> I' the sway of your own will.   Is he array'd?
>   *Gentleman.* Ay, madam; in the heaviness of sleep
> We put fresh garments on him.
>   *Phys.* Be by, good madam, when we do awake him;
> I doubt not of his temperance.
>   *Cor.*   Very well.
>   *Phys.* Please you, draw near.   Louder the music there."

This seems a bold experiment, and one not unfraught with danger. The idea that the insane mind is beneficially influenced by music is, indeed, an ancient and general one; but that the medicated sleep of insanity should be interrupted by it, and that the first object presented to the consciousness should be the very person most likely to excite profound emotion, appear to be expedients little calculated to promote that tranquility of the mental functions, which is, undoubtedly, the safest state to induce, after the excitement of mania. A suspicion of this may have crossed Shakespeare's mind, for he represents Lear in imminent danger of passing into a new form of delusion. The employment of music in the treatment of the insane would form an interesting chapter in the history of ancient and modern psychology. The earliest note of it is in Holy Writ : "And it came to pass, when the evil spirit from God was upon Saul, that David took an harp and played with his hand, so Saul was refreshed, and was well, and the evil spirit departed from him" (1 Sam. xvi.) In Elisha it produced inspiration : he called for a minstrel, and "when the minstrel played, the hand of the Lord came upon him" (2 Kings iii.) Asclepiades effected many cures of insane persons by this means ; and Galen reports that Æsculapius did the same. "Jason Pratensis (cap. De maniâ) hath many examples how Clinias and Empedocles cured some desperately melancholy, and some mad, by this, our music."— *Burton.* But there is danger in its use, "for there are some whom," saith Plutarch, "*musica magis dementat quam vinum.*" In modern times, the greatest advocate for music in the treatment of insanity has been Dr. Mason Cox, who employed it systematically, and, as he relates, with the best effect. Frank also employed it, and he relates the instance of a young person affected with periodical insanity, who, every time he heard the sound of music, was seized with a furious paroxysm of mania. Dr. Knight had seen its tranquilizing and beneficial effects in numerous cases, and had never seen it do harm; but yet he could not think its employment safe in excited and recent cases. Guislain distinguishes its use—1st, as exercising the mind of the patient who executes; and 2nd, when played by others, as producing effects upon the nervous system through the emotions. In the first of these modes, its employment is, undoubtedly, beneficial as a means of recreation; but modern physicians appear to have little faith in its effects when simply listened to. Either the nerves are less delicately strung than formerly, or the quality of music has deteriorated, or the power of medical faith has decayed; of which explanations the latter is, probably, the true one. Still, credence is given to its power in certain conditions; for instance, the national melodies of mountain countries are said to possess a most wonderful influence on the nerves. The *ranz des vaches* causes melancholy in the Switzer; and Locheil, in the screams and groans of the bagpipe, is said to produce the occasional effect of making the Scotchman desire to return to his own country. Shylock records another remarkable consequence of listening to the Highland music, namely, the unpleasant result which ensues in some men "when the bagpipe sings in the nose."

Esquirol attributes a considerable amount of power

both for good and evil to the influence of music on the insane.

"I have often employed music, but have very rarely obtained any success thereby. It calms and composes the mind, but does not cure. I have seen insane persons whom music rendered furious : one was so, because all the notes appeared false ; another, because he thought it frightful that the people should amuse themselves in the presence of so miserable a being. I believe the ancients exaggerated the effects of music, while the facts recorded by modern writers are not sufficiently numerous to determine under what circumstances it possibly may be of benefit. This means of treatment however is precious, especially in convalescence, and ought not to be neglected, however indeterminate may be the principles of its application, and however uncertain may be its efficacy."

When Lear awakes with the loud music ringing in his ears, and finds himself once more in royal state and apparel, and with Cordelia at his feet, fancy flashes upon him the idea that he has passed the dread bourne of life. Remembrance fails, and even personal identity needs verification.

> *Lear.* You do me wrong to take me out o' the grave :
> Thou art a soul in bliss ; but I am bound
> Upon a wheel of fire, that mine own tears
> Do scald like molten lead.
>   *Cordelia.*   Sir, do you know me ?
>   *Lear.* You are a spirit, I know : when did you die ?
>   *Cor.* Still, still, far wide !
>   *Phys.* He's scarce awake : let him alone awhile.
>   *Lear.* Where have I been ? Where am I ? Fair daylight ?
> I am mightily abused. I should e'en die with pity,
> To see another thus. I know not what to say.
> I will not swear these are my hands : let's see ;
> I feel this pin prick. Would I were assured
> Of my condition !

Q

> *Cor.*   O, look upon me, sir,
> And hold your hands in benediction o'er me :
> No, sir, you must not kneel.
>   *Lear.*   Pray, do not mock me :
> I am a very foolish fond old man,
> Fourscore and upward, not an hour more nor less ;
> And, to deal plainly,
> I fear I am not in my perfect mind.
> Methinks I should know you, and know this man ;
> Yet I am doubtful : for I am mainly ignorant
> What place this is ; and all the skill I have
> Remembers not these garments ; nor I know not
> Where I did lodge last night.   Do not laugh at me ;
> For, as I am a man, I think this lady
> To be my child Cordelia.
>   *Cor.*   And so I am, I am.
>   *Lear.* Be your tears wet ? yes, 'faith.   I pray, weep not :
> If you have poison for me, I will drink it.
> I know you do not love me ; for your sisters
> Have, as I do remember, done me wrong :
> You have some cause, they have not."
>   "*Physician.* Be comforted, good madam : the great rage
> You see, is kill'd in him : and yet it is danger
> To make him even o'er the time he has lost.
> Desire him to go in ; trouble him no more
> Till further settling.
>   *Cor.* Will't please your highness walk ?
>   *Lear.*   You must bear with me :
> Pray you now, forget and forgive : I am old and foolish."

The idea that death is past is half a delusion, half a dream, in which the objects of sense are visible while the judgment is not sufficiently alert to interpret them.   When he does awake, the mind, suffering from the weakness which follows fierce excitement, cannot comprehend the new circumstances which surround him—the unknown place and the royal robes.   But,

first of all, the poor patient would assure himself that
he is a living sentient being, and not a soul in torture,
as the fearful dream has represented. The half-timid
enquiries into his state and surroundings represent
both exhaustion and calmness. This self-examination
and interrogation is a common feature in convalescence from insanity; although it must be admitted
that the transactions here represented, and as the exi-
gences of the drama perhaps require that they should
be represented, are more sudden and distinct than the
real operations of nature. Lear's timid consciousness
of infirmity of mind, " I fear I am not in my perfect
mind," is in fine contrast to the energetic assertion
of his frantic state : " Let me have surgeons, I am cut
to the brains." The statement of his age affords
a delicate touch of that intellectual weakness which
accompanies the state of repose and exhaustion. He
does not see that fourscore and upward is not an
exact, but an inexact statement. " Be your tears
wet ?" seems a return to the half-dream, half-delusion;
he still doubts the personality of Cordelia ; and when
he attains conviction on the point, the idea that she
will avenge her wrongs upon him does not at once
forsake him ; and yet it lasts not long, and he desires
her to forget and forgive. The physician wisely ap-
prehends danger from the weak mind throwing itself
back upon the memory of its injuries and sufferings,
and interrupts the colloquy. The high honour and
worth with which Shakespeare invests the physician

here and elsewhere, deserves notice. In Macbeth, although the angry king rejects an agency which cannot work social and political cures, the physician is represented as a wise and dignified person. In this play of Lear the character is still more exalted ; and it would be easy to prove that throughout Shakespeare's writings there is no character held in more honour than that of the physician. Shakespeare, in this respect, presents a remarkable contrast to Molière, with whom the physician of his day was the favourite butt of ridicule ; but Shakespeare's esteem for physic was founded upon knowledge, while Molière's contempt of it was founded upon ignorance ; for while the latter sets up the manners and pretensions of the medical pedant as the butt of his ridicule, there is not a passage in his writings which indicates the slightest knowledge of the art or science of the profession which he so assiduously covers with contempt. The gibberish of dog-latin pretended prescriptions is his nearest approach to it. Shakespeare, on the other hand, evinces so surprising and minute a knowledge of both, that it would be no difficult task to prove from his writings that he had been a diligent student of the healing art, and thence it might be inferred that he had been a doctor's apprentice, with a probability not much below that which has been so ingeniously developed by the Lord Chief Justice, to prove that he was an attorney's clerk. I yield, indeed, to Mr. Payne Collier's theory as argued by Lord

Campbell, the precedence of probability, inasmuch as Shakespeare's knowledge of law is technical, while his knowledge of medicine is general, and such as he might have more readily acquired outside the professional limits. His knowledge of law is that which a clerk might possess; his knowledge of medicine is evidently the acquirement of a riper age, capable of resolving observation into principle; a very different thing to the inventory of an apothecary's shop, which Lord Campbell justly scouts as evidence of more than casual remark and faithful memory. The more modest and probable conclusion, however, would seem to be, not that which the lawyer may compliment himself with, nor that which the doctor or the sailor might respectively arrive at, in consequence of the poet's knowledge of medical and nautical affairs; but simply, that in Shakespeare the world possessed a man who, like Aristotle, was endowed with all the knowledge of his time, combined with the divine gift which the Greek did not possess, of making it available in the most gorgeous employment of fancy and language. He was a naturalist in the widest sense, and a poet in the highest. Infinitely more than Goëthe he merited the title of the Allsided One.

Let us conclude this somewhat professional digression by expressing the opinion, that Shakespeare's prescription for Gloucester's empty and bleeding orbits, " flax and the whites of eggs," is good domestic surgery.

When Lear next appears a prisoner with Cordelia, his mental state has again undergone great change. The weakness of exhaustion has disappeared, and the delusion and incoherency of the preceding excitement has yielded to the good influences with which this daughter, thrice blessed in her devoted affection, has balmed the wounded soul. Lear has returned as nearly as possible to his state of mind before the storm, and the shock of physical suffering and exposure. Medical treatment and physical comfort, and the blessed influences of affection, have soothed his intellectual frenzy. But the moral disturbance remains, with this notable difference however, that he now gives vent to passionate love, as he formerly did to passionate anger and hate. There is no measure or reason in his love for Cordelia, as there was none in his hatred of Goneril. He forgets his age in one as in the other. In prison he will wear out sects of great ones; his enemies shall die and rot before he will part with Cordelia or weep at sorrow which has lost its sting now she is with him.

"*Lear.* Upon such sacrifices, my Cordelia,
The gods themselves throw incense. Have I caught thee?
He that parts us shall bring a brand from heaven,
And fire us hence like foxes. Wipe thine eyes;
The good-years shall devour them, flesh and fell,
Ere they shall make us weep: we'll see 'em starve first."

This is not mania, but neither is it sound mind. It is the emotional excitability often seen in extreme age, as it is depicted in the early scenes of the drama, and it is precisely true to the probabilities of the mind history, that this should be the phase of infirmity displaying itself at this moment. Any other dramatist than Shakespeare would have represented the poor old king quite restored to the balance and control of his faculties. The complete efficiency of filial love would have been made to triumph over the laws of mental function. But Shakespeare has represented the exact degree of improvement which was probable under the circumstances, namely, restoration from the intellectual mania which resulted from the combined influence of physical and moral shock, with persistence of the emotional excitement and disturbance which is the incurable and unalterable result of passion exaggerated by long habitude and by the malign influence of extreme age.

The last scene, in which Lear's tough heart at length breaks over the murdered body of his dear child, is one of those masterpieces of tragic art, before which we are disposed to stand silent in awed admiration. The indurated sympathies of science, however, may examine even the death scene. The first thing to remark is, that there is no insanity in it, that Lear might have spoken and acted thus if his mind had never wandered. He has found Edmund's mercenary murderer hanging Cordelia, so as "to lay the blame upon her own despair." He kills the slave, and with the last remnant of strength carries the dear body into the midst of that heart-struck conclave, where

the sisters, who "desperately are dead," already lie.
At first he is under the excitement of mental agony,
expressing itself in the wild wail:

> "Howl, howl, howl, howl!   O, you are men of stones:
>   Had I your tongues and eyes, I'ld use them so
>   That heaven's vault should crack.   She's gone for ever!"

Then follows the intense cruel anxiety of false hope,
followed by quick resolve and reasonable action: the
demand for the looking-glass: the trial of the feather,
to ascertain if any faint imperceptible breath remains.
Then, the sustaining but fatal excitement over, leaden
grief settles upon the heart, and benumbs the feelings
to every sense, save one.   Noble Kent comes too late
with the prepared surprise of his discovery.   The
wreck of kinghood sits in the midst, with no eyes, no
thoughts for living friend or dead foe, for no object
save one, the voided temple of his love, now a limp
carcase in his nerveless lap.   What a group for a
sculptor, Lear and Cordelia, types of manly grandeur
and female grace, with but half a life between the
two!   The feather test has failed, and the sweet
breath refuses to mist or stain the clear surface of the
stone; conviction arrives that "now she's gone for
ever," and there is no fire left in the once ardent
heart for one more angry word, no thought except
the passing one of satisfied revenge.   She's gone for
ever—doubt of the stern fact is past, and death
presses on his own heart; feeling is mercifully blunted
and thought obscured; imagination is the last to con-

geal ; desire, father to the thought, makes the dear lips move, and the soft voice invite to follow :

" Cordelia, Cordelia ! stay a little.   Ha !
   What is't thou say'st ?   Her voice was ever soft,
   Gentle, and low, an excellent thing in woman."

The loyal friends around, Albany and Kent and Edgar, strive to arouse his attention from the gathering stupor, which they do not yet recognize as that of death ; and in banished Kent, now reinstated in the appurtenances and lendings of his rank, an object bound to stimulate attention and curiosity is at hand. But he has put off the revelation of his faithful service until it is too late to be understood.   The king recognizes his person, indeed, even through the gathering mists of death, which, beginning at the heart, weakens the circulation through the brain and dims the sight.   How constantly does the dying man complain that the room is dark, or that he cannot see. "Where is your servant Caius ?" brings a mechanical thought, trifling as it seems, but in true place.   The unreflecting movement of the mind, the excito-motory action of the brain, as some would call it, a thought of simple suggestion, which is the last kind of thought the dying brain can entertain, just as involuntary muscular action endures after voluntary power of movement is lost.   The new idea, that Caius and Kent are one, cannot be entertained ; this requires comparison and a greater power of cerebration than

the feeble tide of blood, which is now percolating the
brain can provide for.

> "*Lear.*   I am old now,
> And these same crosses spoil me.   Who are you?
> Mine eyes are not o' the best : I'll tell you straight.
>   *Kent.* If fortune brag of two she loved and hated,
> One of them we behold.
>   *Lear.* This is a dull sight.   Are you not Kent?
>   *Kent.*   The same,
> Your servant Kent.   Where is your servant Caius?
>   *Lear.* He's a good fellow, I can tell you that ;
> He'll strike, and quickly too : he's dead and rotten.
>   *Kent.* No, my good lord ; I'm the very man,—
>   *Lear.* I'll see that straight.
>   *Kent.* That, from your first of difference and decay,
> Have follow'd your sad steps.
>   *Lear.*   You are welcome hither.
>   *Kent.* Nor no man else : all's cheerless, dark, and deadly.
> Your eldest daughters have fordone themselves,
> And desperately are dead.
>   *Lear.*   Ay, so I think.
>   *Albany.* He knows not what he says : and vain it is
> That we present us to him.
>   *Edgar.*   Very bootless."

Very bootless—and yet stupified by dire mis-
chance, they are blind to the near approach of the
"veiled shadow with the keys," who is at hand to
release this loved and hated one of fortune from his
eminence of care.   Albany proceeds to make state
arrangements, to promise the wages of virtue and the
cup of deservings to friends and foes, and to resign
his own absolute power to the old majesty, whose
heart is beating slower and fainter, whose face is
blanching, and whose features are pinching as the life

current passes on its way in ever slower and smaller waves, until at length the change of aspect suddenly strikes the dull Duke, and he exclaims, "O! see, see!" and then one flicker more of reflecting thought, one gentle request, "Pray you undo this button," expressing the physical feeling of want of air; one yearning look on her who'll "come no more," and the silver thread is loosed, the golden bowl for ever broken.

"*Lear.* And my poor fool is hang'd! No, no, no life!
Why should a dog, a horse, a rat, have life,
And thou no breath at all? Thou'lt come no more,
Never, never, never, never, never!
Pray you, undo this button: thank you, sir.
Do you see this? Look on her, look, her lips,
Look there, look there!
   Edgar.   He faints! My lord, my lord.
   Kent. Break, heart; I prithee, break!
   Edgar.   Look up, my lord.
   Kent. Vex not his ghost: O, let him pass! he hates him
      much
That would upon the rack of this tough world
Stretch him out longer."

TIMON OF ATHENS.

"I am Misanthropos, and hate mankind."

THE remarkable difference between Timon and all
the other dramas, both in construction and general
idea, has been a subject of much difficulty with the
literary critics. It has been generally supposed to be
one of Shakespeare's latest works transmitted to us
in an unfinished state; but the explanation of Mr.
Knight appears far more probable, that it was originally produced by an inferior artist, and that Skake-
speare remodeled it, and substituted entire scenes of
his own; this substitution being almost wholly confined to the character of Timon. That of Apemantus,
however, bears unmistakeable impressions of the same
die.

It certainly is not like the sepia sketch of a great
master, perfect so far as it goes; nor yet like an unfinished picture which shews the basis of the artist's
work; nor yet like those paintings of the old masters,
in which the accessories were filled in by the 'prentice
hands of their pupils, while the design and prominent
figures indicated the taste and skill of high genius.
It is rather an old painting, retouched perhaps in all

its parts, and the prominent figures entirely remodeled by the hand of the great master, but designed and originally completed by a stranger.

Of the type of Timon's character there can be no doubt. He is unmistakeably of the family of Hamlet and Lear. The resemblance to Lear especially is close ; like him at first, full of unreasoning confidence ; like him at last, full of unreasoning hate. In Lear's circumstances, Timon might have followed closely in his steps. The conditions of rank and age and nation do indeed direct the course of the two in paths wide apart, but in actual development of character they are to some extent parallel.

Timon is very far from being a copy from Plutarch's sketch, "a viper, and malicious man unto mankind." He is essentially high-minded and unselfish. His prodigality is unsoiled with profligacy ; indeed, it takes to a great degree the form of humane and virtuous generosity, satisfied with the pleasure of doing good, the luxury of giving, without view of recompense. Even his profuse feasting is represented as noble and dignified hospitality, alloyed by no grossness. His temper is sweet and serene ; even Apemantus cannot ruffle it.

With all this goodness of heart he is no fool ; his remarks on all occasions shew refined and educated intellect. He has sense on all points except two, namely, in the ability to appreciate character, and the knowledge of the relation of things, as represented by the counters which transfer them. He has all kind of sense except that which is current—common sense. How such a character could be produced in the out-of-door life of Athens, where every citizen had his wits sharpened by contact with those of his neighbours, it would be difficult indeed to conjecture; but the character of Lord Timon in his prosperity is one which may any day be found in the ranks of the English aristocracy. A young man is born to a great name and estate, he inherits a generous disposition and an ardent temper; he is brought up as a little prince, and is never allowed to feel the wholesome pain of an ungratified wish. Can it be matter of wonder that in such a hotbed the growth of mind should be luxuriant and weak. Fortunately for our golden youth they generally undergo the rough discipline of public school and college; their sensibilities are indurated, and their wits sharpened, in societies where, if they find sycophant spirits, they also find independent and even tyrannical ones. But young Crœsus, brought up at home, what must be his destiny in these latter days? When the twenty-first birthday emancipates him from mamma and the mild tutor, well for him if reckless hospitality be his worst offence against prudence; well for him if that old man of the woods, the land steward, does not suffocate him in his tenacious embrace; well for him if the turf and the card-table do not attract his green state of social initiation, devour wealth and destroy morality. Men who most need knowledge of the selfishness of their fellow men have too often the least of it. Bred up on the sunny parterres of life, they have no experience of the difficulties and dangers of the rough thicket. The human pigeon has not even the resource of fear and swift flight to save him from the accipitres of his race. The fascination of false confidence lends him a willing victim to their talons, and under the chloroform of self-esteem he does not even feel being rent and devoured. So it is with Timon : with intelligence quick enough on all other matters, he is utterly incapable of seeing his relation to men and theirs to him, of appreciating the real value of deed and motive. The kind of knowledge most imperatively needed to guide our conduct is that of relation. It is the first to which the mind opens. The child under ever recurring penalties is compelled to acquaint himself with the relation existing between his person and the physical world ; he burns himself, and thereafter dreads the fire. The man under penalties more sharp and lasting must discover his moral relations in this world, must learn to estimate himself and those around him according to the actualities of motive. As the child ascertains that fire and blows cause pain, so the man must learn that flattery is not friendship, that imprudence exacts regret, that the prevalent philosophy of this selfish world is that taught by Lear's unselfish fool, " Let go thy hold when a great wheel runs down a hill, lest

it break thy neck with following ; but the great one
that goes upward, let him draw thee after ;" or by
Timon's poet, who laboriously conveys the same idea
that flashes from the fool :

> "When Fortune in her shift and change of mood
> Spurns down her late beloved, all his dependents
> Which labour'd after him to the mountain's top
> Even on their hands and knees, let him slip down,
> Not one accompanying his declining foot."

Timon, however, takes a widely different view of
life. To him society is a disinterested brotherhood
in which to possess largely is but to have the greater
scope for the luxury of giving, and in which want
itself may be but a means to try one's friends and
to learn their sterling value. His first act of bounty,
not less noble than reasonable, is to pay the debt on
which his friend Ventidius is imprisoned. It is done
with graceful freedom, and his liberated friend is invited to him for further help in the fine sentiment,
that

> "'Tis not enough to help the feeble up,
> But to support him after."

The dowry of the servant Lucilius, to satisfy the
greed of the old miser whose daughter he courts, is
more lavish and less reasonable. Timon will counter-
poise with his fortune what the old man will give
with his daughter, though he feels the burden of the
task.

> "To build his fortune I would strain a little,
> For 'tis a bond of men."

His inquiries are of the shortest. He has no hesitation, no suspicion, but gives away fortunes as if his means were exhaustless, and his discrimination infallible. He acts in fervent disbelief of his opinion immediately afterwards expressed, that since

> " Dishonour traffics with man's nature,
> He is but outside."

Timon conducts himself as if all men on the contrary were true to the core like himself, deriving enjoyment from the happiness of others. Life to him is a poet's dream of goodness and beauty. All men are deserving of his bounty, even as he is deserving of the love and gratitude of all.

But there is more than this reasoning bounty acting upon a false estimate of man's goodness. Timon gives for the very love of giving; he scatters without motive, further than the pleasure of doing so affords.

> " He outgoes the very heart of kindness.
> He pours it out; Plutus, the god of gold,
> Is but his steward; no meed, but he repays
> Sevenfold above itself.

He scatters jewels, and horses, and costly gifts among the rich, even as he distributes fortunes among the needy. He will have nothing back. Ventidius succeeds to the wealth of his father, and seeks to return the talents which freed him from prison, but Timon will have none of the gold.

> " I gave it freely ever; and there's none
> Can truly say he gives, if he receives."

R

This squandering disposition would appear to be the converse of what phrenologists denote acquisitiveness. To coin a word, it is *dis*quisitiveness, and in some men would seem to be an innate bias of the disposition. It is to give, for the pleasure of giving ; to spend, for the pleasure of spending, without esteem for the things procured in return.   Probably, like the opposite desire of accumulating, it is a secondary mental growth. The love of gold in itself would be as absurd as the love of iron ; but after having been first esteemed for its attributes, its ability to confer pleasure and power, it becomes valued for itself, and the mere love of hoarding, without the slightest reference to the employment of the hoard, takes possession of the mind. So in the opposite mental state, the first pleasures of distributing wealth are, no doubt, derived from the gratification it affords in various ways ; in contributing to the happiness of others ; in purchasing esteem or the semblance of it for one's self; in apparently raising one's self above the level of those on whom the benefits are conferred, and thus gratifying vanity ; or in the more direct gratification of the senses.   The pleasure of enjoyment from these sources is at length unconsciously transferred to the mere act of distribution. To give and to spend for the mere pleasure of doing so, combined with the love of change, are the attributes of many a prodigal who is no profligate, of many a man who, in a stricter sense than that usually applied to the saying, is no one's enemy but his own

—very strictly this can never be said, for in civilized society no man can be his own enemy without injuring others.

Such a man is Timon represented. He appears to have had no strong attachment either to men or things. The jewel recklessly purchased is lavishly thrown to the first friend he meets. His fortune is at every one's command, not only of the old friend in prison, and of the old servant aspiring to fortune, but at that of the flatterers of his own rank, empty in head and heart, who have no real wants or claims.

Timon has indeed a noble theory of friendship, but there wants in it all those heartlights which prove the reality of the thing, as it existed between Hamlet and Horatio, or Celia and Rosalind in the other sex. There is, however, a noble freedom of welcome in his introduction to his first feast :—

> " *Timon.* Nay, my lords, ceremony was but devised at first
> To set a gloss on faint deeds, hollow welcomes,
> Recanting goodness, sorry ere 'tis shown ;
> But where there is true friendship, there needs none.
> Pray, sit ; more welcome are ye to my fortunes
> Than my fortunes to me."

In his table speech, his explanation of his own profuseness, and his reliance upon a return in kind from his friends, is almost communist in the expression of the idea, that the fortunes of all should be at the service of each :—

> "Why, I have often wished myself poorer, that I might come nearer to you. We are born to do benefits : and what

better or properer can we call our own than the riches of
our friends? O, what a precious comfort 'tis, to have so
many, like brothers, commanding one another's fortunes!
O joy, e'en made away ere 't can be born! Mine eyes
cannot hold out water, methinks: to forget their faults,
I drink to you."

He gives more entertainment, distributes more jewels,
showers presents on those who bring them and on
those who do not, and, without knowing it, all "out
of an empty coffer." What he bespeaks is all in
debt, he owes for every word. Honest Flavius seeks
to apprise him, but since "it's a word which concerns
him near," he will not listen. Even Apemantus, who
seems to entertain a surly liking for him, and who
seeks to inspire in him some suspicion that friendship
has its dregs, tenders advice which this time is not
quite railing. He admits him to be honest though
a fool.

"Thus honest fools lay out their wealth on court'sies."

He'll not be bribed lest that should shut his mouth,
and Timon would then sin the faster; Timon will
give so long that soon he will give himself away in
paper; but Timon will have none of his warning, it
is railing on society; and Apemantus rebuffed at the
only moment when he is tolerable, turns on his heel
with his rejected advice:

"O, that men's ears should be
To counsel deaf, but not to flattery!"

Timon's profuseness is pourtrayed in the steward's
terse account of his debts, and the ever motion of

his raging waste; but the desire which prompts it
is best given in his own words of farewell to his
guests:

> "I take all and your several visitations
> So kind to heart, 'tis not enough to give;
> Methinks I could deal kingdoms to my friends,
> And ne'er be weary."

But now the time of reckoning approaches, in which
it is prophesied that

> "When every feather sticks in his own wing,
> Lord Timon will be left a naked gull,
> Which flashes now a phœnix."

He is beset with the clamorous demands of creditors,
and turns with reproachful enquiry to the one honest
man who has been seeking so long to check the ebb
of his estate and this great flow of debts; and when
he at length gives ear to the importunity that can no
longer be avoided, his debts double his means, and
all his vast lands are engaged or forfeited. No estate
could support his senseless prodigality,

> "The world is but a word:
> Were it all yours to give it in a breath,
> How quickly were it gone!"

Flavius, like Apemantus, refers the motive of
Timon's profusion to vanity and the love of compliment:

> "Who is not Timon's?
> What heart, head, sword, force, means, but is lord Timon's?
> Great Timon, noble, worthy, royal Timon!
> Ah, when the means are gone that buy this praise,

The breath is gone whereof this praise is made :
Feast-won, fast-lost ; one cloud of winter showers,
These flies are couch'd."

This however is not quite the whole truth.   There
is doubtless much vanity in Timon's ostentation, but
there is also a magnanimous disregard of self, and
a false judgment of others founded upon it.   His
bounty,

> " Being free itself, it thinks all other so."

Now comes the real trial, the test of man's value.
Riches are gone, but the noble heart is "wealthy in
his friends"; it were lack of conscience to think otherwise.

> " *Timon.*   Come, sermon me no further :
> No villanous bounty yet hath pass'd my heart ;
> Unwisely, not ignobly, have I given.
> Why dost thou weep ? Canst thou the conscience lack
> To think I shall lack friends ?   Secure thy heart ;
> If I would broach the vessels of my love,
> And try the argument of hearts by borrowing,
> Men and men's fortunes could I frankly use
> As I can bid thee speak."

The trial is made, the bubble bursts ; one after
another the friends find characteristic and ingenious
excuses.   To one, bare friendship without security is
nothing ; another is in despair that he hath not fur-
nished himself against so good a time ; another puts
on the semblance of anger that he was not sent to
first, and pretending that his honour hath thus been
abated, he refuses his coin.

The world turns dark with Timon, he is struck down by his friends' desertion.

"Thy lord leans wondrously to discontent, his comfortable temper has forsook him; he is much out of health and keeps his chamber."

The period of depression which would naturally intervene between that of confidence and enraged defiance is concealed from view, and only alluded to in the above sentence. Here, as in Lear and Constance, the poet takes care to mark the concurrence of physical with moral causes of insanity. Mere bodily disease is no subject for dramatic representation; and the fact of its existence is lightly enough indicated, but it is indicated, and that is sufficient to preserve the exact natural verisimilitude of the diseased mind's history. When Timon re-appears, the re-action of furious indignation possesses him. He rushes wildly forth from the house in which his loving servants have sought to retain him. Must his very house also be his enemy, his gaol?

"The place where I have feasted, does it now,
Like all mankind, shew me an iron heart?"

At the door he is beset with a crowd of dunning creditors, adding fuel to the flame of his rage.

"*Philotus.* All our bills.
Timon. Knock me down with 'em : cleave me to the girdle.
Luc. Serv. Alas, my lord,—
Tim. Cut my heart in sums.
Titus. Mine, fifty talents.
Tim. Tell out my blood.

Luc. Serv. Five thousand crowns, my lord.
Tim. Five thousand drops pays that.
                              What yours?—and yours?
Tim. Tear me, take me, and the gods fall upon you !
Hortensius. 'Faith, I perceive our masters may throw their caps at their money : these debts may well be called desperate ones, for a madman owes 'em.
                    [*Timon drives them out and re-enters.*
Tim. They have e'en put my breath from me, the slaves. Creditors ?—devils."

He gives orders for his farewell feast, although Flavius reminds him of his absolute want of means, and says that in doing so

    " You only speak from your distracted soul."

However, Timon and the cook will provide. The feast is toward. The expression of rage is controlled, and the infinite sarcasm of the inverted benediction is pronounced before the guests know what it means. The ambiguity of the language is of course intended to conceal for a moment its true meaning—that men are all villains and women no better ; that even their piety is selfishness, so that if the Gods gave all, even they would be despised like Timon ; but all being amiss, let all be suitable for destruction.

The dishes uncovered are full of warm water, which Timon throws into the faces of his mock friends, whose perfect nature "is but smoke and lukewarm water." He overwhelms them with a torrent of curses by no means lukewarm, throws the dishes at them, and driving them from the hall, takes his own farewell of house and home, bursting with rage and general hate.

> " Burn, house ! sink, Athens ! henceforth hated be,
> Of Timon man and all humanity !"

The conclusion of the "smiling, smooth, detested parasites" is the same as that already arrived at by the servants, namely

> " Lord Timon's mad."

Nothing, indeed, is less safe than to adopt the opinion of some of Shakespeare's characters upon others. He makes them speak of each other according to their own light, which is often partial and perverted, obscured by ignorance, or blinded by prejudice. The spectator sees the whole field, and experiences difficulty of judgment, not from narrowness of vision, but from its extent. In Timon, as in the early parts of Lear, the psychological opinion is embarrassed by the very circumstance which constitutes the difficulty in many cases of dubious insanity, namely, that the operations of diseased mind are not retrograde to those of normal function, but merely divergent from them, in the same general direction.

Timon's eloquent declamations against his kind are identical in spirit with those of 'Lear.' They are, indeed, interrupted by no vagrancy of thought, but are always true to the passion which now absorbs him, namely, intense hatred of the human race, in whom he believes baseness and wickedness inherent.

Here lies his great intellectual error which may indeed be called delusion ; that, because some few men have been base and thankless parasites, the whole race is steeped in infamy. His emotional being is absorbed by indignation, and this, re-acting on the intellect, represents human nature in the darkest colours of treachery and villany. It is not clearly made out to what degree Timon is influenced by spite. In the imprecation upon Athens, "Let me look back upon thee" etc., he invokes social disorder of every kind as the punishment for his own treatment, and does not represent it as actually existing, and as the cause of his fierce anger. There is some uncertainty in this passage, some confusion of thought between the depraved state of Athens which merits dire punishment, and the social disorders which in themselves constitute such punishment. The wall of Athens is thought to girdle in a mere troop of human wolves. To avenge his own injuries, he prays that the matrons may turn incontinent, that obedience may fail in children, and so forth, recognizing that the contrary has existed, and that social disorder is invoked as the punishment of demerit towards himself. He acknowledges that "degrees, observances, customs, and laws" have held their place, and that their "confounding contraries" would be a new state of things due to that human baseness which is now obvious to his distempered vision through the medium of his own wrongs. In the following scene, where he apostrophises "the blessed breeding sun" in vehement declamation, he does not so much invoke curses upon man, as describe man's actual state as in itself a curse; since he depicts moral depravity in its existing colors.

> "*Timon.* O blessed breeding sun, draw from the earth
> Rotten humidity; below thy sister's orb
> Infect the air! Twinn'd brothers of one womb,
> Whose procreation, residence, and birth,
> Scarce is dividant, touch them with several fortunes;
> The greater scorns the lesser: not nature,
> To whom all sores lay siege, can bear great fortune,
> But by contempt of nature.
> Raise me this beggar, and deny 't that lord;
> The senator shall bear contempt hereditary,
> The beggar native honour.
> It is the pasture lards the rother's sides,
> The want that makes him lean. Who dares, who dares,
> In purity of manhood stand upright,
> And say 'This man's a flatterer'? if one be,
> So are they all; for every grise of fortune
> Is smooth'd by that below: the learned pate
> Ducks to the golden fool: all is oblique;
> There's nothing level in our cursed natures,
> But direct villany. Therefore, be abhorr'd
> All feasts, societies, and throngs of men!
> His semblable, yea, himself, Timon disdains:
> Destruction fang mankind! Earth, yield me roots!"

Instead of roots he finds gold, yellow, glittering, precious gold, and he comments upon it in terms which still further prove that the social curses he invokes upon the detested town he has quitted are those which he believes to exist. There is no honesty, no nobility in man, proof against this yellow slave, this damned earth which will "knit and break religions, bless the accursed, make the hoar leprosy

adored, place thieves on high and give them titled
approbation." This belief in the existence of man's
utter unworthiness is of prime importance in estimating Timon's character. It is needful to vindicate
his misanthropy from being that of miserable spite.
There is no doubt a mixture of personal resentment
in his feeling, but his deep-rooted disparagement and
contempt of man are founded upon a fixed belief in
man's utter worthlessness. If men were noble and
good, or if Timon could believe them so, he would
not hate them ; but they are all to his distempered
mind either base in themselves or base in their sub-
serviency to baseness. "Timon Atheniensis dictus
interrogatus cur omnes homines odio prosequeretur :
Malos, inquit, merito odi ; cæteros ob id odi, quod
malos non oderint."—*Erasmus.* This is not to hate
man as he ought to be, nor even as he is, but as he
appears in the false colours of mental derangement.

The character of Apemantus is skilfully managed
to elicit the less selfish nature of Timon's misanthropy.
In the one it is the result of a bad heart, in the other
that of a perverted reason. If all men were true and
good they would be the more offensive to the churlish
disposition of Apemantus, who is an ingrained misanthrope, and as such is recognized and abhorred
by Timon himself. He seeks Timon to vex him—
"always a villain's office, or a fool's." He attributes
Timon's conduct to the meanest motives,—a madman
before, he is now a fool :

> "This is in thee a nature but infected,
> A poor unmanly melancholy sprung
> From change of fortune."

He recommends Timon to play the part he was undone by—that of a base flatterer; and that he should turn rascal to have his wealth again, that he might again distribute it to rascals. He accuses him of being an imitator—"Thou dost affect my manners;" —of putting on the sour cold habit of nakedness and melancholy from mere want, and of the capacity to be a courtier, were he not a beggar. Timon estimates the curish spirit which thus attacks him at its true value. "Why shouldst thou hate men? they never flattered thee?" He replies,

> "If thou hadst not been born the worst of men,
> Thou hadst been a knave and flatterer."

Apemantus, indeed, is a real misanthrope, who judges of man by his own bad heart. It was necessary to the drama that he should speak his thoughts, but naturally such a man would only express his antagonism to mankind in his actions. Such misanthropes are too common; every malevolent villain being, in fact, one of them, although selfishness in league with badness may counsel hypocrisy. Boileau recognises this in his lines on the malignant hypocrite of society :

> "En vain ce misanthrope, aux yeux tristes et sombres,
> Veut, par un air riant, en éclaircir les ombres :
> Le ris sur son visage est en mauvaise humeur ;
> L'agrément fuit ses traits, ses caresses font peur ;

> Ses mots les plus flatteurs paroissent des rudesses,
> Et la vanité brille en toutes ses bassesses."

Lord Shaftesbury, in the Characteristics, takes a view of misanthropy, which strictly accords with the character of Apemantus. He places it among "those horrid, monstrous, and unnatural affections, to have which is to be miserable in the highest degree." He writes :

> "There is also among these a sort of hatred of mankind and society ; a passion which has been known perfectly reigning among some men, and has had a peculiar name given to it, misanthropy. A large share of this belongs to those who have habitually indulged themselves in a habitual moroseness, or who, by force of ill-nature and ill-breeding, have contracted such a reverse of affability, and civil manners, that to see or meet a stranger is offensive. The very aspect of mankind is a disturbance to 'em, and they are sure always to hate at first sight."

Timon's contempt of the treasure of gold, which he discovers in his naked and houseless misery, marks his changed nature less than his entire disregard of the invitation of the senators to rank and power, and to be captain of Athens. Riches, for their own sake, he always placed at the lowest value. He now distributes them as moral poison. To Alcibiades, whom, following Plutarch's hint, he hates less than others, he gives it to whet the sword which threatens his country. To the courtezans he gives it, because they are the infecting curses of man.

>   "There's more gold ;
> So you damn others, and let this damn you,
> And ditches grave you all !"

To Flavius he gives it tempting him to misanthropy; to the contemptible poet and painter, because they are villains; to the thieves, that in the poison of wine it may destroy them.

> "Here's gold. Go, suck the subtle blood o' the grape,
> 'Till the high fever seethe your blood to froth,
> And so 'scape hanging."

Gold, which has been his own curse, has become in his eyes the curse of all. It is "the common whore of mankind." His contemptuous distribution of the "yellow slave," the "damned earth," the "strong thief," with blows and maledictions to the mean wretches who seek it from him, is the keenest satire upon the state of society, which for want of it has thrown him from its bosom.

It has been said both by Schlegel and Hazlitt that Timon is more a satire than a drama. This idea may have been derived from the limited development of character which it exhibits. Each character is placed clear and definitely formed in the page, and remains so. Timon's alone undergoes one radical change, of which we see the effect rather than the transition. During the fourth and fifth acts the movements of the drama are solely devised with the intention of bringing the several personages under Timon's withering denunciation.

There are, however, some passages which hint of change, and are more important than the more prominent and eloquent ones in affording an estimate of

Timon's mental state. By the other personages he is evidently regarded as mad. Alcibiades thus excuses his anathemas on the ladies of pleasure :

> " Pardon him, sweet Timandra ; for his wits
> Are drown'd and lost in his calamities."

The good steward expresses wondering grief at the change in his appearance, the pregnant sign of the mind's disease :

> "*Flavius.*   O you gods !
> Is yond despised and ruinous man my lord ?
> Full of decay and failing ?   O monument
> And wonder of good deeds evilly bestow'd !
> What an alteration of honour
> Has desperate want made !
> What viler thing upon the earth than friends
> Who can bring noblest minds to basest ends !"

Even before this, life-weariness has suggested the intention of suicide ; the life-weariness of true mental disease, which is distinct from misanthropy, and has reference only to the individual. Misanthropy of opinion may be robust, egotistical, resisting, full of life. The misanthropy of melancholia is despairing and suicidal.

> " I am sick of this false world, and will love nought
> But even the mere necessities upon 't.
> Then, Timon, presently prepare thy grave ;
> Lie where the light foam of the sea may beat
> Thy grave-stone daily : make thine epitaph
> That death in me at others' lives may laugh."

It is, however, not certain whether Timon dies directly by his own hand, or indirectly by the misery which he inflicts upon himself. The exposure described in such noble poetry by Apemantus out of place as it seems in his churlish mouth, "What, think'st that the bleak air thy boisterous chamberlain" etc., is in itself a kind of suicide, which has many a time and oft been resorted to by the insane. Indeed, of all forms of voluntary death, that of starvation is the most frequently attempted by them. Timon, however, does not actually refuse food; he digs for roots and eats them, while he regrets the necessity

> "That nature being sick of man's unkindness
> Should yet be hungry."—

Although his exposure to "desperate want," which hath made him almost unrecognizable to the loving eyes of his faithful steward, may from the first have been adopted for a suicidal purpose, it seems probable that the manner of his death was still more voluntary; for, however sensibly he might feel his failing health drawing to a close, it is not likely that on the day when he supported the animated dialogue with the senators he should be able positively to foretell his death from exhaustion on the morrow.

> "Why, I was writing of my epitaph;
> It will be seen to-morrow: my long sickness
> Of health and living now begins to mend,
> And nothing brings me all things."

After mocking the senators with the pretended patriotism of a public benefit, copied from the short notice

s

to be found in Plutarch, the invitation forsooth to the
Athenian citizens to stop their afflictions by hanging
themselves upon his tree, Timon takes his farewell of
men and their deeds, in words pointing to a voluntary
death, in a predetermined time and place :

> " Come not to me again : but say to Athens,
> Timon hath made his everlasting mansion
> Upon the beached verge of the salt flood ;
> Who once a day with his embossed froth
> The turbulent surge shall cover : thither come,
> And let my gravestone be your oracle.
> Lips, let sour words go by and language end :
> What is amiss plague and infection mend !
> Graves only be men's works and death their gain !
> Sun, hide thy beams !   Timon hath done his reign."

Suicide had not that place of honour among the
Greeks which it afterwards obtained among the
Romans, and at the present day has among that remote and strange people, the Japanese.   Yet the duty
of living and bearing one's burden manfully was not
fully recognized until a better religious faith instructed
us that this life is but a state of preparation for another.   The suicide of Timon, however, whether it
is effected by exposure and want, or by more direct
means, has no motive recognized even by the ancients
as an excuse, and can only be attributed to the suggestions of a diseased mind.

Whether Shakespeare intended in Timon to describe the career of a madman is a question on which
it is difficult, perhaps impossible, to come to a definite
conclusion.   The chief objection to the affirmative

would be, that all satire upon the hollowness of the world would lose much of its point if it came from the lips of an undoubted lunatic. This objection, however, loses somewhat of its validity, when it is remembered that in Lear Shakespeare actually has put such satire in the mouth of the maddest of his characters during the height of the disease ; and that in his devotion to the truth of nature he would have represented such misanthropy as Timon's as a monstrous growth of the mind, if it be so.

Is it possible even in a state of disease? Is it actually met with? Undoubtedly, yes. Making allowance for the difference between the adorned descriptions of poetry and plain matter of fact, putting on one side the power of eloquent declamation, which belongs indeed not to the character but to the author, the professed misanthrope in word and in deed is met with among the insane, and, probably, among the insane only. This malignant and inhuman passion, for such it is, takes divers forms. Sometimes it is mere motiveless dislike ; every one is obnoxious with or without cause, like Dr. Fell in the adage. This is the malignity of Apemantus expressing itself in conduct rather than in frank confession. The explanation of it is best given by Timon himself, that

> "*Ira brevis furor est*,
> But this man 's always angry."

If anger be identical with madness, except in its duration, this form of madness may be said to be a life-long and universal anger.　Another form of insanity, not uncommon in and out of lunatic asylums, approaches more nearly to the misanthropy of Timon ; namely, that form of chronic mental disease, whether it be called mania or melancholia, which constantly torments itself and others by attributing evil motives, not like Timon's to all ranks and classes of society, but to every individual with whom the unhappy being comes in contact.　The poetical misanthropy of Timon is generalized, and cannot be said to point at any individual, unless it be Apemantus.　The misanthropy of reality is individualized ; it points to all persons in turn, but to one only at a time.

This form of misanthropy may, and indeed often does, exist with none of the attributes of Insanity, but as the expression of that misleading influence which evil dispositions exercise over the judgment.　In not unfrequent instances, however, it passes the limits of sanity, and presents all the features of mental disease. Hate and suspicion become constant and uncontrolable emotions ; belief in the misconduct of others develops into delusions, representing the commission of actual crimes ; and with these mental symptoms the physical indications of brain disease are not wanting. No task of psychological diagnosis, however, is so arduous as that of determining the point at which exaggerated natural disposition of any kind becomes actual disease ; but when the boundaries of sane mind are far left behind, difficulty and doubt vanish.

When sane malignity has developed into insane misanthropy, a remarkable change is sometimes seen in the habits of the man, resembling the self-inflicted miseries of Timon. The author once knew a gentleman whose educated and acute intellect occupied itself solely in the invention of calumnies against every person with whom he was brought into contact. This habit of mind was associated with utter negligence of the proprieties of life, and indeed of personal decency, so that it became absolutely requisite, for his own sake, that he should receive the protection of an asylum. A more close approximation to the misanthropy represented by the dramatist, because more general and uninfluenced by malign feeling, was, however, presented in the case of a poor creature, in whose expulsion from that which served for his cave the author took some part. For several years he had frequently passed by a desolate-looking house, which was believed to be uninhabited. Any strange thing, accompanied by change, strikes one's attention, but stranger things not so accompanied pass by unnoticed. So it was that this house remained in this state for years, without anyone asking why it was so. At length information was received that an insane person was incarcerated within its desolate-looking walls. In company with a Justice of the Peace the author obtained admission into the house, and, by forcing a door, into the chamber of the anchorite. Here in gloomy mistrust and dislike of all mankind he had

secluded himself for five years.   Little of his history
was known, except that he had travelled in all parts
of the world, had returned to find great domestic
affliction, and from that time had shut himself in one
room ; the bare necessaries of life being supplied to
him by relatives who connived at his eccentricity, one
of whom, scarcely more sane than himself, also occupied a room in this strange house.   It is astonishing
that, with a penurious diet and absence of all comfort,
and an absolute want of fresh air and exercise, he
retained health for so long a time.   Had it not been
for this self-inflicted misery and incarceration, it would
have been difficult to certify that this poor man was
insane.   He disliked his fellow men, and shut himself
up from them ; that was all.   Although not a rich
man, he had property ; and while it was under contemplation how he could be rescued from his voluntary
misery, some relations took him under their kind
protection.   Had this man possessed the passionate
eloquence of Timon, and been exposed to severe
incitements to its use, by irritating invasions on his
misanthropic privacy, he might have declaimed as
Timon did—if Timon•indeed did declaim ; if silence
indeed is not the natural state of misanthropy, and
all the eloquence of this drama that of the author
rather than of the character.

The character which Shakespeare has delineated
in Timon is remarkably enough the subject of the
chef d' œuvre of French comedy.   The Misanthrope

of Molière, however, is in many respects a very distinct personage from that of Shakespeare. So far from being susceptible to flattery and to the blandishments of prosperity, more than half of his quarrel with society is founded upon his abhorrence of this social falsehood. Although he loudly condemns general vices, and thus accounts for his retirement from the world,

> " La raison, pour mon bien, veut que je me retire ;
>   Je n'ai point sur ma langue un assez grand empire,"

yet he detests private scandal, and reproaches his mistress for indulging in it. The dishonest praise and blame of individuals are equally hateful to his ears. The reason he assigns for his misanthropy, and its extent, are identical with those which Erasmus attributed to Timon ; in his anger he says that his aversion to man admits of no exception :

> " Non, elle est générale, et je hais tous les hommes ;
>   Les uns, parcequ'ils sont méchants et malfaisants,
>   Et les autres, pour être aux méchants complaisants."

He hates all mankind, because they all come under the category of rogues or flatterers. He is, however, elevated above Timon in this, that the personal injuries he himself receives are not the cause of this hatred ; on the contrary, he treats them with a noble indifference. The character of Alceste is, on the whole, that of a magnanimous, truth-loving, truth-speaking man, misplaced in a court where servility and corruption are triumphant. His very defects, his anger at vice and duplicity, and his promptness to express it, are those of a noble soul.

Rousseau has taken this view of the character in a severe criticism, to which he has exposed Molière for degrading the dramatic art, to pander to the corrupt morals of his age, in covering virtue with ridicule, and vice with false attractions. Other French writers have generally dissented from this condemnation, but Rousseau's letter to D'Alembert is a fine example of analytic criticism, not to be set aside by the sneering assertion, that he identified himself with this noble character, and felt his own vanity wounded in its unworthy treatment. Rousseau's estimate of it is irrefragably just and logical. If he has erred at all, it is in the opinion of the impression which the character of Alceste is calculated to make. His imprudent magnanimity may have been a subject of ridicule to the *parterre* of Molière's time, and doubtless was so ; but this view of the character would be due less to the manner in which it is delineated, than to the corrupt morals and taste of that age. In better times it would be difficult to throw ridicule upon that which is intrinsically and morally excellent. An interesting anecdote, related by St. Simon, attests that this view of the character was even taken in Molière's own time by the person most interested in estimating it justly. The Duc de Montausier was generally recognized to be the original of the misanthrope, and was so indignant at the supposed insult that he threatened to have Molière beaten to death for it. When the king went to see the play, M. Le Duc was compelled to go with him as his governor. After the performance the Duke sent for Molière, who was with difficulty brought to him, trembling from head to foot, expecting nothing less than death. M. Montausier, however, gave him a very different reception from that which he expected ; he embraced him again and again, overwhelmed him with praises and thanks, for " if he had thought of him in drawing the character of the misanthrope, which was that of the most perfectly honest man possible, he had done him an honour which was only too great, and which he should never forget."

Rousseau seems to think not only that Alceste was not a misanthrope in the proper sense of the word, but that no sane man can be such.

"One may say that the author has not ridiculed virtue in Alceste, but a true fault ; that is to say, hatred of mankind. I reply, that it is not true that he has endowed his character with this hatred. The mere name of misanthrope must not be understood to imply that he who bears it is the enemy of the human race. A hatred of this kind would not be a defect, but a depravity of nature, and the greatest of all vices, since all the social virtues are connected with benevolence, and nothing is so directly contrary to them as inhumanity. The true misanthrope, if his existence were possible, would be a monster who would not make us laugh ; he would excite our horror."

The true misanthrope, in fact, is such a character as Iago, a malevolent devil, without belief in any human goodness, without human sympathies, one who has said in his heart, " evil, be thou my good." But the very nature of such inhuman hatred would impose not only silence as to evil thoughts, but hypocritical expression of humane sentiment. The honest wide-mouthed misanthropy of Timon is wholly explicable on neither of these theories. It is neither the rough garb of sincerity and virtue, as in Alceste, nor of inhuman hatred as in Iago. It is a medium between the two, inconsistent with sane mind, and explicable alone as a depravity and perversion of nature arising from disease. It is a form of insanity.

Aretæus, describing the conduct of maniacs " in the height of the disease," remarks, " some flee the haunts of men, and going into the wilderness live by themselves."

In Caius Cassius there is a fine psychological delineation of another character, who estimates man and his motives depreciatingly. Cassius is robustly sane and self-possessed, and therefore has little in common with Timon. He would approximate more closely to Jaques, did not the strong intermixture of spleen pickle him as it were from the contagion of melancholy. In Cæsar's unfriendly but graphic description he figures as the type of cynicism, except that the envy of ambition is attributed to him which the true cynic would despise.

> "*Cæsar.* Let me have men about me that are fat :
> Sleek-headed men and such as sleep o'nights :
> Yond Cassius has a lean and hungry look ;

He thinks too much : such men are dangerous.
 Antony. Fear him not, Cæsar ; he's not dangerous ;
He is a noble Roman and well given.
 Cæs. Would he were fatter ! But I fear him not :
Yet if my name were liable to fear,
I do not know the man I should avoid
So soon as that spare Cassius. He reads much ;
He is a great observer and he looks
Quite through the deeds of men ; he loves no plays,
As thou dost, Antony ; he hears no music ;
Seldom he smiles, and smiles in such a sort
As if he mock'd himself and scorn'd his spirit
That could be moved to smile at any thing.
Such men as he be never at heart's ease
Whiles they behold a greater than themselves,
And therefore are they very dangerous."

However true the dangerous nature of such men
may be, in times when despotic power can only be
attacked by conspiracy, it can scarcely be so when
eloquence is the most formidable assailant of estab-
lished authority. Sleep o' nights is needful to sustain
the energy of the day, and a fat body is often associated with a well-nourished brain of best quality.
The greatest orators and some of the greatest de-
magogues have at least indicated a proclivity to
Falstaffian proportions ; witness Danton, Fox, O'Con-
nell, John Bright, and the Bishop of Oxford. Falstaff,
indeed, himself says, " Give me spare men and spare
me great ones," but this was only for soldiers.

CONSTANCE.

CONSTANCE is delineated with Greek simplicity. The grandeur of one great passion is weakened by no subordinate parts of character on which the mind can rest and feel relief. All is simple and clear, like the one thrilling note of a trumpet, rising higher or falling lower, but never altering its tone. The wondrous eloquence in which the passion clothes itself does but display its force. Its unity and directness of purpose remain unchanging and unchangeable. Passion is not seen except when transformed into action. Like a great wind, it would be voiceless except for opposition; it would be viewless except for its effects. These may be a few tossed leaves, or a whirling cloud-rack, or the crash of forests. The invisible force remains the same, measured most imperfectly by the casualties of resistance.

But this passion itself, single in its onward force, is not altogether so in its nature and origin. It wears the garb of maternal affection, of the strong love a widowed mother bears to her only child; but, as in Queen Margaret, the fury of ambition is added: ambition for herself as much as for her son, which Elinor perceives, and with wounding truth expresses:

" Out, insolent ! thy bastard shall be king,
That thou mayst be a queen, and check the world !"

This fierce desire of power and place, which is but
coldly expressed in the word ambition, is as undeniable in Constance as her mother's love. Had she
no child she would be ambitious for herself. Having
one, she is more vehemently ambitious for him, and
indirectly for herself. The tenderness of love alone
would have led her to shun contention and to with-
draw her child from danger; as Andromache sought
to withhold her husband from the field of honour with
unalloyed womanly apprehension. But love influenced by ambition, and ambition stimulated by love,
produced that compound passion which incurred all
risks, braved all dangers. Combined passions are
weak or strong, according to their perfection of union
and singleness of purpose. If concurrent desires are
but half of one mind, they pull diverse ways, and
give rise to the weakness of inconsistency; but if they
are thoroughly of one accord, chemically combined
as it were, the product acquires new and irresistible
strength. This force of compound emotion is finely
developed in Constance, in contrast with the other
female characters of the drama. Ambitious without
love, she would have possessed the hard vigour of
Elinor ; loving without ambition, she would have been
tenderly devoted like Blanch. Under the lash of the
combined passion she is a fury, whom her boundless
love and her deep woe barely suffice to redeem from
our horror.

The first words of Constance are those of prudent
advice, the suggestion of a strong vehement nature
against the first move in the dread game of war.
They contrast well with the ready boasts of coward
Austria and feeble France :

> " Stay for an answer to your embassy,
>   Lest unadvised you stain your swords with blood."

It is the only tranquil speech which the poor woman
is permitted to utter. The scolding match into which
she immediately precipitates herself with Queen Elinor
develops the irritability and vehemence of her temper.
To Elinor's taunt of unchastity she replies with acrid
tu quoque invective. She fairly overwhelms the queen-
mother with vituperation, and does her best to merit
the contemptuous entreaty of John, " Bedlam, have
done!" and at length to earn the expostulations of
her own friend.

> "*Elinor.* Thou unadvised scold, I can produce
> A will that bars the title of thy son.
>   *Constance.* Ay, who doubts that? a will! a wicked will;
> A woman's will; a canker'd grandam's will!
>   *K. Philip.* Peace, lady! pause, or be more temperate:
> It ill beseems this presence to cry aim
> To these ill-tuned repetitions."

She has already incurred the remonstrance of her
gentle son.

> "*Arthur.*   Good my mother, peace !
> I would that I were low laid in my grave :
> I am not worth this coil that's made for me."

Her very tenderness to her child is fierce, like that

of some she-beast of prey. Had there been no motive in the mother's heart but that of love, this appeal might well have checked not only the unbridled use of speech, but the dangerous course of action into which Constance throws herself. But at this period ambition is stronger than love, and it would be hard to say to what extent ambition for herself was not mixed up with that for her son. The scene affords clear insight into the natural character of Constance, as a proud ambitious woman, of irritable and ungoverned temper. The flight of her imagination, like that of her passion, is yet comparatively low. She roundly scolds her opponents indeed, but not until later is her unrivalled power of invective fully developed.

In nothing is Shakespeare's master-hand more evident than in the manner in which he lays a true and consistent foundation for his characters. To have built such an one as that of Constance on the basis of the common female virtues would have been monstrous. Constance, in whom fierce passion is not the result, but the cause of madness, could only have been from the beginning, what she is plainly shewn to have been, a haughty irascible woman, whose tongue and temper were dreaded by friend and foe.

Although accurate history has little to do with dramatic representation of character, it is worthy of remark, that the imperious claim of Constance to the crown of England for her son was not founded upon

that indefeasible right which would have been recognized at a later period. Mr. Foster in his *Historical
Essays* remarks that,

"In England, while some might have thought Arthur's
hereditary claim superior to his uncle's, there was hardly a
man of influence, who at this period would have drawn the
sword for him on any such principle as that the crown of
England was heritable property. The genius of the country
had been repugnant to any such notion. The Anglo-Saxon
Sovereignty was elective, that people never sanctioning a
custom by which the then personal and most arduous duties
of sovereignty, both in peace and war, might pass of right
to an infant or imbecile prince; and to the strength of this
feeling in the country of their conquest the Normans heretofore had been obliged to defer."

When the alliance between John and Philip has
been determined, the latter enquires for Constance,
and the Dauphin replies,

"She is sad and passionate in your highness' tent."

Philip thinks the peace "will give her sadness very
little cure," and in real apprehension asks his brother
of England, "how we may content this widow lady?"
John proposes to give up Bretagne and other dignities
and powers to Arthur, and trusts in this manner to
appease if not to satisfy her ambition and avert her
vituperation:

"I trust we shall,
If not fill up the measure of her will,
Yet in some measure satisfy her so
That we shall stop her exclamation."

John, however, had reckoned without his host; the
lady's will was not to be so readily satisfied, nor her

passionate exclamation so easily stopped. When
Salisbury bears to her the message of the kings, and
the information of their new compact, her rage knows
no bounds, and the expression of it is as vehemently
eloquent as that of her passionate grief when she has
really lost all. Those who in deference to the sacred
virtues of womanhood attribute all the language and
conduct of Constance to the all-sanctifying motive of
maternal love, will do well to remark that this passionate scene takes place while her son is with her
and free from danger, except that which her own
ambition prepares for him. Her rage arises from the
thought that Blanch shall have those provinces instead
of her son :

> "Gone to be married ! gone to swear a peace !
> False blood to false blood join'd ! gone to be friends !
> Shall Lewis have Blanch, and Blanch those provinces ?
> It is not so ; thou hast misspoke, misheard ;
> Be well advised, tell o'er thy tale again :
> It cannot be ; thou dost but say, 'tis so :
> I trust I may not trust thee ; for thy word
> Is but the vain breath of a common man :
> Believe me, I do not believe thee, man ;
> I have a king's oath to the contrary.
> Thou shalt be punish'd for thus frighting me,
> For I am sick and capable of fears,
> Oppress'd with wrongs and therefore full of fears,
> A widow, husbandless, subject to fears,
> A woman, naturally born to fears ;
> And though thou now confess thou didst but jest.
> With my vex'd spirits I cannot take a truce,
> But they will quake and tremble all this day."

> " O, if thou teach me to believe this sorrow,
> Teach thou this sorrow how to make me die,

T

> And let belief and life encounter so
> As doth the fury of two desperate men
> Which in the very meeting fall and die.
> Lewis marry Blanch! O boy, then where art thou?
> France friend with England, what becomes of me?
> Fellow, be gone: I cannot brook thy sight:
> This news hath made thee a most ugly man."

In this violent language the spirit of disappointed ambition is paramount: ambition not only for Arthur but for herself, "What becomes of me?" The attack on Salisbury, the innocent messenger, so unworthy of a lady and a princess, can only be excused on the supposition that she is beside herself with fruitless rage, and vents it on any one within reach. It wants but little that she should turn her tongue or her hands even upon Arthur. When, alarmed by her fury, he interposes, "I do beseech you, madam, be content," she replies with a strange sophistry, which a true mother's heart would never employ, that if he were "grim, ugly, and slandrous to his mother's womb," etc.,

> "I would not care, I then would be content,
> For then I should not love thee, no, nor thou
> Become thy great birth nor deserve a crown."

When was true mother's love ever measured by the beauty of her child? When did it not rather increase with the child's imperfections? Sacred miracle of nature, a mother's love hangs not on such casual gifts as form and beauty. The crétin idiot, hideous and half human, claims and receives more than its share. Even moral deformities cannot exhaust this unselfish all-enduring fount of love; as the reprobate son, the outcast of the family, knows full well, feeling that there is a bond holding him to one pure heart which can never loosen. But the love of Constance is alloyed with pride, and ambition, and selfishness. Not simply because Arthur is her son is he dear to her, but also because he is rightful heir to a crown, and because his beauty flatters her pride:

> " Of Nature's gifts thou mayst with lilies boast
> And with the half-blown rose."

With the true selfishness of intense pride, she attributes the sufferance of all Arthur's injuries to herself. She alone feels and must underbear the woes of disappointed ambition. She calls upon the peer whom she has so insolently and causelessly abused to assist in her vituperations:

> " Tell me, thou fellow, is not France foresworn?
> Envenom him with words, or get thee gone,
> And leave those woes alone which I alone
> Am bound to underbear."

She will not go with Salisbury to the Kings. Did they know her truly they would never send for her. She is in an ecstasy of passion, which she miscalls grief and sorrow. The idea that she will make the huge firm earth the throne of this great emotion carries one beyond the earth in its grandeur. The intensity of her passion is almost satanic. Her humanity is alone vindicated by her subjection to its powers. Such passion in a questionable cause, moving a strong nature, would excite only fear and abhorrence ; endured by a weak one it excites our extremest pity. Insanity alone redeems such passion to the kindred of womanhood, and is already foreshadowed in that culminating point where the extremes of pride and grief meet in the dust.

> "I will instruct my sorrows to be proud ;
> For grief is proud and makes his owner stoop.
> To me and to the state of my great grief
> Let kings assemble ; for my grief 's so great
> That no supporter but the huge firm earth
> Can hold it up : here I and sorrow sit ;
> Here is my throne, bid kings come bow to it."

There is one word in the above quotations which must not pass without comment. Constance avows herself in ill health. "For I am *sick*." This point of physical disturbance is rarely omitted by Shakspeare in the development of insanity. It may be referred to in this instance in the most casual and careless manner, for the drama can take little cognizance of the physical imperfections of our nature. Still, however skilfully and imperceptible, the point is made. In a sick frame, passion like that of Constance would have fuller sway. The irritable nerves and the irritated mind would act and re-act on each other. Emotion would obtain more complete and disastrous empire.

When Constance, unobserved before, rises from the ground amidst the congratulating court, with the dignified and solemn denunciation of kingly treachery, one of the finest possible dramatic effects is produced with the simplest means. Her eloquence throughout this scene is magnificent. The interests even of kingdoms seem below its lofty aim. The truth of kings, and, as a minor term, the truth of all other men, is counterfeit. The invocation to the Heavens, that they should arm for her, and be husband to her, and set discord betwixt these perjured kings, is the climax of eloquence. To Austria's entreaty, " Lady Constance, peace ;" she replies in utter forgetfulness of all miseries except her own :

"War ! war ! no peace ! peace is to me a war."

No idea of the Pythoness, or of any woman inspired by good or evil influences, ever represented a more extatic state of eloquent emotion. The poet's own representation of inspired insanity, Cassandra in Troilus and Cressida, is tame and indistinct in comparison :

"Cry Trojans, cry ! Lend me ten thousand eyes
  And I will fill them with prophetic tears," etc.

Constance descends from this exalted strain to wither Austria with her unmatched powers of vituperation, in which she does not even disdain a ridiculous image :

"Thou wear a lion's hide ! doff it for shame,
  And hang a calf's-skin on those recreant limbs."

The war she invokes is near at hand in the "holy errand" of the Legate. When this clerical despot pours the vials of the church's wrath on the head of John, who "blasphemes" in terms of English patriotism and protestantism, Constance must vie with the curses of authority, for which there's "law and warrant."

> "*Constance.*   O, lawful let it be
> That I have room with Rome to curse a while !
> Good father cardinal, cry thou amen
> To my keen curses ; for without my wrong
> There is no tongue hath power to curse him right."

Afterwards she only contributes short sentences to the dialogue, so pregnant with mighty interest ; but they are artfully conceived to incline the wavering mind of King Philip and Lewis to the warlike decision she so ardently desires, and they are expressed with fierce unity of purpose. As she has imprecated from heaven the bloody arbitrament of battle, she invokes hell itself to alarm the timid soul of Philip :

> "Look to that, devil ; lest that France repent,
> And by disjoining hands, hell lose a soul."

Lewis she taunts with his unfledged bride, and the coyness of his honour. Her passion stimulates her lofty intellect, and enables her to suggest in the strongest possible manner to each person the motive likely to weigh most.

She gains her purpose, and the issue of war is to decide her rights. Blanch, with true woman's heart, laments for the sake of those she loves simply and for themselves. To her,

> "The sun's o'ercast with blood."

But Constance, to whom peace is war, war is of all things most welcome, as the means to the end of her ambition, her fiendish ambition. May those who seek for war ever bear its heaviest penalties. May the general murderer feel the truth of Pandulph's assertion of the particular one:

> "For he that steeps his safety in true blood,
>   Shall find but bloody safety and untrue."

So it is with Constance. She loses her cause and her son, and the passion of ambitious love now appears in the form of grief, perhaps of remorse.

When all purpose of ambition is at an end, and even the chief object of it lost, its instigations are no longer predominant in the poor woman's heart. In the prostrating grief she now endures there is no thought of the lost kingdom; one monster grief, like Aaron's rod, devours all smaller ones; there is from henceforth only one thought, one feeling, one mental object, one fixed idea,—that her son is for ever lost. King Philip recognizes in her one already dead to the world:

> "Look, who comes here! a grave unto a soul!
>   Holding the eternal spirit, against her will,
>   In the vile prison of afflicted breath."

Constance taunts him with his and her own calamities as the result of his peace, whereas they were in reality the issue of her war. This is the only point on which her quick intellect ever trips. She shews no signs of bending, though her spirit is wounded unto death.

Her invincible pride rejects all comfort, all solace. The charnel-house ideas of her invocation to death is poetic delirium, the frenzy of imagination. Juliet's imagination, embracing the same ideas, is feeble and prosaic compared with this horror :

> " No, I defy all counsel, all redress,
> But that which ends all counsel, true redress,
> Death, death ; O amiable lovely death !
> Thou odoriferous stench ! sound rottenness !
> Arise forth from the couch of lasting night,
> Thou hate and terror to prosperity,
> And I will kiss thy detestable bones
> And put my eyeballs in thy vaulty brows
> And ring these fingers with thy household worms
> And stop this gap of breath with fulsome dust
> And be a carrion monster like thyself :
> Come, grin on me, and I will think thou smilest
> And buss thee as thy wife.   Misery's love,
> O, come to me !"

In her fierce unconquerable pride she would make death itself obey her as a vassal, and would shake the world even in leaving it :

> " O, that my tongue were in the thunder's mouth !
> Then with a passion would I shake the world,
> And rouse from sleep that fell anatomy."

Pandulph tells her plainly that she is mad, and rouses that eloquent defence of her reason, in which she repeats the test of madness which Lear applies to himself, the recognition of personal identity, and in which she expresses the same idea of madness as a refuge from sorrow, which Gloucester does :

> "*Pandulph.* Lady, you utter madness, and not sorrow.
> *Constance.* Thou art not holy to belie me so ;

I am not mad : this hair I tear is mine ;
My name is Constance ; I was Geffrey's wife ;
Young Arthur is my son, and he is lost :
I am not mad : I would to heaven I were !
For then, 'tis like I should forget myself :
O, if I could, what grief should I forget !
Preach some philosophy to make me mad,
And thou shalt be canonized, cardinal ;
For being not mad but sensible of grief,
My reasonable part produces reason
How I may be deliver'd of these woes,
And teaches me to kill or hang myself :
If I were mad, I should forget my son,
Or madly think a babe of clouts were he :
I am not mad ; too well, too well I feel
The different plague of each calamity."

This supposed test of sanity, the preservation of
the sense of personal identity, is used in the same
manner by Sebastian in Twelfth Night, to assure
himself that in the strange enjoyment of Olivia's
favours he is neither dreaming nor doting.

"*Sebastian.* This is the air ; that is the glorious sun :
This pearl she gave me, I do feel 't, and see 't ;
And though 'tis wonder that enwraps me thus,
Yet 'tis not madness. Where 's Antonio, then ?
I could not find him at the Elephant :
Yet there he was ; and there I found this credit,
That he did range the town to seek me out.
His counsel now might do me golden service ;
For though my soul disputes well with my sense,
That this may be some error, but no madness,
Yet doth this accident and flood of fortune
So far exceed all instance, all discourse,
That I am ready to distrust mine eyes
And wrangle with my reason that persuades me
To any other trust but that I am mad
Or else the lady's mad ; yet, if 't were so,

She could not sway her house, command her followers,
Take and give back affairs and their dispatch
With such a smooth, discreet and stable bearing
As I perceive she does : there's something in 't
That is deceivable."

It is however no better a test of madness than
that applied by Cassio to prove his state of sobriety :

" Do not think, gentlemen, I am drunk : this is my Ancient ;
This is my right hand, and this is my left."

Angrily as Constance rejects the idea of madness,
yet she is mad ; the very type of acute reasoning
mania.   In real life the intellect would scarcely be
so consistent and consecutive in its operations ; but
in real life neither sane nor insane people talk blank
verse, and express even their deepest emotions in the
magnificent imagery which great poets use.   The
raving of maniacal frenzy, in which the emotions are
exclusively involved, would be represented by short
and broken sentences, in which every link in the idea
chain would not be expressed, and which would
therefore represent, more or less, the features of incoherence.   The poet fills up these chasms in the
sense, and clothes the whole in the glowing language
of excited intellectual power ; and thus we have in
Constance the representation of a frenzied woman,
speaking with more arrangement of ideas than frenzy
really permits.   King Philip bids her bind up her
tresses, which she has been madly tearing with her
own hands to prove herself not mad.   These tresses,

" Where but by chance a silver drop hath fallen,"

she will bind up as she is bid ; she will even do this in fanciful reference to the one subject of all thought, her son's imprisonment :

> "I tore them from their bonds, and cried aloud
> 'O that these hands could so redeem my son,
> As they have given these hairs their liberty !'
> But now I envy at their liberty,
> And will again commit them to their bonds,
> Because my poor child is a prisoner."

The despairing cry of overwhelming misery, which can apprehend no hope even in heaven, expresses itself in the fancy that she can never again see her son even beyond the grave, for canker sorrow will change him :

> "And so he'll die ; and, rising so again,
> When I shall meet him in the court of heaven
> I shall not know him : therefore never, never
> Must I behold my pretty Arthur more."

Her last words indicate a state of hallucination. Grief represents her son's voice and figure to her senses. Or if this be not taken literally, it at least represents one manner in which hallucination is produced. An absorbing emotion constantly directs the attention to one idea-image. This creation of the mind at length becomes accepted by the sense as a reality, and the hallucination of insanity exists. This differs however, in its origin and its significance, from the form of hallucination arising from some abnormal state of the nerves of sense merely, which may exist, as it did in Ben Jonson and Nicolai, without

any deviation from a sound state of mental health.
If the lively representation of Arthur's presence be
not intended to convey the idea of actual hallucination, it at least expresses the complete dominion
which an absorbing emotion attains over the attention
and mental conception.

> "*K. Philip.* You are as fond of grief as of your child.
> *Constance.* Grief fills the room up of my absent child,
> Lies in his bed, walks up and down with me;
> Puts on his pretty looks, repeats his words,
> Remembers me of all his gracious parts,
> Stuffs out his vacant garments with his form;
> Then, have I reason to be fond of grief?
> Fare you well: had you such a loss as I,
> I could give better comfort than you do.
> I will not keep this form upon my head,
> When there is such disorder in my wit.
>   [*Tearing off her head-dress.*
> O Lord! my boy, my Arthur, my fair son!
> My life, my joy, my food, my all the world!
> My widow-comfort, and my sorrow's cure!
>   *K. Phi.* I fear some outrage, and I'll follow her."

The frightful spectacle of acute mania pursuing
its course to a fatal end was no fit subject for
dramatic representation. Shakespeare exhibited the
growing horror to the extreme limit which decent
regard to human weakness permitted, and then mercifully drew the veil. The spectacle of sleepless nights
and restless days, of fierce raving and desperate outrage until exhausted nature sinks, this he could not
well exhibit to the public gaze. In one short line
alone he tells the end,

> "The Lady Constance in a frenzy died."

This concealment of the horrors of furious mania, although their existence is indicated, has its parallel in the treatment of the death of the Queen in Cymbeline. The strong mind of this bad woman, one who "bears down all with her brain," is lost in maniacal frenzy, brought on by the disappointment of her schemes. She lies "upon a desperate bed," with

> "A fever from the absence of her son ;
> Madness of which her life's in danger."

The horror of the desperate bed is withheld. Its termination only is recorded with the frenzied confession of her wickedness. In the flush of victory the King is accosted by Cornelius, the good and discreet physician, who had baffled the Queen's intended poisonings.

> "Hail, great king !
> To sour your happiness, I must report
> The queen is dead.
> *Cymbeline.* Whom worse than a physician
> Would this report become? But I consider,
> By medicine life may be prolong'd, yet death
> Will seize the doctor too. How ended she?
> *Cornelius.* With horror, madly dying, like her life,
> Which, being cruel to the world, concluded
> Most cruel to herself."

The death of the noble-minded wife of Brutus is a distant terror like that of Constance. Impatience at the absence of her husband, and grief at the growing power of his enemies, induce the frenzy of despair and suicide :

> "With this she fell distract,
> And her attendants absent, swallowed fire."

In all the deaths of all the plays, a long bill of mortality indeed, there is only one instance in which all the horrors of a bad end are laid bare, namely, in that of the Cardinal Beaufort. In King John's death physical anguish alone is expressed, and this with such beauty and force of language as to veil the foul reality of death by a corrosive poison.

Constance even more than Lear establishes the fact that Shakespeare held the origin and nature of insanity to be emotional. Until the last there is no delusion, scarcely a deviation from correct reasoning, and yet she is conducted through a tempest of emotional disturbance into the very midst of maniacal excitement. All the causes of her disease are purely emotional. The predisposing cause is her fiercely passionate disposition. The exciting cause is grief. The symptoms are the same as the causes, transformed into abnormal conditions of degree. Disorder in the wit is felt, but scarcely exhibited. Loss of control over the operations of the intellect is manifested in the last speech only, or perhaps also in the disconnected expression preceding, "To England if you will." Nature is above art, as Lear says, and a truth now appreciated by science needs not the support of opinion even from so great an artist as Shakespeare. But perfect art is founded upon science, the science of exact observation at least, and to such a test there can be little doubt that this character was submitted in the crucible of the poet's great brain, before it was moulded into that form of fierce power and beauty in which it excites our admiration and awe. The wondrous eloquence of Constance is second to that of no other character except Lear. It would seem that Shakespeare revels in the free swing of fancy, in the repudiation of all mental restraint which madness justifies. He uses these characters as the motley favourites of old courts were often used, to speak bitter truth without fear or favour, without hesitation or retention, without prudential subtraction or self-seeking after thought. The madmen of Shakespeare are his broadest exponents of humanity.

In the development of the insanity of Constance the power of passion finds a potent ally in that of imagination. Imagination, that creative faculty which paints in the mind's eye those images which in health may be dismissed at will, but which in disease haunt the oppressed brain with their importunate presence. The faculty of forming sensational ideas without the intervention of the external senses, is one which, if not kept in subjection to a sober judgment, is more perilous to mental health than aught else except unbridled passion. In actual insanity this function runs riot, and the world of reality is supplanted by that of fancy. This idea is most beautifully expressed in *Midsummer Night's Dream :*

    " 'Tis strange, my Theseus, that these lovers speak of.
      Theseus. More strange than true : I never may believe
    These antique fables, nor these fairy toys.
    Lovers and madmen have such seething brains,

Such shaping fantasies, that apprehend
More than cool reason ever comprehends.
The lunatic, the lover, and the poet
Are of imagination all compact :
One sees more devils than vast hell can hold,
That is, the madman : the lover, all as frantic,
Sees Helen's beauty in a brow of Egypt :
The poet's eye, in a fine frenzy rolling,
Doth glance from heaven to earth, from earth to heaven ;
And as imagination bodies forth
The forms of things unknown, the poet's pen
Turns them to shapes and gives to airy nothing
A local habitation and a name.
Such tricks hath strong imagination,
That, if it would but apprehend some joy,
It comprehends some bringer of that joy ;
Or in the night, imagining some fear,
How easy is a bush supposed a bear ?"

The best commentary on this is again to be found
in the pages of that acute and original thinker, the
author of the *Characteristics*, who directly traces the
origin of insanity to this very excess of the imaginative
faculty uncorrected by the judgment.

"This, indeed, is but too certain; that as long as we
enjoy a mind, as long as we have appetites and sense, the
fancies of all kinds will be hard at work; and whether we
are in company or alone, they must range still, and be
active. They must have their field. The question is,
whether they shall have it wholly to themselves ; or whether
they shall acknowledge some controller or manager. If
none, 'tis this I fear which leads to madness. 'Tis this, and
nothing else which can be call'd madness, or loss of reason.
For if fancy be left judge of anything, she must be judge of
all. Everything is right, if anything be so, because I fancy
it. 'The house turns round. The prospect turns. No,
but my head turns indeed, I have a giddiness; that's all.
Fancy would persuade me thus and thus, but I know better.'

'Tis by means therefore of a controller and corrector of fancy, that I am saved from being mad. Otherwise, 'tis the house turns, when I am giddy. 'Tis things which change (for so I must suppose) when my passion merely or temper changes. But I was out of order. I dreamt. Who tells me this? Who besides the correctrice, by whose means I am in my wits, and without whom I am no longer myself?"

There are many passages in Shakespeare sufficiently illustrative of these remarks.

> " And so, with great imagination
> Proper to madmen, led his powers to death
> And winking leap'd into destruction."
>
> *King Henry IV.*, II.

> " He that is giddy thinks the world turns round."
>
> *Taming the Shrew.*

This distinction between the mind directed by fancy under the sway of the senses, and the appeal from thence to reason, is directly asserted in the *Winter's Tale.*

> "*Camillo.* Be advised.
> *Florizel.* I am, and by my fancy : if my reason
> Will thereto be obedient, I have reason ;
> If not, my senses, better pleased with madness,
> Do bid it welcome."

What is this corrector or controller of fancy ? It is somewhat begging the question to reply that it is the reason ; for reason is often held to include all the intellectual operations, and among them the one to be controlled. The real umpire appears to be the faculty of comparison, by which the unrealities of imagination, or the misrepresentations of perverted

U

sensation, are contrasted with the knowledge derived from experience. Shakespeare somewhere remarks, that after one has looked fixedly at the sun, all things appear green. If this appearance continued, the mental preservative against belief in its reality would be, the comparison of present impressions with the memory of the past, the testimony of others, and a grounded belief in the unchangeability of nature.

In the greater number of delusive appearances one sense corrects another ; but when all the senses and all the circumstances of time and place combine to affirm the reality of some transaction, it is difficult to see from whence the corrective may come. If the sensations of dreaming were as clear and consistent as those of the waking state, how would men be able to distinguish the memory of their dreams from those of their real actions? There is a curious passage bearing on this point in *Troilus and Cressida.* The young lover has just witnessed the falsehood of his mistress. He cannot at first believe the evidence of his senses, and argues against his misery, by combating the testimony of his eyes and ears with that of his affections.

> "*Ulysses.* All's done, my lord.
> *Troilus.*   It is.
> *Ulyss.*   Why stay we, then?
> *Tro.* To make a recordation to my soul
> Of every syllable that here was spoke.
> But if I tell how these two did co-act,
> Shall I not lie in publishing a truth?

Sith yet there is a credence in my heart,
An esperance so obstinately strong,
That doth invert the attest of eyes and ears,
As if those organs had deceptious functions,
Created only to calumniate.
Was Cressid here?
   Ulyss.   I cannot conjure, Trojan.
   Tro. She was not, sure.
   Ulyss.   Most sure she was.
   Tro. Why, my negation hath no taste of madness.
   Thersites. Will he swagger himself out on 's own eyes?
   Tro. This is not she.   O madness of discourse,
That cause sets up with and against itself!
Bi-fold authority! where reason can revolt
Without perdition, and loss assume all reason
Without revolt : this is, and is not, Cressid.
Within my soul there doth conduce a fight
Of this strange nature that a thing inseparate
Divides more wider than the sky and earth,
And yet the spacious breadth of this division
Admits no orifice for a point as subtle
As Ariachne's broken woof to enter."

The arguments of Macbeth against the unreal
mockeries of the phantom rest upon a like foundation ;
but somehow or other, and despite of all the philosophy
of Bishop Berkeley, there does exist in the same mind
means of distinguishing between appearance and
reality. And the mode of reasoning is generally very
simple.

    " The Spanish fleet you cannot see because
     It is not yet in sight."—*The Critic.*

THE MELANCHOLY JAQUES.

"And melancholy marked him for her own."

"The melancholy Jaques" is another phase of the Hamlet character, contemplated under totally different circumstances. There is the same contemplative cast of thought on the frailties of man exercising itself in obedience to a depressed state of emotion. In Jaques this has not been the result of sudden revulsion of feeling, of some one great grief, which has, as it were, overspread the heavens with a pall. It is of more gradual and wholesome growth, the result of matured intellect and exhausted desire. Jaques is an "old man," or at least old enough to be called so by the rustic lass in her anger of disappointment; and he himself indirectly attributes his melancholy to his wide knowledge of the world.

"It is a melancholy of mine own, compounded of many simples, extracted from many objects, and indeed the sundry contemplation of my travels, in which my often rumination wraps me in a most humorous sadness." "Yes, I have gained my experience."

It is thus he hath gained knowledge, but not

wisdom ; unless wisdom be truly described in that line of the poet, which says that it enables us

"To see all others' faults and feel our own."

He does indeed suffer from more than intellectual depreciation of man's sensuality. He has wallowed in it himself, and if he feels not the acute sting of remorse, he endures the dull ache of exhaustion. To use a term now almost naturalized among us, he is thoroughly *blasé* with licentious freedom. He has squandered his means and exhausted his powers of enjoyment ; having been forgetful that moderation is the true epicureanism of enjoyment, he will now rail upon the pleasures of the world in the false stoicism of disgust. Falstaff says that old men "measure the heat of our livers by the bitterness of their own galls ;" but in Jaques it is the heat of his own liver which has embittered the gall of his opinion. He says

"Invest me in my motley ; give me leave
 To speak my mind, and I will through and through
 Cleanse the foul body of the infected world,
 If they will patiently receive my medicine.
    Duke. Fie on thee ! I can tell what thou wouldst do.
    Jaques. What, for a counter, would I do but good ?
    Duke. Most mischievous foul sin, in chiding sin :
 For thou thyself hast been a libertine,
 As sensual as the brutish sting itself ;
 And all the embossed sores and headed evils,
 That thou with license of free foot hast caught,
 Wouldst thou disgorge into the general world."

The contrast of this philosophy with the nobler one of the banished Duke, which leads him to discover

the sweet uses of adversity, and to find good in everything, is all in favour of the latter; for the loving
humanity of the Duke, as contemplative in its way as
the cynicism of Jaques is felt to be that of goodness,
and nobleness, and truth; while that of Jaques is
made to throw, not only on his thoughts, but on
himself, that tinge of ridicule which belongs to perverse exaggeration. His general cynicism, however,
is combined with tenderness of heart; he grieves even
at the physical pain endured by brutes; and the
moral evil of the world, which he sees through and
through, pains and distresses him. The selfishness
which makes worldlings bequeath wealth to the rich,
and which makes "misery part the flux of company,"
and the prosperous to look with contempt upon the
wretched, is to him not a source of hatred, but of
sorrow.

> "Most invectively he pierceth through
> The body of the country, city, court,"

but his invectives are half erased with tears. Jaques'
melancholy is no affectation, though he "loves it better
than laughing," "and can suck it out of a song, as
a weasel sucks eggs." Although his intimate knowledge of mankind, and his sententious power of expression, and his perverse ingenuity in representing
things awry, make his company an intellectual feast,
so that the Duke says,

> "I love to cope him in these sullen fits,
> For then he's full of matter,"

he feels no vain pleasure in the display, and avoids
the disputation and collision of wit which the Duke
so much enjoys.

"*Jaques.* And I have been all this day to avoid him. He
is too disputable for my company : I think of as many matters
as he, but I give heaven thanks and make no boast of
them."

He is as far from being unsocial as he is from
being really misanthropic. He delights in the gay
Amiens and his songs, though he does suck melancholy from them. He fancies Orlando, sees no fault
in him, except "to be in love," and invites his companionship "to rail against our mistress the world
and all our misery." He almost solicits friendship
with Rosalind ; and to Touchstone he cleaves as to
a grotesque image of his own thoughts. There is no
trace in him of that terrible selfishness which distinguishes melancholy when it has become disease.
The sensual sources of selfishness have been dried up
in him, and the intellectual ones are frozen by his
ingrain cynicism. He is more disposed to solitude
than disputation, to silence than to intellectual display,
seeing that "'tis good to be sad and say nothing."
The most subtle of all vanities, that of mental power,
is absent, and the two or three long speeches he
makes are but the spontaneous expression of his
contemplation. If this contemplation paints itself in
sad colours, it is singularly free from personal ani-
mosity. This is finely expressed in his reply to the

accusation of the Duke, that he would commit sin in
chiding sin.

> *"Jaques.* Why, who cries out on pride,
> That can therein tax any private party?
> Doth it not flow as hugely as the sea,
> Till that the weary very means do ebb?
> What woman in the city do I name,
> When that I say the city-woman bears
> The cost of princes on unworthy shoulders?"

The motive for this general censure of vice is,
indeed, as wide apart from that of individual slander,
as benevolence is from malice. The tenderest love of
which the world's history bears record, denounced and
unsparingly lashed all vice, but the woman taken in
adultery was told to "go and sin no more."

The Duke always appears unduly severe in his
estimate of Jaques' humour. He has accused him of
"sullen fits," of being "compact of jars," of deriving
his disgust of life from used-up libertinism; and after
Orlando's famishing appeal for pity and sustenance,
he does him the injustice to refer the cause of his
sadness to the feeling of personal misery.

> *"Duke.* Thou seest we are not all alone unhappy:
> This wide and universal theatre
> Presents more woeful pageants than the scene
> Wherein we play in."

Jaques replies in that epitome of life in twenty-
eight lines, describing the seven ages of man, the
condensed wisdom of which has become "familiar as
household words." It affords a complete though indirect refutation to the Duke's implied reproach, and

distinctly lays the wide basis of his philosophy on
human life at large. It is to be remarked that there
is neither anger nor malice in this description of life.
It merely represents the shady side of truth. The
weakness of infancy, the pains of education, the woes
of love, the dangers of glory, the pedantry of mature
authority, the meanness of aged frugality, and the
wretchedness of decay, these are the aspects of life
given in brief sentences, each of which is like a picture
in outline from the pencil of Retzsch. But life has
another aspect : infancy has its pleasures of sense and
its beauty ; boyhood, its buoyancy and fun ; love, its
joys ; war, its glory ; and age, its honourable worth.
Only in the last scene of all, when decay and rotten-
ness claim the yet living ruins of mind and body, is
there no redeeming compensation :

> "Last scene of all,
> That ends this strange eventful history,
> Is second childishness and mere oblivion,
> Sans teeth, sans eyes, sans taste, sans every thing."

But how few who start in life reach this melancholy
part of the course, more painful to behold perhaps
than to endure. Infancy mewling and pewking, or
crowing with laughter, is abundant as flowers in
spring, but the living decay of second childhood is
a prodigy.

The delight which Jaques takes in the quaint
humour of Touchstone is partly owing to the attrac-
tion which that singular compound of wit and folly

has for one whose curiosity to know all varieties of character is as keen as that of an antiquarian or a naturalist for some strange or new thing, and partly to the satire on human life expressed in the fool's sallies. Touchstone is second only in the aristocracy of Shakespeare's fools, subordinate only to him, hight of Lear, whose younger brother he might well be, more robust in health and coarse in humour, but with the selfsame faculty of turning wisdom into folly and folly into wisdom, of levelling pretension by ridicule, and exposing the naked absurdity of false honour. The philosophy of folly is more broad, uncleanly, and rabelaisian in the expression which it receives from Touchstone than from the fool in Lear, but it is the same in effect, and as such is delightful to Jaques. He delights in him, and entreats the Duke to do so likewise. "Good my Lord, like this fellow." He goes out of his way to counsel him against his false marriage and its effects, when the wood so greenly put together will warp, warp.

Jaques indeed displays a greedy appetite for all knowledge of human nature. He hunts after peculiarities and revels in the chase ; as Shakespeare himself must have done, to have acquired that wonderful collection of game and vermin which he has transmitted to us in the vast museum of his dramas. That Jaques, with all his contempt of mankind in general, really loves man in the particular, is proved by his last speech :

"*Jaques.* Sir, by your patience. If I heard you rightly,
The duke hath put on a religious life
And thrown into neglect the pompous court?
   Jaq. de Boys. He hath.
   Jaq. To him will I : out of these convertites
There is much matter to be heard and learn'd.
[*To Duke*] You to your former honour I bequeath ;
Your patience, and your virtue well deserves it :
[*To Orlando*] You to a love that your true faith doth merit :
[*To Oliver*] You to your land and love and great allies :
[*To Silvius*] You to a long and well-deserved bed :
[*To Touchstone*] And you to wrangling ; for thy loving voyage
Is but for two months victuall'd.   So, to your pleasures :
I am for other than for dancing measures."

In this he does full justice to all, even to poor Touchstone, whose perverse match he has not been able to
prevent.   If he is not for dancing measures, it is because the gay cloak of ceremonious amusement would
conceal that which he hungers after, the heart of man ;
because it would afford a less fruitful field of observation than the words and works of the Duke, so recently
converted from the wicked enjoyment of worldly power.
Jaques really has no thorough want of belief in
human goodness, and in his own heart there is so
much of it that he is quite unable to support con-
sistently the part of scoffer, much less that of misanthrope.

> " With too much knowledge for the sceptic's side,
>   With too much weakness for the stoic's pride,
>   He hangs between ;"

between his general theory of man, painted in the
sombre colours of his own emotional sadness, and

his love of individual men. Instigated not less by his own goodness of heart than by his profound knowledge of the strength and weakness of men, their good and evil, their virtue and vice, mixed human nature receives from him more pity than contempt.

Jaques leaves upon the mind the impression that he was not insane. In him judgment remained master of the direction of thought, and the dilatation of feeling. It is true he cherished his melancholy, but if he had thought fit to do so, he retained the power to oppose, if not to repress it. Herein appears to exist the psychical distinction between the sane and the insane melancholist; a distinction which it may often be very difficult if not impossible to establish, but the only one which can be safely propounded, and which must be constantly borne in mind and sought for even when it cannot be found. The still more essential difference, that in one case there is cerebral disease, and that in the other there is not, can only be proved by the symptoms of disease, which are often obscure or concealed.

But if Jaques was sane, it cannot also be said that he was safe. The voluntary indulgence of melancholy is a perilous experiment. Health may carry a man through it, as it will carry one through the miasm of a marsh reeking with ague, or through the pestilential breath of a fever ward. But if under any change of circumstances health should fail, or the virulence of the poison be increased, the resistance would in one

case, as in the other, be eventually overpowered. If
Jaques had fallen on the bed of sickness, or under the
dark shadow of real grief, it is probable that his fan-
tastic melancholy would have been converted into the
melancholia of disease, which, assimilating all things
unto itself, would first have defied, and finally have
subjugated the reason, and have given him cause to
exclaim with Messala :

> " O hateful error, melancholy's child,
>   Why dost thou shew to the apt thoughts of men
>   The things that are not."

There are few words which have been used both
by Shakespeare and others in such various and different senses as *melancholy*. The history of words
is the history of thought, and a complete account of
the life and adventures of this word, from its birth in
Greek physics, its development through philosophy
and poetry, to its present state of adult vigour in the
prose of every-day life, would be an interesting ex-
ercitation, but neither an easy nor a brief one. Originally employed to express a medical theory of the
ancients on the origin of madness, it has singularly
enough been used to denote the most opposite emotional states. Choler signifies anger, a meaning upon
which Shakespeare frequently quibbles ; but melan-
choler, black choler, means the opposite of anger,
namely emotional depression. It has however only
recently settled into this signification. The learned
Prichard asserts that the ancient writers attached to

it no idea of despondency, but only that of madness in general. Dr. Daniel Tuke, however, points out that in this opinion Prichard has not displayed his usual accuracy. "Hippocrates in one of his aphorisms says, "If fear or distress continue for a long time, this is a symptom of melancholy.' And in other places he distinguished melancholy from mania by the absence of violence; at other times, however, he applies the word to madness in general. Modern writers before Esquirol used the word melancholy to convey the idea of derangement on some particular point, whether accompanied by gloom or mirth. Thus Cullen included under melancholy 'hallucinations about the prosperous' as well as 'the dangerous condition of the body'; and Dr. Good speaks of 'a self-complacent melancholy.'" Other writers appear to have used the term in a non-medical sense, with equal diversity of meaning. Thus Henry More makes melancholy synonymous with enthusiasm:

"It is a strong temptation with a melancholist when he feels a storm of devotion and zeal come upon him like a mighty wind—all that excess of zeal and affection, and fluency of words is most palpably to be resolved into the power of melancholy, which is a kind of natural inebriation"—"the vapour and fumes of melancholy partake of the nature of wine."

Milton uses the word melancholy in the sense of contemplative thought, and invokes and deifies the emotion in *Il Penseroso:*

"But hail thou goddess, sage and holy,
Hail divinest melancholy."

Since then the term has been gradually settling down into its present meaning of emotional dejection. It is not however properly used even now to signify a morbid state, unless periphrasis for that purpose be made use of; and care should be taken, which is not always done, to distinguish between melancholy and melancholia, the latter being the proper technical term applied to a form of mental disease.

Shakespeare uses the word melancholy with many modifications in its meaning, but with far less of laxity than that employed by other authors, and in a sense more approaching that of melancholia. In *Love's Labour Lost*, the grandiloquent Spaniard in his letters to the King uses the term in its strictly medical sense :

"Besieged with sable-coloured melancholy, I did commend the black-oppressing humour to the most wholesome physic of thy health-giving air."

In the following scene the question is actually mooted, though unfortunately not determined, of the difference between sadness and melancholy.

"*Armado.* Boy, what sign is it when a man of great spirit grows melancholy?

Moth. A great sign, sir, that he will look sad.

Arm. Why, sadness is one and the selfsame thing, dear imp.

Moth. No, no; O lord, sir, no.

Arm. How canst thou part sadness and melancholy, my tender juvenal?

Moth. By a familiar demonstration of the working, my tough senior."

King John, in that fine scene where he tempts
Hubert to the murder of his nephew, says :

> "Or if that surly spirit, melancholy,
> Had baked thy blood and made it heavy-thick,
> Which else runs trickling up and down the veins,
> Making that idiot, laughter, keep men's eyes
> And strain their cheeks to idle merriment."

In *Twelfth Night* the surly spirit is supposed to
perform another culinary process. Fabian says, "If
I lose a scruple of this sport, let me be boiled to
death with melancholy."

In *Taming the Shrew*, the physicians are said to
recommend the pleasant comedy to Christopher Sly,
on the grounds that,

> "Seeing too much sadness hath congeal'd your blood,
> And melancholy is the nurse of frenzy :
> Therefore they thought it good you hear a play
> And frame your mind to mirth and merriment,
> Which bars a thousand harms and lengthens life."

In Viola's touching description of the effects of
concealed love, the black spirit is made to assume
a new livery, in a manner which proves Shakespeare
to have been conversant with the appearances at least
of chlorosis or green sickness, the *febris amatoria* as
it has also been called :

> "She never told her love,
> But let concealment, like a worm i' the bud,
> Feed on her damask cheek : she pined in thought,
> And with a green and yellow melancholy
> She sat like patience on a monument,
> Smiling at grief."

The alliance, or rather the resemblance, existing between pride and melancholy, is noted in *Troilus and Cressida.* Speaking of Achilles, the enquiry is made "Is he not sick?" Ajax replies:

"Yes, lion sick of a proud heart: you may call it melancholy, if you will favour the man; but by my head it is pride."

But the melancholy which approaches most nearly to that of Jaques is that of Antonio, the merchant of Venice. In his noble simplicity he does not parade it like Jaques, who rather prides himself on the sable plumage of his disposition. Antonio merely calls his depression sadness, and attempts not to account for it.

"In sooth, I know not why I am so sad:
It wearies me; you say, it wearies you;
But how I caught it, found it, or came by it,
What stuff 'tis made of, whereof it is born,
I am to learn;
And such a want-wit sadness makes of me,
That I have much ado to know myself."

His friends endeavour to account for the emotional phenomenon in various ways, more or less unjust. His "mind is tossing on the ocean," and "fear of misfortune makes him sad," or he is in love. "Fie, fie!" that folly at least is not to be imputed to the staid nobleness of his character. Then it must be constitution and the work of nature; he's sad because he is not merry; "Nature hath framed strange fellows in her time;" some will grin at anything, and others

X

will smile at nothing; "Though Nestor swear the jest be laughable."

Gratiano is still less complimentary, and attributes the sadness of his friend to the desire to gain the world's opinion for wisdom. The downright unreserved frankness of these men to Antonio is, however, an indirect testimony to the goodness of his heart and the sweetness of his temper.

> "*Gratiano.* You look not well, Signior Antonio;
> You have too much respect upon the world:
> They lose it that do buy it with much care:
> Believe me, you are marvellously changed.
>   *Antonio.* I hold the world but as the world, Gratiano;
> A stage where every man must play a part,
> And mine a sad one.
>   *Gra.*　　　Let me play the fool:
> Why should a man, whose blood is warm within,
> Sit like his grandsire cut in alabaster?
> Sleep when he wakes and creep into the jaundice
> By being peevish?
> There are a sort of men whose visages
> Do cream and mantle like a standing pond,
> And do a wilful stillness entertain,
> With purpose to be dress'd in an opinion
> Of wisdom, gravity, profound conceit,
> As who should say, *I am Sir Oracle,*
> *And, when I ope my lips let no dog bark!*
> *　　*　　*　　*　　*　　*
> But fish not with this melancholy bait,
> For this foolgudgeon, this opinion."

A most unjust imputation, for there are few characters in all these dramas less self-seeking than that of this princely merchant. The more probable cause of his unexplained melancholy would seem to be that of *ennui,* arising from unruffled prosperity. Man is not born only to trouble, but a certain amount of it is good for his mental health. Without some motion of the elements, the waters of life stagnate. Antonio's melancholy has its origin in his prosperity, his unself-ish disposition, and sweet temper. To have spat upon old Shylock's gaberdine was as little indication of the contrary, as to have kicked a vicious cur when he was worrying helpless children. He delivered those who made plaint to him from the Jew's forfeit-ures, and he despised and spat upon the wretched usurer. When real trouble comes upon him, his melancholy disappears, and he will gladly release himself from the penalties of the bond. The apparent submission to his fate, because he is "a tainted wether of the flock," and will by death avoid "the hollow eye and rumpled brow and age of poverty," all this is spoken in the magnanimous desire to relieve the wretchedness of his friends; but when the wealth, of which he was formerly so careless, is regained there is no expression of melancholy in its reception.

"Sweet lady, ye have given me life and living."

Monotonous prosperity is the cause of his morbid sadness; a strong dose of adversity its cure. The more wholesome condition is that of the middle state prayed for by the wise Agur, "Give me neither poverty nor riches, feed me with food convenient for me."

The melancholy of the Queen in King Richard the
Second bears a strong resemblance to that of Antonio.
A new element, however, is added, in the vague
apprehension of coming evil. The sadness of the
Queen, like that of Antonio, is partly constitutional,
and arises in the midst of prosperity ; but, unlike it,
it does not rest in the present, but throws its dark
shadow into the future. This union of sadness and
fear is constantly met with among the insane ; very
frequently, indeed, groundless fear is the sole apparent
cause of melancholia, or rather its only prominent
feature. In the following passage, the Queen's explanation of the origin of sadness from fear, and
Bushy's rejoinder upon the origin of fear from sadness,
is a wonderful example of psychological acumen. It
is remarkable that in Richard's Queen, as in Antonio,
the real stroke of adversity is described as adverse to
the melancholy which had free sway in prosperous
times ; for when the King is led in humiliation through
London, the Queen's spirit is roused, and she en-
courages her depressed Consort to lion-like resistance.

> "*Bushy.* Madam, your majesty is too much sad :
> You promised, when you parted with the king,
> To lay aside life-harming heaviness
> And entertain a cheerful disposition.
> *Queen.* To please the king I did ; to please myself
> I cannot do it ; yet I know no cause
> Why I should welcome such a guest as grief,
> Save bidding farewell to so sweet a guest
> As my sweet Richard : yet again, methinks,
> Some unborn sorrow, ripe in fortune's womb,
> Is coming towards me, and my inward soul

With nothing trembles : at something it grieves,
More than with parting from my lord the king.
 Bushy. Each substance of a grief hath twenty shadows,
Which shows like grief itself, but is not so :
For sorrow's eye, glazed with blinding tears,
Divides one thing entire to many objects ;
Like perspectives, which rightly gazed upon
Distinguish proper form,—but eyed awry
*Show nothing but confusion,—*So your majesty,
Looking awry upon your lord's departure,
Find shapes of grief, more than himself, to wail ;
Which, look'd on as it is, is nought but shadows
Of what it is not. Then, thrice-gracious queen,
More than your lord's departure weep not ; more's not seen :
Or if it be, 'tis with false sorrow's eye,
Which for things true weeps things imaginary.
 Queen. It may be so ; but yet my inward soul
Persuades me it is otherwise : howe'er it be,
I cannot but be sad ; so heavy sad
As, though on thinking on no thought I think,
Makes me with heavy nothing faint and shrink."

In the above quotation I have ventured with
diffidence to alter the lines in italics from the original,
in which, by some accident of writing or printing, the
sense appears to have been perverted to the very
contrary of that which it seems to me evident that it
was intended to convey. In the original, the perspective or telescope, when rightly gazed upon, is said to
shew confusion, and when eyed awry, to distinguish
form aright ; a statement opposed both to the context
and to the fact. The text in both Collier's and
Knight's editions stands thus :

> " Like perspectives, which rightly gazed upon
> Shew nothing but confusion,—eyed awry,
> Distinguish form : so your sweet majesty," etc.

The old authors commonly used the word 'perspective' for telescope, and by Bishop South the word is not only used in this sense, but is employed in a simile closely parallel to the above ; disturbed position being substituted for disturbed refraction.

"It being as impossible to keep the judging faculty steady in such a case, as it would be to view a thing distinctly and perfectly through a *perspective* glass held by a shaking paralytic hand."—Vol. iii., Serm. 2.

Thus, in different characters, Shakespeare has referred to melancholy as the cause, or the consequence, or the accompaniment of various and very different emotions. The villain-melancholy described by John, the love-melancholy by Viola, the melancholy of pride in Achilles, of prosperity in Antonio, of constitution and timidity in the Queen of Richard II., of contemplation in Jaques, have their several anatomies opened to view with more skill, if less labour, than that employed by the quaint and learned diligence of old Burton, the professed dissector of the passion. In *Cymbeline*, this diversity of melancholy's habitation is positively though poetically expressed :

"O melancholy !
Who ever yet could find thy bottom? find
The ooze, to show what coast thy sluggish crare
Might easiliest harbour in ?"

There is but one step from *melancholy* to *music*. There is but one step from delicacy of pleasure to that of pain, and from that of pain to pleasure. Highly strung sensibility is the common term, or

rather the common condition of both. Internal or
external circumstance, the events or humours of life,
determine to which side the balance shall temporarily
or permanently incline. According to existing state
or bias, the same thing may cause or allay emotional
depression. This is most remarkable in the influence
exercised by music upon persons of melancholic
tendency. Melancholy may be said to be the minor
key of the soul, and, in finely strung organisms, the
internal vibration responds to the external concord
of sweet sounds. It is only the uncontemplative man
of action, like Harry Hotspur, who would

> "rather be a kitten, and cry mew,
> Than one of those same metre ballad-mongers."

Jaques, on the contrary, "can suck melancholy out
of a song, as a weazel sucks eggs," and finds as much
enjoyment in the process. His delight in music may
be correlated with many passages in the other dramas
to the same effect. The most obvious and beautiful
of these perhaps are to be found in the *Merchant of
Venice* and *Twelfth Night.* In the former, not only
is the sentiment expressed, but the reason for it is
given :

> "*Jessica.* I am never merry when I hear sweet music.
> *Lorenzo.* The reason is, your spirits are attentive."

This reason is illustrated by the effect which a trumpet
sound produces upon a herd of wild colts, and the
conclusion is indicated that the melancholy moved by
music is that of sensibility, and is opposed to the

darker melancholy which is referred to in King John as that fit for a base action.

> " The man that hath no music in himself,
> Nor is not moved with concord of sweet sounds,
> Is fit for treasons, stratagems, and spoils ;
> The motions of his spirit are dull as night,
> And his affections dark as Erebus :
> Let no such man be trusted."

In *Twelfth Night* the Duke uses music with another psychological purpose :

> " If music be the food of love, play on ;
> Give me excess of it, that, surfeiting,
> The appetite may sicken, and so die."

The same idea is expressed by Cleopatra,

> " Give me some music, music moody food
> Of us that trade in love."

It is invoked by Queen Catherine to dispel sadness :

> " Take thy lute, wench ; my soul grows sad with troubles :
> Sing and disperse them if thou canst."

In some sad moods, however, it cannot be endured, as when in deep misery Richard II. exclaims :

> " This music mads me ; let it sound no more ;
> For though it have holp madmen to their wits,
> In me it seems it will make wise men mad."

In Ariel's counter incantation it is used, as in Lear, to cure madness.

> " A solemn air, and the best comforter
> To an unsettled fancy, cure thy brains,
> Now useless, boiled within thy skull ! There stand, etc.
> . . . . The charm dissolves apace ;
> And as the morning steals upon the night,

Melting the darkness, so their rising senses
Begin to chase the ignorant fumes that mantle
Their clearer reason."

But enough of this: it would be wearisome to
quote all Shakespeare's references to this most refined
of sensual pleasures, of which it cannot be doubted
that he was passionately fond. Collins's Ode, in which
music is made to express in turn the voice of all the
passions, does not indicate so sensitive an ear, and
so true an appreciation of its influence on the mind,
as that which pervades the dramas of Shakespeare.

MALVOLIO.   CHRISTOPHER SLY.
COMEDY OF ERRORS.

IN the times when Shakespeare wrote, and of which he wrote, the "Imputed Lunatics' Friend Society" had not beeen organised.   At least there are no records of its existence, and not even a tradition thereof.   Is it possible that one of the members may have immolated the Secretary on a funeral pyre of the proceedings, and thus converting the whole into the baseless fabric of a vision, left not a wreck behind.   If so, the more's the pity ; for if the writings of Shakespeare may be taken as a guide, it was more needed then than it is now ; inasmuch as the false imputation of insanity appears at that time to have been quite a common incident.

These characters of imputed insanity were needful to bring Shakespeare's psychological delineations "full circle round."   The various phases of real and feigned insanity, which he has depicted with such marvellous skill and truthfulness, needed this one link to complete the chain.   In its way it is perfect, as representing not only a masterly and most amusing sketch of the fabrication of imputed lunacy, but also of the treatment thought to be suitable for the insane in

those days. Some incidental references to the usual
treatment of the insane are to be found in several of
the dramas. Thus Cominius says to Coriolanus,

> "If 'gainst yourself you be incensed, we'll put you,
> Like one that means his proper harm, in manacles."

In *Romeo and Juliet* is the following :

> "*Benvolio.* Why, Romeo, art thou mad?
> *Romeo.* Not mad, but bound more than a madman is;
> Shut up in prison, kept without food,
> Whipp'd and tormented."

In *As you Like it*, Rosalind incidently refers to the
treatment of insanity :

> "Love is merely a madness, and, I tell you, deserves as
> well a dark house and a whip as madmen do: and the
> reason why they are not so punished and cured is, that the
> lunacy is so ordinary that the whippers are in love too."

So also in the *Comedy of Errors:*

> "*Pinch.* Mistress, both man and master is possess'd;
> I know it by their pale and deadly looks :
> They must be bound and laid in some dark room.
> *Adriana.* O, bind him, bind him! let him not come near
> me."

Again, in *Merry Wives of Windsor:*

> "*Page.* Why this passes, Master Ford; you are not to
> go loose any longer, *you must be pinioned.*
> *Evans.* Why this is lunatics, this is mad as a mad dog."

And in *Much Ado About Nothing:*

> "Fetter strong madness in a silken thread."

Malvolio only gets the half of Rosalind's recipe,
which he endures without exciting much commisera-
tion; a fact which may lead to the reflection that the
ill-treatment of a real madman is an offence of very

different colour to a frolic, however mischievous, with a vain egotistical coxcomb like Malvolio, or a drunken humorist like Sly. A sane man who has behaved himself like a madman deserves some sort of punishment, while the misfortune of real disease claims ever enduring forbearance and kindness; from whence it results that the interests of an insane person, who has really suffered ill-treatment, and those of a sane person who has brought upon himself the imputation of insanity, are very far from being identical.

In the frolic of *Twelfth Night*, Shakespeare prefaces the character fit for the imputation of madness with the same skill he has elsewhere displayed in laying the ground-plan for the reality. The unalloyed egotism of the major-domo at first vents itself in a querulous attack on the Fool, and on those who laugh at his folly. He is one of those men to whose self-important gravity every jest is an insult. Olivia gives the key-note of his disposition; a testy temper measuring all things by the rule of his narrow self-esteem.

"O, you are sick of self-love, Malvolio, and taste with a distempered appetite. To be generous, guiltless, and of free disposition, is to take those things for bird-bolts that you deem cannon-bullets."

Though he has right on his side in objecting to Sir Toby's saturnalia, the same priggish vanity is evident in the method of reproof, bringing down upon him the pungent sarcasm of that moist moralist:

"Art thou any more than a steward? Dost thou think because thou art virtuous there shall be no more cakes and ale?"

He offends Maria also with his Jack-in-office re-proofs. Maria, the "wittiest piece of Eve's flesh in all Illyria," instantly forms the plan of consummate revenge, namely, to "gull him into a nay-word, and make him a common recreation." She has taken the exact guage of his self-esteem, and knows every pebble in the hover of vanity where the great trout lies, which she will lure into her grasp with tickling falsehoods.

"*Maria.* I will drop in his way some obscure epistles of love; wherein, by the colour of his beard, the shape of his leg, the manner of his gait, the expressure of his eye, fore-head, and complexion, he shall find himself most feelingly personated. I can write very like my lady your niece: on a forgotten matter we can hardly make distinction of our hands.

Sir Toby. Excellent! I smell a device.

Sir Andrew. I have 't in my nose too.

Sir Toby. He shall think, by the letters that thou wilt drop, that they come from my niece, and that she 's in love with him."

Malvolio has made enemies on every side by the tale-bearing arts of upper-servant diplomacy, so that recruits to the ambuscade of frolic are easy to find. Fabian will be boiled to death with melancholy "rather than lose a scruple of the sport," and Sir Toby will "fool him black and blue." The poor victim's proclivity to folly is smoothed and tended before Maria's wicked device of the letter makes the cup brim o'er.

" He has been yonder i' the sun practising behaviour to his own shadow this half hour : observe him, for the love of mockery ; for I know this letter will make a contemplative idiot of him."

Malvolio's egregious vanity expressed in his overheard soliloquy is so preposterously flagrant, that it scarcely needed the dish of poison dressed for him in the feigned letter from the Countess, to bring it to a climax so closely resembling madness that Olivia should accept the fact without further proof than the absurd demeanour which the poor " baffled fool" puts on before her :

" *Malvolio.* 'Tis but fortune ; all is fortune. Maria once told me she did affect me : and I have heard herself come thus near, that, should she fancy, it should be one of my complexion. Besides, she uses me with a more exalted respect than any one else that follows her. What should I think on 't ?"

The steward's conceit has not the common companionship of goodnature to redeem it. He is testy and quarrelsome among his fellow-servants, and a willing tell-tale of their failings, an ill-disposed sheep-dog of the domestic flock, a " niggardly rascally sheep-biter," as Sir Toby calls him. He is a man who has no pity for others, having himself put into prison the captain who rescued Viola, for some unspecified offence. His adhesion to Olivia is founded upon selfishness alone. He not only displays no real affection for her, not even that of a faithful servant, but from the first he treats her with that off-handed upper-servant want of respect, which seems to say that she is honoured by

his service. The folly of his aspiration to her hand
has not therefore a breath of excuse or palliation.
He can love no one but himself, and the demeanour
which he puts on in consequence of Maria's letter, is
but the expression of his own previous thoughts and
aspirations. He dons himself in yellow stockings,
a colour which Olivia abhors, cross-garters himself,
a fashion she detests, and presents himself before—
not the goddess of his idolatry, but the stepping-stone
to his ambition, with the apish manners of an under-
bred dandy: Maria having previously prepared her
mistress's mind for the most obvious explanation of
his absurdities.

"*Maria.* He's coming, madam; but in very strange
manner. He is, sure, possessed.

Olivia. Why, what's the matter? does he rave?

Mar. No, madam, he does nothing but smile: your lady-
ship were best to have some guard about you, if he come;
for, sure, the man is tainted in 's wits.

Oli. Go call him hither. [*Exit Maria.*] I'm as mad as he,
If sad and merry madness equal be.
How now, Malvolio!

Malvolio. Sweet lady, ho, ho.

Oli. Smilest thou?
I sent for thee upon a sad occasion.

Mal. Sad, lady! I could be sad: this does make some
obstruction in the blood, this cross-gartering; but what of
that? if it please the eye of one, it is with me as the very
true sonnet is, 'Please one, and please all.'

Oli. Why, how dost thou, man? what is the matter
with thee?

Mal. Not black in my mind, though yellow in my legs.
It did come to his hands, and commands shall be executed:
I think we do know the sweet Roman hand.

Oli. God comfort thee! Why dost thou smile so and kiss thy hand so oft?

Mar. How do you, Malvolio?

Mal. At your request! yes; nightingales answer daws.

Mar. Why appear you with this ridiculous boldness before my lady?

Mal. 'Be not afraid of greatness:' 'twas well writ," etc.

"*Oli.* Why, this is very midsummer madness."

In what midsummer madness is supposed to differ from that of the rest of the year is not certain, unless it may be that the heat of the weather may be thought to increase that of the brain, and render its vagaries more rampant. Olivia's injunction to Maria, to "let this fellow be looked to," and that the people should have special care of him, though immediately following the expression of her opinion that he is mad, has so little the effect of opening his eyes, dimmed with the scales of egotism, that he draws from the half contemptuous expression a perverse and flattering meaning:

"'Let this fellow be looked to'; fellow! not Malvolio, nor after my degree, but fellow. Nothing that can be, can come between me and the full prospect of my hopes."

Not even the direct accusations of the conspirators that he is mad can excite a suspicion of the foolery of which he is both the agent and the butt. They are idle shallow things, not of his element; they will know more shortly, and have reason to behave more respectfully. This bantering scene is pregnant with comicality, and with reference to the old-fashioned

ideas of madness and disease. While Sir Toby and
Maria wickedly refer the cause of the supposed
insanity to demoniacal possession, Fabian hits the
more sensible explanation afforded by humoral pathology.

"*Fabian.* Here he is, here he is. How is't with you,
sir? how is't with you, man?

Malvolio. Go off; I discard you: let me enjoy my
private: go off.

Maria. Lo, how hollow the fiend speaks within him!
did not I tell you? Sir Toby, my lady prays you to have
a care of him.

Mal. Ah, ha! does she so?

Sir Toby. Go to, go to; peace, peace; we must deal
gently with him: let me alone. How do you, Malvolio?
how is't with you? What, man! defy the devil: consider,
he's an enemy to mankind.

Mal. Do you know what you say?

Mar. La you, an you speak ill of the devil, how he
takes it at heart! Pray God, he be not bewitched!

Fab. Carry his water to the wise woman.

Mar. Marry, and it shall be done to-morrow morning, if
I live. My lady would not lose him for more than I'll say.

Fab. No way but gentleness; gently, gently: the fiend
is rough, and will not be roughly used.

Sir Toby. Why, how now, my bawcock! how dost thou,
chuck?

Mal. Sir!

Sir Toby. Ay, Biddy, come with me. What, man! 'tis
not for gravity to play at cherry-pit with Satan: hang him,
foul collier!

Mar. Get him to say his prayers, good Sir Toby, get
him to pray.

Mal. My prayers, minx!

Mar. No, I warrant you, he will not hear of godliness.

Mal. Go, hang yourselves all! you are idle shallow
things: I am not of your element: you shall know more
hereafter."

Y

The unscrupulous tormentors have some apprehension that he may verily go mad, from the complete
success of their device. Sir Toby at first thinks that
he may become actually insane from disappointment,
when he finds that the castle-building of his ambition
is all in the clouds. "Why, thou hast put him in
such a dream that when the image of it leaves him
he must run mad." Now, however, they think that
the very excess of his morbid vanity will bring him
to this consummation.

> "*Fabian.* Why, we shall make him mad indeed.
> *Maria.* The house will be the quieter.
> *Sir Toby.* Come, we'll have him in a dark room and
> bound.   My niece is already in the belief that he's mad:
> we may carry it thus, for our pleasure and his penance, till
> our very pastime, tired out of breath, prompt us to have
> mercy on him: at which time we will bring the device to
> the bar, and crown thee for a finder of madmen."

He is put in the dark room and bound; and to
carry on the riotous fun, an exorcist is provided in
the Clown, representing Sir Topas the Curate.

> "*Clown.* What, ho, I say! peace in this prison!
> *Malvolio.* [*Within*] Who calls there?
> *Clo.* Sir Topas the curate, who comes to visit Malvolio
> the lunatic.
> *Mal.* Sir Topas, Sir Topas, good Sir Topas, go to my
> lady.
> *Clo.* Out, hyperbolical fiend! how vexest thou this man!
> talkest thou nothing but of ladies?
> *Sir Toby.* Well said, master Parson.
> *Mal.* Sir Topas, never was man thus wronged: good
> Sir Topas, do not think I am mad: they have laid me here
> in hideous darkness.
> *Clo.* Fye, thou dishonest Satan! I call thee by the

most modest terms; for I am one of those gentle ones that will use the devil himself with courtesy: sayest thou that house is dark?

Mal. As hell, Sir Topas.

Clo. Why, it hath bay windows transparent as barricadoes, and the clear-stories toward the south north are as lustrous as ebony; and yet complainest thou of obstruction?

Mal. I am not mad, Sir Topas: I say to you, this house is dark.

Clo. Madman, thou errest: I say, there is no darkness but ignorance; in which thou art more puzzled than the Egyptians in their fog.

Mal. I say, this house is as dark as ignorance, though ignorance were as dark as hell; and I say, there was never man thus abused. I am no more mad than you are: make the trial of it in any constant question.

Clo. What is the opinion of Pythagoras concerning wild-fowl?

Mal. That the soul of our grandam might haply inhabit a bird.

Clo. What thinkest thou of his opinion?

Mal. I think nobly of the soul, and no way approve his opinion.

Clo. Fare thee well. Remain thou still in darkness: thou shalt hold the opinion of Pythagoras ere I will allow of thy wits, and fear to kill a woodcock, lest thou dispossess the soul of thy grandam. Fare thee well."

This interview represents a caricature of the idea that madness is occasioned by demoniacal possession, and is curable by priestly exorcism. The idea was not merely a vulgar one in Shakespeare's time, and was maintained even long afterward by the learned and the pious. More than a trace of it, indeed, remains to the present day in Canon LXXII. of the Church, which provides, that no Minister without the license of the Bishop of the Diocese shall "attempt, upon any pretence whatsoever, either of possession or obsession, by fasting and prayer, to cast out any devil or devils, under pain of the imputation of imposture or cosenage, and deposition from the ministry."

The exorcism of the false Sir Topas is supposed to be proceeded with in the proper place, namely, the Church, and hence the reference to the bay windows and to the clerestories. This ceremonial must have been of no uncommon occurrence in Shakespeare's time. In Catholic countries it is still resorted to ; and in the lunatic colony of Gheel, in Belgium, it appears to be, or was but recently, the usual active treatment to which recently-admitted patients are subjected.

There is nothing new under the sun, at least, in human nature ; to this conclusion a careful study of Shakespeare must inevitably lead, for either, from contemplation or observation, he seems to have known all the absurdities and all the shades of man's intellectual weakness and pride. Could he arise again, would he not find this century rather dull and uninteresting, compared with his own? Material improvements excepted, would he not find the world rather worse for wear, more crowded and less merry, more pretentious and less truthful, more knowing and less wise ; and would he not find existing follies as numerous as old ones, only less picturesque?

If the old-world system of exorcism is caricatured by the false Sir Topas, one of the modern tests of

insanity is also keenly quizzed. The idea of testing
the existence of insanity by questions on the doctrine
of transmigration, may find its counterpart in more
than one recent legal investigation, in which it has
been argued by very learned counsel, and maintained
by very eminent physicians, that, because an educated
gentleman retains some knowledge of his previous
acquirements, it is impossible that he can be insane.

It is noteworthy that Shakespeare does not introduce the exorcist in the grave and tragic instances of
insanity, but only to cope with the comic instances
of falsely imputed madness, in Malvolio and the
Antipholi.

The Clown puts off the character of the reverend
exorcist, and appears in his own. He well advises
Malvolio to "endeavour thyself to sleep and leave thy
vain bibble babble;" and in the very acme of pretended good faith, he exhorts the victim, "tell me
true, are you mad indeed? or do you but counterfeit?"
and in reply to the strenuous denial of both, he closes
the argument with the assertion which might have
prevented it, "nay, I'll never believe a madman 'till
I see his brains."

The Clown provides the poor dupe with materials
and means to write a letter, and undertakes to carry
it to Olivia, whom Malvolio thinks the cause of his
ill-usage. The Clown, however, does with the letter
much as the letters of insane patients are too often
used at the present time. He detains it until the

writer comes in question respecting the imprisonment of Viola's friend, the sea-captain, and then presents it with the remark that "a madman's epistles are no gospels, so it skills not much when they are delivered."

The Duke rightly thinks that the letter "savours not much of distraction." Malvolio comes into the presence, and gives a temperate account of the treatment by which he has been "made the most notorious geck and gull that e'er invention played on."

It is to be feared, however, that if the steward's vanity is diminished under treatment, the gall and malice of his disposition are increased. He takes leave with the threat, "I'll be revenged on the whole pack of you," foreshadowing a criminal information for conspiracy, or at the very least an action for assault and false imprisonment.

The theme of Christopher Sly's imputed madness in the Induction of Taming the Shrew turns on the old point of undistinguished identity. The frolic, to "practise on the drunken man" by letting him awake from the insensibility of his liquor surrounded by the circumstances of a lord, at once suggests the old question,

"Would not the beggar then forget himself?"

Sly, we fear, is a sad rogue, though he denies it. "The Sly's are no rogues. Look in the Chronicles, we came in with the Conqueror." But descent bareth not bad qualities, and a great man's lineage may have "crept through scoundrels ever since the flood." He would almost barter his birthright for a pot of small ale, and it is not therefore surprising that he should readily enough give up his identity when bribed with an atmosphere of sensual gratification. Consciousness and conscientiousness are not merely allied in sound. There is exquisite drollery, if there is also some inconsistency in making Sly, who is sane, accept this oft-repeated test of alienation. Sly's readiness to submit to a change of identity is proof positive, if other proofs were wanting, that this test is not trustworthy. He is at first very positive.

"What, would you make me mad? Am I not Christopher Sly, old Sly's son of Burton-heath, by birth a pedlar, by education a card-maker, by transmutation a bear-herd, and now by present profession a tinker? Ask Marian Hacket, the fat ale-wife of Wincot, if she know me not: if she say I am not fourteen pence on the score for sheer ale, score me up for the lyingest knave in Christendom. What! I am not bestraught!"

Here is identification with circumstance: but, alas, the tempter comes to prove all this is but a strange lunacy, and to proffer the delights of lordly luxury, and the sensualist gives up his past existence to embrace that of the sybarite. After all it is but a change of manner.

"Am I a lord? and have I such a lady?
Or do I dream? or have I dream'd till now?
I do not sleep: I see, I hear, I speak;

> I smell sweet savours and I feel soft things :
> Upon my life, I am a lord indeed
> And not a tinker nor Christophero Sly.
> Well, bring our lady hither to our sight;
> And once again, a pot o' the smallest ale."

Self-identification is, indeed, no test of sanity or insanity. An insane man, who fancies himself made of butter or of glass, is not convinced to the contrary by fire not melting him or blows not breaking him, and is not likely to be convinced by the persistence of ordinary sensation in a substance which ought to be senseless. The power of the delusion which overlooks the attributes of that which it believes to exist, is not likely to succumb to the attributes of that which it believes not to exist. Moreover, sensation may be defective or perverted, while emotion and intellect remain sound. The prick of Lear's pin might be inflicted on a limb which had lost the sense of feeling ; and if the organs of vision had been affected, Sebastian might neither have seen the glorious sun nor the pearl, or might have seen them multiplied or distorted.

> "This is the air; that is the glorious sun :
> This pearl she gave me, I do feel't and see't :
> And though 'tis wonder that enwraps me thus,
> Yet 'tis not madness.
> For though my soul disputes well with my sense,
> That this may be some error, but no madness,
> Yet doth this accident and flood of fortune
> So far exceed all instance, all discourse,
> That I am ready to mistrust mine eyes,
> And wrangle with my reason that persuades me
> To any other trust, but that I am mad ;
> Or else the lady's mad, yet, if 'twere so,

She would not sway her house, command her followers,
Take and give back affairs, and their despatch,
With such a smooth, discreet, and stable bearing,
As I perceive she does : there's something in't
That is deceivable."

Twelfth Night.

In the *Comedy of Errors,* madness is imputed to
four of the principal characters, namely, to the two
pairs of twins. There is more of fanciful incident than
of delineation of character in this piece. The idea of
insanity first presents itself to the mind of the
courtesan to whom Antipholus of Ephesus denies the
ring he has had from her. The idea once suggested
is eagerly seized upon by his shrewish wife and her
partisans to interpret the violent and absurd conduct
of her lord. Mistaken identity is again the pivot of
the imputed madness, but in this instance the mistake
is not made by the subject of it, but by the public.
Adriana procures the assistance of a conjuring exorcist, Pinch. The marks of anger are interpreted
into the signs of madness.

" Alas, how fiery and how sharp he looks !"
" Mark, how he trembles in his exstasy !"
"*Pinch.* Give me your hand and let me feel your pulse.
Ant. E. There is my hand, and let it feel your ear.

[*Striking him.*

Pinch. I charge thee, Satan, housed within this man,
To yield possession to my holy prayers,
And to thy state of darkness hie thee straight :
I conjure thee by all the saints in heaven !"

This of course adds fuel to the fire of the angry
man's excitement ; discussion leads to violence ; master

and man overpowered and bound together are put in a dark and damp vault.

Antipholus and Dromio of Syracuse, the other halves of the identity, as they may be called, take refuge from their persecutions in the sanctuary of the cloister. The interview of the Abbess with the zealous and jealous wife is the fine passage of the play. Adriana must have drawn upon her fancy for the account of the premonitory symptoms, or have thus interpreted the ill-humour caused by her own shrewish temper. The Abbess makes a wrong guess or two at the cause, but her keen eye reads the only probable one in the feature language of the wife. The manner in which she inveigles the latter into self-accusation, and then describes the distracting effect of domestic cark and worry is finely graphic.

> "*Abbess.* How long hath this possession held the man?
> *Adriana.* This week he hath been heavy, sour, sad,
> And much different from the man he was;
> But till this afternoon his passion
> Ne'er brake into extremity of rage.
> *Abb.* Hath he not lost much wealth by wreck of sea?
> Buried some dear friend? Hath not else his eye
> Stray'd his affection in unlawful love?
> A sin prevailing much in youthful men,
> Who give their eyes the liberty of gazing.
> Which of these sorrows is he subject to?
> *Adr.* To none of these, except it be the last;
> Namely, some love that drew him oft from home.
> *Abb.* You should for that have reprehended him.
> *Adr.* Why, so I did.
> *Abb.*   Ay, but not rough enough.
> *Adr.* As roughly as my modesty would let me.

Abb. Haply, in private.
Adr.   And in assemblies too.
Abb. Ay, but not enough.
Adr. It was the copy of our conference :
In bed he slept not for my urging it ;
At board he fed not for my urging it ;
Alone, it was the subject of my theme ;
In company I often glanced it ;
Still did I tell him it was vile and bad.
   Abb. And thereof came it that the man was mad :
The venom clamours of a jealous woman
Poison more deadly than a mad dog's tooth.
It seems his sleeps were hindered by thy railing ;
And therefore comes it that his head is light.
Thou say'st his meat was sauced with thy upbraidings :
Unquiet meals make ill digestions ;
Thereof the raging fire of fever bred ;
And what's a fever but a fit of madness ?
Thou say'st his sports were hinder'd by thy brawls :
Sweet recreation barr'd, what doth ensue
But moody and dull melancholy,
Kinsman to grim and comfortless despair,
And at her heels a huge infectious troop
Of pale distemperatures and foes to life ?
In food, in sport and life-preserving rest
To be disturb'd would mad or man or beast :
The consequence is then thy jealous fits
Have scared thy husband from the use of wits."

The imputation of disordered mind is cast upon
many other characters in these dramas, but in no
other is there a discussion or, so to say, an inquisition
upon the truth of the fact, except in *Measure for
Measure*, when Isabella throws herself before the
Duke, praying for justice upon his hypocrite deputy,
the saintly Angelo. The imputation of disordered
intellect is here made in all seriousness, to discredit

the accuser and avert the punishment of crime.
Angelo replies to the maiden's denunciation.

> "*Angelo.* My lord, her wits, I fear me, are not firm :
> She hath been a suitor to me for her brother
> Cut off by cause of justice,—
>   *Isabel.*   By cause of justice !
>   *Angelo.* And she will speak most bitterly and strange.
>   *Isabel.* Most strange, and yet most truly, will I speak."

The accusation is made, and the Duke answers in
well-assumed belief in Angelo's truth and Isabella's
distractedness ; thus eliciting from her that discrimination between the impossible and the improbable,
which ought never to be lost sight of, in estimating
dubious statements of suspected minds.

> " *Duke.*   Away with her ! Poor soul,
> She speaks this in the infirmity of sense.
>   *Isabel.* O prince, I conjure thee, as thou believest
> There is another comfort than this world,
> That thou neglect me not, with that opinion
> That I am touch'd with madness ! Make not impossible
> That which but seems unlike."

The Duke accepts the distinction, and applies the
best possible test to the reasonableness of the statement, namely, the just consequence of one idea on
another, the "dependency of thing on thing."

> "*Duke.*   By mine honesty,
> If she is mad,—as I believe no other,—
> Her madness hath the oddest frame of sense,
> Such a dependency of thing on thing,
> As e'er I heard in madness.
>   *Isabel.*   O gracious duke,
> Harp not on that, nor do not banish reason
> For inequality ; but let your reason serve
> To make the truth appear where it seems hid."

This imputation of insanity to smother truth is as old as the time when it was replied to by the great apostle of truth, in the very spirit of Isabella's appeal : " I am not mad, most noble Festus, but speak forth the words of truth and soberness." The test which the Duke applies is the only one valid in regard to the reason, although it is opposed to Locke's theory that madmen reason right on wrong premises. But the right statement of the premises is a great part of the reasoning process : the dependency of one premise on another being duly set forth, the conclusion follows as a matter of course. Hence it follows, that although it may be needful to apply other tests to ascertain the soundness of other functions of the mind, that of the reason, strictly so called, must ever be estimated by the due sequence of ideas, the " dependency of thing on thing."

THE END.

CAMBRIDGE :—PRINTED BY JONATHAN PALMER.